Better Homes and Gardens®

Amazing Desserts
for Every Occasion

Meredith® Books
Des Moines, Iowa

Meredith Books
1716 Locust Street
Des Moines, Iowa 50309-3023
www.meredithbooks.com

First Edition. Printed in the United States of America
ISBN: 0-696-23526-9
Excerpted from *Better Homes and Gardens® New Baking Book*

CONTENTS

Pictured on the front cover: *top left,* Lemon Tea Cakes (page 113), *top right,* Mini Molten Chocolate Cakes (page 177), *bottom left,* Chocolate-Hazelnut Cookie Torte (page 180), *bottom right,* Jam Thumbprints (page 146)

Pictured on page 4: *top left,* Sour Cream, Raisin, and Pear Pie (page 66) *lower left,* Crème Brûlée, (page 194) *right,* Pistachio Cake with White Chocolate Buttercream (page 103)

INTRODUCTION

Sure, it's easier to buy cakes, cookies, and other baked goods from the bakery or the grocery store. But home baking comes from the heart. It connects you with family and friends as well as traditions— handed down, learned, or new. In creating this book, we wanted to capture the rich, emotional experience of baking while presenting our largest, most comprehensive collection of baking recipes and information.

So, we asked people nationwide why they still choose to pull out a rolling pin and heat up the oven. "Baking is fun, cooking is everyday," said one individual. Another baker added, "It's rewarding when your kids get excited and say your cookies are the best, even if you burn a batch."

Now, *Better Homes and Gardens*® *Amazing Desserts for Every Occasion* puts all the pleasures of baking between two covers. With hundreds of recipes, including must-have basics and hundreds of new ideas, this book will challenge seasoned cooks while inspiring novices. Count on instructional photos and tips throughout, too. Whatever your specialty, you will find it here: from cobblers and crisps to pies and pastries, from cakes and cookies to showy desserts, and holiday classics for every occasion—including breakfast, dinner, snack time, high tea, and parties.

Better Homes and Gardens® *Amazing Desserts for Every Occasion* truly becomes yours once you have pressed your fingertips into dough and caught aromas wafting from the kitchen and throughout the house. After all, these recipes—with their marvelous flavors and textures—are personal gifts to lovingly shape and bestow.

baking basics

BAKING BASICS

You wouldn't build a house without a good set of plans, an understanding of the materials and techniques, and the right tools. Mastering the art of baking is no different. Whether you're making your first cake or your hundredth batch of peanut butter cookies, there's no substitute for a trusted recipe and a good resource tool to rely on when you have questions. This chapter is full of information about common ingredients, measuring methods, mixing techniques, equipment, and bakeware that can help make your baking successful the first time—and every time.

Many of the recipes in this book are marked with one of the following symbols. These symbols designate recipes that are Best-Loved favorites, Low-Fat, and Easy to prepare, helping you choose recipes that fit your preferences, time limits, and dietary needs.

 A Best-Loved recipe is one that is either so outstanding it gained instant favor among our food editors and Test Kitchen home economists or has been in the *Better Homes and Gardens*® archives for many years and is a classic.

 A Low-Fat recipe is just that: low in fat, which by our definition, means it contains 3 to 5 grams of fat per serving.

An Easy recipe is a comparatively simple one when you consider the entire collection of recipes in the chapter. It might have relatively few ingredients or might require only one bowl to prepare, for instance.

NUTRITION FACTS

With each recipe, we give important nutrition information. The calorie count of each serving and the amount, in grams, of fat, saturated fat, cholesterol, sodium, carbohydrates, fiber, and protein will help you keep tabs on what you eat. You can check the levels of each recipe serving for vitamin A, vitamin C, calcium, and iron. These are noted in percentages of the Daily Values. The Daily Values are dietary standards determined by the Food and Drug Administration (FDA).

HOW WE ANALYZE

Our Test Kitchen uses a computer analysis of each recipe to determine the nutritional value of a single serving. Here's how:

■ When ingredient options appear in a recipe (such as milk or half-and-half), we use the first one mentioned for analysis. The ingredient order does not mean we prefer one ingredient.

■ When milk is an ingredient in a recipe, the analysis is calculated using 2-percent milk.

■ The analysis does not include optional ingredients.

■ We use the first serving size listed when a range is given (such as "Makes 4 to 6 servings.")

RECIPE TIME ESTIMATES

The timings listed with each recipe should be used as general guidelines. Consider the following points as well.

■ Preparation (Prep) times with recipes are rounded to the nearest 5-minute increment.

■ Listings include the time to chop, slice, or otherwise prepare ingredients.

■ When a recipe gives an ingredient option, the calculations use the first ingredient.

■ Timings assume some steps are performed simultaneously.

■ The preparation of optional ingredients is not included.

EQUIPMENT

Using the right equipment is one way to guarantee a successful and enjoyable baking experience.

■ **Electric mixers.** These machines make life in the kitchen a whole lot easier. Portable (handheld) electric mixers are perfect for light jobs and short mixing periods, like whipping cream. For heavy-duty jobs and long mixing periods, a freestanding electric mixer works best, and it leaves you free to proceed with another part of the recipe.

■ **Food processors.** Food processors can blend, chop, and puree as does a blender, but they also slice and shred. Some brands can even mix batters and blend pastry (check your owner's manual to see what your model can do).

■ **Bakeware.** Bakeware is made in a range of materials: aluminum, tin, stainless steel, black steel, glass, and pottery. Both the material and the finish affect the final product. Shiny bakeware reflects heat, slowing the browning process. On the other hand, dark and dull-finish bakeware absorbs more heat, increasing the amount of browning. Here are some rules of thumb: Shiny bakeware, including aluminum, tin, and stainless steel, will result in thinner cake crusts and softer-set cookies that spread more. Dark or dull-finish bakeware, including dull aluminum or tin and glass, will give you heavier cake crusts, piecrusts that are evenly browned underneath as well as on top, crisp and nicely browned crusts, and crisper

cookies. Black steel pans create a crisp dark crust. Essential bakeware includes:

Baking pans: 9×9×2-inch, 11×7×1½-inch, 13×9×2-inch

Baking sheets: 15×12-inch

Cake pans (round): 8×1½-inch, 9×1½-inch

Casserole dishes: in various sizes

Custard cups: 6 ounces each

Glass baking dishes: 1½-quart, 2-quart, 3-quart

Jelly-roll pan: 15×10×1-inch

Loaf pans: 8×4×2-inch, 9×5×3-inch

Muffin pan

Pie plate: 9-inch

Pizza pan or stone

Rectangular pans: 12×7×1½-inch, 13×9×2½-inch

Springform pan: 8- or 9-inch

Square pan: 8×8×2-inch or 9×9×2-inch

Tube pan: 10-inch (plain and fluted)

MEASURING

Baking is both an art and a science. To satisfy the scientific part, you must be correct and consistent when measuring ingredients. Not all ingredients are measured the same way.

■ **Liquids.** Use a glass or clear plastic liquid measuring cup on a level surface. Bend down so your eye is level with the marking on the cup (see photo, below left). When a liquid is measured in a measuring spoon, fill the spoon

to the top, but don't let it spill over. Don't pour liquid ingredients over the other ingredients, in case you spill.

■ **Sugar.** Granulated or powdered sugar should be spooned into a dry measuring cup and leveled off. Brown sugar, on the other hand, is pressed firmly into a dry measure so it holds the shape of the cup when it is turned out (see photo, below).

■ **Flour.** Proper measuring of flour is critical. Too much flour can cause baked goods to turn out dry or sauces to become too thick. To measure flour, stir it in the bag or canister to lighten it. Except for cake flour, sifting is not necessary. Gently spoon flour into a dry

measuring cup or a measuring spoon. Level it off the top with the straight side of a knife (see photo, above).

■ **Shortening.** Solid shortening is measured by pressing it firmly into a dry measuring cup or spoon with a rubber scraper (see photo, right), then leveling the excess off with a straight edge.

■ **Butter.** Butter is often packaged in stick form, with markings on the paper or foil wrapper indicating tablespoon and cup measures. Use a sharp knife to cut off the amount needed (see photo, below). If the wrapper isn't marked, measure it as you would shortening.

■ **Spices.** Lightly fill the correct spoon just to the top with spice. A dash is less than ⅛ teaspoon, which is the smallest amount you can measure accurately using a standard measuring spoon. A dash often is used when calling for dry seasonings or salt. Shake or sprinkle the ingredient into the palm of your hand so you can see how much you have; add it to suit your taste.

BAKING AT HIGH ALTITUDES

Baking at high altitudes requires some adjustments to standard recipes.

HIGH-ALTITUDE ADJUSTMENTS

Ingredient	3,000 feet	5,000 feet	7,000 feet
Liquid: add for each cup	1 to 2 tablespoons	2 to 4 tablespoons	3 to 4 tablespoons
Baking powder: decrease for each teaspoon	⅛ teaspoon	⅛ to ¼ teaspoon	¼ teaspoon
Sugar: decrease	0 to 1	0 to 2	1 to 3

■ **Cakes.** If you live at or more than 3,000 feet above sea level, use the chart above to adjust the cake ingredients listed. Try the smaller amounts first; make any necessary adjustments next time around. When baking a cake, increase the oven temperature about 20 degrees and decrease the baking time slightly to keep it from expanding too much. For cakes leavened by air, such as angel food, beat the egg whites only to soft peaks. Otherwise, your cakes may expand too much (because the air pressure is less). If you're making a cake that contains a large amount of fat or chocolate—a cup or more—you may need to reduce the shortening by 1 to 2 tablespoons and add an egg to prevent the cake from falling. The leavening, sugar, and liquid in cakes leavened with baking powder or baking soda may need adjustment, too (see chart, above).

■ **Cookies, biscuits, and muffins.** Cookies, biscuits, and muffins are more stable than cakes and need little adjustment at high altitudes. If you feel it is necessary, experiment by slightly reducing the sugar and baking powder and increasing the liquid. For cookies, increase the oven temperature about 20 degrees and slightly decrease the baking time. This will keep your cookies from drying out.

■ **Yeast doughs.** If you're working with a yeast dough, allow unshaped dough to rise according to recipe directions; punch dough down. Repeat rising step once more before shaping dough. If dough seems dry, add more liquid and reduce the amount of flour the next time you make the recipe. Because flours tend to be drier at high altitudes, sometimes they absorb more liquid.

■ **Further information.** For more information on cooking at high altitudes, contact your county extension agent or write: Colorado State University Food Science Extension Office Fort Collins, CO 80523–1571. (Please use this address only for questions related to high-altitude cooking.)

EGGS

■ **Separating eggs.** To separate a yolk from the white, use an egg separator (see photo, below). Separating the egg yolk from the egg white by passing the yolk from shell to shell is not considered safe.

■ **Egg safety.** Eating uncooked or slightly cooked eggs can be hazardous, especially to people vulnerable to salmonella such as the elderly, infants, children, pregnant women, and the seriously ill. Commercial forms of egg products are safe because they are pasteurized, which destroys salmonella bacteria.

■ **Using egg substitutes.** Refrigerated or frozen egg substitutes are easy to use, readily available, and enable anyone on a cholesterol-restricted diet to enjoy great baked goods that contain eggs. These products are based on egg whites and contain no fat or cholesterol. When baking with an egg substitute, use ¼ cup of either refrigerated or frozen egg product for each whole egg called for in the recipe for most cookies, cakes, and muffins. Do not, however, use an egg substitute when the recipe you are making relies on air being whipped into eggs to leaven it, such as a sponge cake.

EGG EQUIVALENCE CHART

If you use an egg size other than large, you may need to increase or decrease the number of eggs you use in our recipes. Use these suggested alternatives:

1 large egg	=	1 jumbo, extra-large, medium, or small egg
2 large eggs	=	2 jumbo, 2 extra-large, 2 medium, or 3 small eggs
3 large eggs	=	2 jumbo, 3 extra-large, 3 medium, or 4 small eggs
4 large eggs	=	3 jumbo, 4 extra-large, 5 medium, or 5 small eggs
5 large eggs	=	4 jumbo, 4 extra-large, 6 medium, or 7 small eggs

■ **Beating eggs.** Beating eggs to the just-right stage is critical for many recipes.

Slightly beaten eggs: Use a fork to beat the whole egg until the yolk and white are combined and no streaks remain (a).

Soft peaks: Place the egg whites in a clean glass or metal bowl (do not use plastic). Beat with an electric mixer on medium speed or with a rotary beater until they form peaks with tips that curl over when the beaters are lifted (b). Be careful as you separate your eggs—even just a tiny speck of fat, oil, or yolk in the bowl will prevent the whites from whipping. For the best results, separate your eggs and let the whites sit at room temperature for 30 minutes.

Stiff peaks: Continue beating egg whites on high speed until they form peaks with tips that stand straight when the beaters are lifted (c).

Beating egg yolks: Beat the egg yolks with an electric mixer on high speed for about 5 minutes or until they are thick and lemon-colored (d).

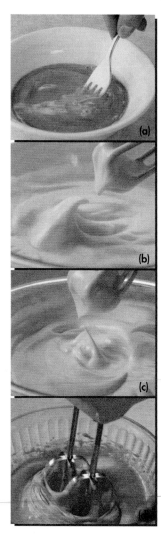

(a)

(b)

(c)

FATS AND OILS

Baked products such as cakes and cookies rely on fats for flavor and tenderness.

■ **Butter.** Nothing beats the flavor and richness that butter adds to baked goods. For all of the recipes in this book, we recommend using butter rather than margarine (see tip, right). What doesn't make a difference is whether you use salted or unsalted butter (although if you use unsalted butter, you may want to increase the amount of salt in the recipe).

■ **Margarine.** Margarine, made from vegetable oil or animal fat, was developed in the late 1800s as a substitute for butter. For all of the recipes in this book, we recommend using butter.

■ **Shortening.** Shortening is a solid fat that has been made from vegetable oils. It's often used for tender, flaky piecrusts and biscuits. It now comes packaged in sticks marked conveniently with tablespoon and cup measurements. Shortening can be stored at room temperature for up to a year. Plain and butter-flavored types are available; use whichever you prefer.

■ **Cooking oils, flavored oils.** For baking, these cannot be used interchangeably with solid fats because they are unable to hold air when beaten. Mildly flavored vegetable oils generally are made from corn, soybeans, sunflower seeds, or peanuts and have a pale color. Nut oils, such as walnut oil, have a pronounced nutty flavor and can be darker in color. Olive oil is used primarily in baking recipes for focaccia, pizza doughs, breads, and the occasional cake.

WHY NOT MARGARINE?

Technically, anything on your supermarket shelf labeled "margarine" must be at least 80 percent vegetable oil or fat, which—if used in baking in place of butter—will provide satisfactory results. However, there are so many margarine look-alikes on the market—and their labeling can be so tricky—it can be confusing as to which is a true margarine. Any margarinelike product that has less than 80 percent vegetable oil or fat contains additional water and milk solids and can make your baked goods soggy or rock-hard. If you do elect to use a true margarine, your rolled cookie dough, for instance, will be softer than if you use butter. You may need to chill it in the freezer to make it workable. Also, it's critical to use butter in baked goods that rely strictly on butter for flavor, such as genoise and pound cake. Shortbread should only be made with butter to retain its characteristic butter flavor, richness, and dense crumb. Streusel toppings, too, shouldn't be made with margarine because they don't crisp up as they do when they're made with butter.

FLOURS AND GRAINS

Flours are essential to many baked products. Many cereals, roots, and seeds are milled to make flour, although wheat is the most popular and contains the gluten necessary to give baked goods their structure. Some flours are made from soft wheats, some from hard wheats, and others are a combination of the two. Each type of flour affects the crumb texture of baked products differently.

■ **All-purpose flour.** This flour is made from a blend of soft and hard wheat flours and, as its name implies, is used as a multipurpose flour in a range of baked goods. However, different manufacturers use varying proportions of hard and soft wheats, so the protein level in all-purpose flours ranges from 9 to 15 grams per cup.

For information on bleached versus unbleached flour, see the tip on page 12.

■ **Cake flour.** Cake flour is made from soft wheat and produces a tender, delicate crumb because the gluten is less elastic. Many bakers use it for angel food and chiffon cakes. All the recipes in this cookbook were perfected using all-purpose flour. If you would like to use cake flour instead, sift it before measuring. Use 1 cup plus 2 tablespoons of cake flour for every 1 cup of all-purpose flour.

■ **Self-rising flour.** Self-rising flour is an all-purpose flour that contains baking powder, baking soda, and salt.

■ **Bread flour.** Bread flour contains more gluten and protein than all-purpose flour, making it ideal for baking breads. When rubbed between your fingers, it feels a bit more granular than all-purpose flour. When used instead of all-purpose flour, you usually need less.

■ **Specialty flours.** Specialty flours, such as whole wheat or graham, rye, oat, buckwheat, and soy, generally are combined with all-purpose flour in baked products because none has sufficient gluten to provide the right amount of elasticity on its own.

■ **Whole wheat.** Whole wheat or graham flours are processed less than plain flour and, therefore, retain more of their nutrients and fiber.

■ **Rye flour.** Rye flour is a traditional ingredient in many breads, cakes, and pastries of Northern and Eastern Europe. The gluten in rye flour adds stickiness to the dough but lacks the elasticity of wheat flour gluten. Using a large proportion of rye flour to wheat flour results in a more compact product.

■ **Oat flour.** Oat flour can be purchased or made by grinding rolled oats to a fine powder in a food processor, ½ cup at a time.

■ **Soy flour.** Soy flour is a cream colored, strong flavored flour that is a rich source of protein and iron and contains no gluten. Baked products made with soy flour brown more quickly, so you may have to reduce the baking temperature depending on the amount used.

■ **Storing flour.** All-purpose flour should be stored in an airtight container in a cool, dry place for up to 10 to 15 months. Whole wheat and other whole grain

---

BLEACHED VS. UNBLEACHED

What's the difference between bleached and unbleached flour? They're both all-purpose, which means they're equally good for making most baked goods. The difference is that bleached flour has been made chemically whiter in appearance than unbleached flour. The bleaching process does compromise some of the flour's nutrients, but they are often added back to the flour. Which flour you choose is a personal preference. Some bakers like their white cake and bread as white as they can be; others prefer their flour to be processed as little as possible.

---

flours may be stored for up to 5 months. For longer storage, refrigerate or freeze the flour in a moisture- and vaporproof container. Be sure to warm chilled flour to room temperature before using in yeast breads so it does not slow down the rising of the bread.

LEAVENINGS

Leavening agents add lightness to baked goods by "raising" them. Common leavens include yeast, baking powder, and baking soda. Steam, which forms when the liquid in the batter or dough heats up, also can cause a product to expand.

■ **Yeast.** Yeast is a one-celled organism that wakes up and goes into action when it's combined with a warm liquid and sugar or starch. It produces little bubbles of carbon dioxide gas that get trapped in your dough and make it rise. There are three forms of yeast available: active dry, quick-rising, and compressed. Active dry yeast is the most popular form. These tiny, dehydrated granules are mixed with flour or dissolved in warm water before they're used. Quick-rising yeast (sometimes called fast-rising or instant yeast) is a more active strain of yeast. It's usually mixed with the dry ingredients before the warm liquids are added. Quick-rising yeast cuts rising time by about one-third. The first rising will take about 10 to 15 minutes less; the second rising will be shortened, too. Quick-rising yeast can be substituted for active dry yeast, except in recipes requiring the dough to rise in the refrigerator and in doughs using sourdough starter. Compressed yeast, also called fresh yeast, comes in small, foil-wrapped square cakes. Soften it in warm water according to the package directions.

■ **Baking powder and soda.** Baking powder and baking soda are chemical leavening agents that produce carbon dioxide just as yeast does. Double-acting baking powder produces gases in two stages: first, when liquids are added and, second, during baking. Baking soda creates carbon dioxide bubbles instantly when it's mixed with acidic ingredients such as buttermilk, sour cream, or fruit juices. Any recipe that uses only baking soda as leaven should be baked immediately, before all those bubbles deflate.

DAIRY PRODUCTS

Milk and milk products are used in baking to provide moisture, flavor, and color and to activate the leavening agents. Because whole, low-fat, and skim milk vary only in fat content, you can use them interchangeably in baking. Whole milk may, however, result in a richer flavor than skim milk.

■ **Buttermilk.** Buttermilk is low-fat or skim milk to which a bacterial culture has been added. It is low in fat, thick, and creamy, with a mildly acidic taste. Sour milk, made from milk and lemon juice or vinegar, can be substituted for buttermilk (see substitutions, page 208).

■ **Whipping cream.** Whipping cream contains between 30 and 49 percent fat and can be beaten to form peaks that retain their shape. To speed up whipping, chill the bowl and beaters first.

■ **Light cream.** Light cream or table cream contains 10 to 30 percent fat, which is not sufficient for whipping.

■ **Half-and-half.** A mixture of milk and cream, half-and-half can be used instead of light cream in most recipes.

■ **Evaporated milk.** Evaporated milk is milk that has had 60 percent of its water removed. It is sold in cans and can be stored at room temperature until opened. Do not use evaporated milk as a substitute for sweetened condensed milk. It

---

WHIPPED CREAM FROSTING

Sweetened whipped cream makes a wonderful frosting on a cake, but unless it's stabilized, it doesn't hold its shape for long once it's piped through a pastry bag. Here's how to make it retain its shape for up to 2 days: In a glass measuring cup stir together 1 tablespoon cold water and ½ teaspoon unflavored gelatin. Let stand for 2 minutes. Place the measuring cup in a saucepan of boiling water. Cook and stir about 1 minute or until the gelatin is completely dissolved. In a bowl beat 1 cup whipping cream and 2 tablespoons sugar with an electric mixer on medium speed while gradually drizzling the gelatin over the cream mixture. Continue beating the cream mixture until stiff peaks form. Makes 2 cups (can be doubled).

---

may be substituted for other milk products if you reconstitute it using 2 parts evaporated milk to 3 parts water (for example, ½ cup evaporated milk to ¾ cup water).

■ **Sweetened condensed milk.** Sweetened condensed milk is milk that has had about 50 percent of its water removed

---

and, like evaporated milk, is sold in cans and can be stored at room temperature until opened. Because sweetened condensed milk also has about 40 percent added sugar, it is not a suitable substitute for other milks.

■ **Nonfat dry milk.** Nonfat dry milk has both the fat and water removed. Mix nonfat milk powder with water according to package directions to form milk. Some of the recipes in this cookbook call for it as a dry ingredient to add richness to baked products.

SWEETENERS

Sweeteners are essential for adding flavor, tenderness, and a bit of browning to baked goods. They may be either granular, as in granulated white and brown sugar, or liquid, as in honey, corn syrup, and molasses.

■ **Granulated, or white, sugar.** Granulated, or white, sugar is the most common sweetener used in baking. It is made from sugarcane or sugar beets. White sugar is most commonly available in what is called fine granulation, but it also comes in superfine (also called ultrafine or caster sugar), a finer grind of sugar that dissolves readily, making it ideal for frosting, meringues, and drinks. Pearl or coarse sugar is just that—a coarser granulation best used for decorating cookies and other baked goods.

■ **Brown sugar.** Brown sugar is a processed mixture of granulated sugar and molasses which gives it its distinctive flavor and color. Brown sugar is available in both light and dark varieties; dark brown sugar has the stronger flavor. Recipes in this cookbook were tested using light brown sugar, unless specified otherwise. You can substitute granulated sugar measure for measure for brown sugar, except in products where color and flavor might be important, such as a caramel sauce. In baked products that use baking powder or baking soda, add ¼ teaspoon more baking soda for each cup of brown sugar used in place of granulated sugar.

■ **Powdered sugar.** Powdered sugar, also known as confectioner's sugar, is granulated sugar that has been milled to a fine powder then mixed with cornstarch to prevent lumping. Sift powdered sugar before using and do not substitute it for granulated sugar.

■ **Honey.** Honey is made by bees from all sorts of flower nectars. It adds moisture, sweetness, and a characteristic flavor to baked goods. Because it caramelizes more quickly and at lower temperatures than sugar, honey causes baked goods to brown more quickly. Although it is available in whipped forms, the recipes in this cookbook refer to pure, unwhipped honey.

■ **Corn syrup.** Corn syrup is a heavy syrup that has half the sweetness of sugar. It is available in light and dark varieties. Like dark brown sugar, dark corn syrup has the stronger flavor.

■ **Molasses.** Although it is primarily used for flavoring gingersnaps and gingerbread, molasses—a thick, dark brown syrup generally made from the juice pressed from sugarcane

---

HOW TO SKIN A HAZELNUT

Hazelnuts—long popular in Europe (especially in combination with chocolate)—have been gaining many fans in North America in the last few years with their rich, sweet taste. For most uses, hazelnuts need to have their bitter brown cloak of skin removed before they're stirred into a cake batter or sprinkled over a tart. Here's how: Spread shelled hazelnuts on an ungreased cookie sheet and toast in a 350° oven for 10 to 15 minutes, stirring occasionally, until the skins begin to flake. Remove from the oven and place a handful of nuts at a time in a clean, dry cotton kitchen towel and rub vigorously until the skins come off.

---

during refining—adds sweetness to baked goods, too. Molasses comes in light and dark varieties. The two forms are interchangeable, so choose one depending on how much molasses flavor you like.

NUTS

Whole or chopped, plain or salted, nuts add an appealing crunch and rich flavor to any baked product.

■ **Almonds.** Almonds are a flat, oval-shaped nut with a reddish brown skin that can be removed by blanching. The smooth, light-colored meat has a mild,

---

yet rich, flavor. Almonds are available whole, sliced, slivered, and chopped.

■ **Brazil nuts.** Brazil nuts (elephant toes to some) are a large nut with a thin, brown skin and an oily, rich flavor.

■ **Cashews.** Crescent-shaped cashews, with their rich, buttery flavor, are a favorite of bakers and snackers. Buy them raw or roasted, salted or plain. Choose roasted cashews for baking unless specified otherwise.

■ **Hazelnuts.** Hazelnuts, also called filberts, are a small, round nut with a mild, sweet flavor. The nut meat is covered with a thin, brown skin that needs to be removed before you use them in baking (see tip, above left).

■ **Hickory nuts.** Hickory nuts resemble walnuts but have a rich, oily flavor similar to that of toasted pecans.

■ **Macadamia nuts.** These tropical nuts taste rich, sweet, and buttery. You can use these small, round nuts wherever you would use cashews.

■ **Peanuts.** America's favorite nut, the peanut, is technically not a nut at all but a legume. Roasting intensifies a peanut's rich, buttery flavor. For baking, it's best to use peanuts that have had their skins removed. Selecting between salted or unsalted peanuts is strictly a personal choice.

■ **Pecans.** Pecans are rich and buttery and have the highest fat content of any nut. Pecans often are substituted for walnuts and vice-versa.

■ **Pine nuts.** Also known as pignolia or piñon, pine nuts actually are seeds from a variety of pine trees. This gives the small, creamy white nut a sweet, faint pine flavor. Pine nuts can be slender and pellet-shaped or more triangular.

■ **Pistachios.** The small pistachio has a pale green meat covered with a paper-thin, brown skin. Their thin, smooth shells, which are split at one end, are often dyed red or green. Their mild, sweet flavor is similar to that of almonds.

■ **Walnuts.** Black walnuts are rich and oily with an intense flavor. Walnuts, other than the black walnut, are called English walnuts. They have a mild flavor that makes them popular in baking.

FRUITS

Dried fruits add flavor, texture, and color to baked goods.

■ **Berries and cherries.** Dried cranberries, blueberries, and cherries are available in larger supermarkets or through catalogs. They have a very sweet taste and chewy texture. These small, flavor-packed gems can be used in breads, desserts, and pies—anywhere you might expect to find raisins.

FRUIT MATH

You're making your favorite recipe, and it calls for 2 cups of mashed bananas. What does that mean in terms of whole bananas? Rest easy. We've done the culinary calculations to answer that question and a few others, too:

1 pound bananas = 3 medium or 4 small = 2 cups sliced = 1 cup mashed

1 pound apples = 4 small, 3 medium, or 2 large = 2¾ cups sliced = 2 cups chopped

1 pound apricots = 8 to 12 whole = 2½ cups sliced

1 pound pears = 3 medium = 3½ cups sliced = 3 cups chopped

1 medium lemon = 3 tablespoons juice = 2 teaspoons shredded peel

---

■ **Apples, etc.** Dried apples, apricots, pears, and peaches can be used whole or chopped. They're readily available at your supermarket.

■ **Dates and figs.** Dates and figs come in lots of forms. Just remember, when a recipe calls for "snipped dates," use cut-up whole dates, not the sugar-coated dates. You can find figs in light or dark varieties.

■ **Candied fruits.** During the holiday season, supermarkets stock up on candied fruits. They add color and flavor to fruit cakes and cookies. Candied fruits are available as citron, peels,

mixed fruit, cherries, pineapple, apricots, mango, and papaya.

■ **Raisins and currants.** In terms of baking, the main point of difference between raisins and currants is their size (currants are smaller than raisins). Both have dark brown, wrinkly skin and are very sweet.

SECTIONING CITRUS FRUIT

Eating all of an orange—including the white membrane that surrounds each segment—may be all right at lunchtime, but when you're baking something special with citrus, the recipe often calls for fruit that has been sectioned or had its segments separated from each other and the white membrane removed. To section a citrus fruit, use a sharp paring knife to remove the peel and white rind. Working over a bowl to catch the juice, cut into the center of the fruit between one section and the membrane. Turn the knife and slide it along the other side of the section, next to the membrane, cutting outward.

CHOCOLATE

Considered to be "food of the gods" to many, chocolate comes in a passel of products on the market. Because chocolate differs in flavor and consistency when it's melted, be sure to use only the type of chocolate called for in a recipe using melted chocolate.

■ **Unsweetened chocolate.** Unsweetened chocolate is the basic type of chocolate from which all others are made. Sometimes called baking or bitter chocolate, unsweetened chocolate is pure chocolate with no sugar or flavoring added.

■ **Semisweet chocolate.** Semisweet chocolate is pure chocolate with cocoa butter and sugar added to it.

■ **Sweet baking chocolate.** Sweet baking chocolate is similar to semisweet chocolate but has a higher sugar content.

■ **Milk chocolate.** Milk chocolate is made of pure chocolate, extra cocoa butter, sugar, and milk solids. Milk chocolate is used mostly for candy bars and other confections. You won't see it called for in too many recipes.

■ **White baking bars.** White baking bars and pieces are often referred to as "white chocolate." But white chocolate isn't really chocolate at all because it lacks pure chocolate (and therefore can't be labeled chocolate in the United States). These products are a blend of sugar, cocoa butter, dry milk solids, and vanilla or vanillin.

■ **Candy coating.** Candy coating is a chocolatelike product with most of the cocoa butter removed and replaced with vegetable fat. You can find it in assorted colors and flavors.

■ **Mexican chocolate.** From our neighbors south of the border comes Mexican-style sweet chocolate. This chocolate starts with roasted cocoa beans ground together with cinnamon and sugar. Ground almonds may also be added. You'll find it in Mexican markets.

■ **Unsweetened cocoa powder.** Unsweetened cocoa powder is made by pressing most of the cocoa butter from pure chocolate, then grinding the remaining chocolate solids into a powder. Dutch-process cocoa powder, also called European-style cocoa powder, is unsweetened cocoa powder that has been treated with alkali to neutralize the naturally occurring acids; its flavor is more mellow and the color redder than unsweetened cocoa powder. These two cocoa powders can be used interchangeably.

■ **Storing chocolate.** Keep your chocolate in a tightly covered container or sealed plastic bag in a cool, dry place. If stored in a too-warm place (higher than 78 degrees), your chocolate may "bloom" or develop a harmless gray film. Keep cocoa powder in a tightly covered container in that same cool, dry place.

■ **Melting chocolate.** Place cut-up chocolate or chocolate pieces in a heavy saucepan. Melt over low heat, stirring often to avoid scorching. When it's necessary that the chocolate set up when it cools, such as when dipping fruits or making chocolate garnishes, before heating, add 1 teaspoon shortening for each ½ cup (3 ounces) of chocolate.

■ **Microwave method:** To melt chocolate in your microwave oven, place ½ cup of pieces or 3 ounces cut-up chocolate in a microwave-safe measuring cup or custard cup. Microwave, uncovered, on high for 60 to 90 seconds or until softened enough to stir smooth, stirring after 1 minute. (Chocolate won't seem melted until stirred.)

■ **Quick-tempering chocolate.** Tempering chocolate is a method of slowly melting chocolate followed by carefully cooling it. This procedure stabilizes the cocoa butter so the chocolate holds its shape. Since tempering chocolate is a lengthy process, we use a method of melting chocolate that produces the same results in less time. We call this method "quick-tempering." Quick-temper chocolate when you will be using it for decorations that must hold their shape at room temperature, such as chocolate leaves or chocolate lace (see photos and instructions on page 17) or when dipping dried fruit or nuts. Follow these step-by-step directions for quick-tempering, and your chocolate will set up crisp and glossy every time.

Step 1: Chop up to 1 pound of bars, squares, or large pieces of chocolate into small pieces. In a 4-cup glass measure or a 1½-quart glass mixing bowl, combine the amount of chocolate and shortening called for in the recipe. (Or, use 1 tablespoon of shortening for every 6 ounces of chocolate.)

Step 2: Pour very warm tap water (100° to 110°) into a large glass casserole or bowl to a depth of 1 inch. Place the measure or

CHOCOLATE GARNISHES

Sweet, seductive, and smooth—chocolate makes the ultimate garnish. Here's everything you need to know to craft simple trims as well as stunning chocolate ornaments.

■ **Grated:** Rub a solid piece of chocolate across the grating section—either fine or large—of a handheld grater.

■ **Shaved:** Using a vegetable peeler, make short, quick strokes across the surface of a solid piece of chocolate.

■ **Lace:** Pipe tempered chocolate from a pastry bag onto a chilled, waxed-paper-lined baking sheet; let dry.

■ **Small curls**: Draw a peeler across the narrow side of a chocolate bar (milk chocolate may be easier for small curls).

■ **Leaves**: Brush tempered chocolate on the underside of nontoxic leaves such as mint, rose, lemon, and strawberry.

■ **Large curls:** Carefully draw a vegetable peeler across the broad surface of a bar of chocolate.

bowl containing the chocolate inside the casserole. Water should cover the bottom half of the measure or bowl containing the chocolate. Adjust the water level as necessary. (Do not splash any water into the chocolate.)

Step 3: Stir the chocolate mixture constantly with a rubber spatula until completely melted and smooth. This takes about 15 to 20 minutes. (Don't rush.)

Step 4: If the water begins to cool, remove the measure or bowl containing the chocolate.

Discard the cool water and add warm water. Return the measure or bowl containing the chocolate to the bowl containing water.

Step 5: Do not allow any water or moisture to touch the chocolate. Just one drop can cause the chocolate to become thick and grainy. If water should get into the chocolate, stir in additional shortening, 1 teaspoon at a time, until the mixture becomes shiny and smooth.

Step 6: When melted and smooth, the chocolate is ready

for dipping or shaping. If the chocolate becomes too thick during handling, repeat Step 4. Stir the chocolate constantly until it again reaches dipping consistency.

Step 7: Let your finished product set up in a cool, dry place. Do not chill your finished product, or the chocolate will lose temper and become soft at room temperature.

DECORATING

Decorations and garnishes turn a simply delicious dessert into a work of art. Here's how to create some classic embellishments.

■ **Piping.** With a pastry bag fitted with a variety of tips and a little practice, you have almost unlimited options for making beautiful designs on your desserts with whipped cream or frosting. A round tip is used for writing and making dots and lines (a). A star tip can be used to make stars, shells, and zigzags (b). Leaf tips are great for making leaves of all shapes and sizes (c).

■ **Two-Tone piping.** Fill your decorating bag with two different colors of frosting or whipped cream to pipe marbled decorations or decorations with tinted edges. For these, use a decorating bag fitted with a

medium or large star tip (about ¼- to ½-inch opening). To make marbled stars, shells, or zigzags, carefully fill each side of the bag with a different color frosting or whipped cream (see photo above, top row). To give tinted edges to stars, shells, or zigzags, use a long metal spatula to spread a thin layer of one color frosting or whipped cream onto the inside of the entire decorating bag. Carefully spoon another color frosting or cream into the bag (see photo above, bottom row).

■ **Edible flowers.** Top almost any dessert with naturally colorful, edible flowers. Scatter small flowers over cakes or tortes, or break off some petals and sprinkle them over desserts.

Choose any edible flower to decorate your dessert. If you plan to eat the flower, select one with a flavor that is compatible with sweets. Some good choices are pansies, violets, rose petals, and dianthus.

Be sure to use only edible flowers around food even if you don't plan to eat them. To be edible, the flower must be free of both naturally occurring and man-made toxins. To find edible flowers, look no farther than your own garden, provided that neither you nor your neighbors use chemical fertilizers or pesticides. Pick the flowers just before using, rinse, and gently

pat dry. Or, look for edible flowers in the produce section of your supermarket. Flowers that come from a florist are usually treated with chemicals and should never be used with food.

■ **Dusting.** Dusting is one of the easiest decorating techniques to master. You can dust over cakes, tortes, cheesecakes, cookies, and even puddings. For toppings, try ground nuts, unsweetened cocoa powder, ground spices, coarse-grain or crystal sugar, extra-fine-grain sugar, cinnamon-sugar, powdered sugar, or powdered sugar mixed with spices, unsweetened cocoa powder, or powdered food coloring. Sift the topping through a sieve or sifter onto the top of the dessert. When selecting the utensil to use, consider the fineness of your topping. A sifter works well for powdered sugar or unsweetened cocoa powder. Ground nuts will require a sieve with a coarser mesh.

To dust a dessert top, spoon the topping of your choice into a sieve or sifter. Hold the utensil over the dessert. With your free hand, gently tap the utensil so a little of the topping comes out. Dust lightly, moving the sieve over the dessert to cover the whole surface. For a heavier coating, dust again.

■ **Stenciling.** Personalize your dessert by stenciling a unique design. It works best on cakes, tortes, and pastries with flat surfaces.

For a stencil, use a purchased doily or a purchased stencil, or make your own stencil from lightweight cardboard. A doily can be cut into small pieces to use part of the design.

To make your own stencil, draw a design on a piece of cardboard (a gift box or a manila folder works well). Then use a crafts knife to cut out the design.

Place the stencil on top of the dessert surface. Sift the desired topping over the stencil, as directed for Dusting (see page 18 and photo below). If your stencil has large designs, use a

clean, dry brush to brush any topping left on the stencil into the holes. This keeps the edges of your design sharp and clean. Carefully lift off the stencil. If you like, brush any remaining topping off your stencil and save the stencil to use another time.

To stencil a design on a plate, choose a stencil with large holes. Place the stencil on the plate and lightly brush melted butter or shortening in the holes (or spray the holes with nonstick spray coating). Sprinkle the desired topping over the stencil as directed for Dusting. Carefully lift off the stencil.

■ **Marzipan.** Marzipan, a creamy almond confection, can be formed into a variety of fanciful shapes and decorations. Marzipan can be found in your

grocery store or a gourmet or specialty store. To tint marzipan, break off a small portion and knead in a little liquid or paste food coloring. Add a tiny bit of food coloring at a time until the marzipan becomes a shade you like. Shape the tinted marzipan into tiny fruits; paint (see Painting, below) or roll out and cut with small cookie cutters into hearts, stars, or other shapes.

■ **Painting.** Paint a colorful design on desserts, such as cookies, pastries, and frosted cakes. For paint, use powdered food coloring or petal dust. (Petal dust is a fine dusting powder that is available in many colors, including gold and silver. Use gold and silver petal dust to give a shimmery, glistening highlight to foods. Petal dust is available through mail-order sources or specialty stores.) You can use powdered food coloring or petal dust either diluted with a little alcohol or in its dry form. If you want a smooth finish, mix a little powdered food coloring or petal dust with a few drops of 90- or 100-proof alcohol. (Do not use rubbing alcohol.) The alcohol will evaporate quickly, so you may need to add a few more drops of alcohol to the coloring while painting. With a clean, small paintbrush, paint designs on your desserts. To give soft highlights to decorations made from marzipan, paint with the dry powdered coloring or petal dust. Use a dry, clean, small paintbrush to brush the coloring on the decoration. You may want to try brushing the powdered coloring or petal dust along the edges of the decorations.

CANDIED FLOWERS

With a luster all their own, candied flowers create a glistening garnish. To make candied flowers, gently wash fresh edible flowers in water. Place them on white paper towels and let them air-dry or gently blot them dry. For large flowers or flowers with petals that are closed tightly, break off the petals and candy the individual petals.

In a small bowl stir together 2 tablespoons water and 1 tablespoon thawed frozen egg substitute. Using a small, clean paintbrush, brush the egg mixture on each side of each petal in a thin, even layer. Sprinkle each flower evenly with superfine-grain sugar. To give the flowers a hint of gold color, mix $\frac{1}{8}$ teaspoon gold petal dust with the sugar before sprinkling it over the flowers. Shake each flower or petal to remove the excess sugar. Let the flowers dry on waxed paper for 2 to 4 hours.

Store candied flowers in an airtight container between layers of waxed paper for up to 4 weeks. For longer storage, freeze the candied flowers in the airtight container for up to 6 months.

BAKING GLOSSARY

■ **Almond paste.** A creamy mixture made of ground blanched almonds and sugar. For the best baking results, use an almond paste without syrup or liquid glucose. Almond paste is used as a filling in pastries, cakes, and confections.

■ **Baker's ammonia.** A compound also known as hartshorn powder that was once used commonly as a leavening agent. It's most often used in Scandinavian baking and is available at pharmacies.

■ **Baking dish.** A coverless glass or ceramic vessel used for cooking in the oven. A baking dish can be substituted for a metal baking pan of the same size. For baked items, such as cakes, the oven temperature will need to be lowered 25 degrees to prevent overbrowning of the food.

■ **Baking pan.** A coverless metal vessel used for cooking in the oven. Baking pans vary in size and may be round, square, rectangular, or a special shape, such as a heart. The sides of the pan are ¾ inch high or more.

■ **Baking stone.** A heavy, thick plate of beige or brown stone that can be placed in the oven. Baking stones can be round or rectangular and can be left in the oven when not in use.

■ **Batter.** A mixture usually made with flour and a liquid, such as milk or fruit juice. It also may include egg, sugar, butter, shortening, cooking oil, leavening, or flavorings. Batters can vary in consistency from thin enough to pour to thick enough to drop from a spoon.

■ **Beat.** To make a mixture smooth by briskly whipping or stirring it with a spoon, fork, wire whisk, rotary beater, or electric mixer.

■ **Blend.** To combine two or more ingredients until smooth and uniform in texture, flavor, and color; done by hand or with an electric blender or mixer.

■ **Boil.** To cook food in liquid at a temperature that causes bubbles to form in the liquid and rise in a steady pattern, breaking on the surface. A rolling boil is when liquid is boiling so vigorously the bubbles can't be stirred down.

■ **Caramelize.** To heat and stir sugar until it melts and browns. Caramelized, or burnt, sugar is used in dessert recipes such as flan, candy-coated nuts, and burnt sugar cake and frosting.

■ **Chill.** To cool a food to below room temperature in the refrigerator or freezer, or over ice.

■ **Chop.** To cut foods with a knife, cleaver, or food processor into smaller pieces.

■ **Coconut.** The large, oval, husk-covered fruit of the coconut palm. Its market forms include canned and packaged coconut that is processed and sold shredded, flaked, and grated in sweetened and unsweetened forms. Flaked coconut is finer than shredded. Fresh and dried coconut pieces also are available.

■ **Cream.** To beat a fat, such as butter or shortening, either alone or with sugar to a light, fluffy consistency. This process incorporates air into the fat so baked products have a lighter texture and better volume.

■ **Créme fraîche.** A dairy product made from whipping cream and a bacterial culture. The culture causes the whipping cream to thicken and develop a sharp, tangy flavor. Créme fraîche is similar to sour cream but is softer and has a milder flavor. Popular in French cooking, créme fraîche is often spooned over fresh fruit or used in recipes as you would sour cream. It is available at specialty food stores. If you can't find it in your area, you can make a substitute by combining ½ cup whipping cream and ½ cup dairy sour cream. Cover the mixture and let it stand at room temperature for 2 to 5 hours or until it thickens. Refrigerate for up to 1 week.

■ **Crimp.** To pinch or press pastry dough together using your fingers, or a fork or another utensil. Usually done for a piecrust edge.

■ **Cut in.** To work a solid fat, such as shortening or butter, into dry ingredients, usually with a pastry blender or two knives.

■ **Dash.** A measure equal to ¹⁄₁₆ teaspoon. Can be measured by filling a ¼-teaspoon measure one-fourth full.

■ **Devonshire cream.** A specialty of Devonshire, England, this extra-thick cream is made by heating whole, unpasteurized milk until a semisolid layer of cream forms on the surface. After cooling, the Devonshire, or clotted, cream traditionally is served atop scones with jam (see recipe, page 192 steps 1–3).

■ **Dissolve.** To stir a solid food and a liquid food together to form a mixture in which none of the solid remains.

■ **Dough.** A mixture of flour and liquid to which other ingredients, such as sweeteners, shortening, butter, egg, or a leavening agent, may be added. A dough is thick and nonpourable; some doughs can be kneaded. Soft doughs have more liquid and generally are used for biscuits, breads, and drop cookies. Stiff doughs are firm enough to be rolled out easily and are used to make items such as piecrusts and cutout cookies.

■ **Dried egg whites.** Dried egg whites can be used where egg white is needed, but not meringue powder, which has added sugar. Dried egg whites also are safer than raw egg whites. One handy use for them is in making egg white glazes for baked goods (no yolk is wasted). Dried egg whites are found in powdered form in the baking aisle of many grocery stores.

■ **Dried fruit.** Fruit that has been depleted of more than half its water content by exposure to the sun or by mechanical heating methods. Dried fruit is chewy and very sweet due to the concentration of sugars during the drying process.

■ **Drizzle.** To randomly pour a liquid, such as powdered sugar icing, in a thin stream over food.

■ **Dust.** To lightly coat or sprinkle a food with a dry ingredient, such as flour or powdered sugar, either before or after cooking.

■ **Extract and oil.** Products based on the aromatic essential oils of plant materials that are distilled by various means. In extracts, the highly concentrated oils usually are suspended in alcohol to make them easier to combine with other foods in cooking and baking. Almond, anise, lemon, mint, orange, peppermint, and vanilla are some of the extracts sold.

■ **Flavoring.** An imitation extract made of chemical compounds. Unlike an extract or oil, a flavoring often does not contain any of the original food it resembles. Some common imitation flavorings available are banana, black walnut, brandy, cherry, chocolate, coconut, maple, pineapple, raspberry, rum, strawberry, and vanilla.

■ **Flute.** To make a scalloped, decorative pattern or impression in food, usually a piecrust.

■ **Fold.** A method of gently mixing ingredients—usually delicate or whipped ingredients that cannot withstand stirring or beating. To fold, use a rubber spatula to cut down through the mixture, move across the bottom of the bowl, and come back up, folding some of the mixture from the bottom over close to the surface.

■ **Food coloring.** Either liquid, paste, or powdered edible dyes used to tint foods.

■ **Frost.** To apply a sweet cooked or uncooked topping to cakes, cupcakes, or cookies that is soft enough to spread but stiff enough to hold its shape.

■ **Ganache.** A rich chocolate icing made of bittersweet chocolate and whipping cream heated and stirred together until the chocolate melts. The mixture is cooled until lukewarm and poured over a cake or torte for a satiny, glossy finish.

■ **Garnish.** To add visual appeal to a finished dish by decorating it with small pieces of food or edible flowers. The term also refers to the items used for decoration.

■ **Ginger.** A semitropical plant whose root is used as a pungent spice. Ginger has a slightly hot flavor and nippy aroma. Ginger comes fresh as gingerroot, powdered, and in candied or crystallized form.

■ **Glaze.** A thin, glossy coating on a food. There are numerous types of glazes. A mixture of powdered sugar and milk can be drizzled on cookies, cakes, or breads for a glaze.

■ **Gluten.** An elastic protein present in flour, especially wheat flour, that provides most of the structure of baked products.

■ **Grate.** To rub food—especially hard cheeses, vegetables, and whole nutmeg and ginger— across a grating surface to make very fine pieces. A food processor may also be used.

■ **Grease.** To coat a utensil, such as a baking pan or skillet, with a thin layer of fat or oil.

■ **Grind.** To mechanically cut a food into small pieces, usually with a food grinder or a food processor.

■ **Ice.** To drizzle or spread baked goods with a thin frosting.

■ **Juice.** To extract the natural liquid contained in fruits and vegetables. This can be done with a juicer or—in the case of citrus fruits—simply by squeezing wedges of fruit over a measuring cup to catch the juice.

■ **Knead.** To work dough with the heels of your hands in a pressing and folding motion until it becomes smooth and elastic; an essential step in developing the gluten in many yeast breads.

■ **Marble.** To gently swirl one food into another; usually done with light and dark batters for cakes or cookies.

■ **Mascarpone cheese.** A very rich cream cheese made primarily of cream. Mascarpone cheese most often is used in Italian desserts. Cream cheese may be substituted for mascarpone.

■ **Mash.** To press or beat a food to remove lumps and make a smooth mixture. This can be done with a fork, potato masher, food mill, food ricer, or an electric mixer.

■ **Meringue.** Sweetened, stiffly beaten egg whites used for desserts. There are two basic types of meringues. Soft meringues are moist and tender and are used for topping pies and other desserts. Hard meringues are sweeter than soft meringues and are baked to form crisp, dry dessert shells or cookies, such as macaroons. Meringue shells often are filled with fresh fruit or puddings.

■ **Peel.** The skin or outer covering of a vegetable or fruit; also called the rind. Also refers to removing the covering.

■ **Pipe.** To force a semisoft food, such as whipped cream, frosting, or mashed potatoes, through a bag to decorate a food.

■ **Plump.** To allow a food, such as raisins or dried cherries, to soak in a liquid.

■ **Proof.** To allow a yeast dough to rise before baking. Also a term that indicates the amount of alcohol in a distilled liquor.

■ **Puree.** To change a solid food into a liquid or heavy paste, usually by using a food processor, blender, or food mill. Also refers to the resulting mixture.

■ **Ricotta.** A fresh, moist, white cheese that is very mild and semisweet. It has a soft, slightly grainy texture. It is available in whole milk, part-skim milk, or fat-free varieties, with the whole milk cheese having a creamier consistency and fuller flavor than the part-skim types.

■ **Roll.** To form a food into a shape. Dough, for instance, can be rolled into ropes or balls. The phrase "roll out" refers to mechanically flattening a food—usually a dough or pastry—with a rolling pin.

■ **Scald.** To heat a liquid, often milk, to a temperature below the boiling point, when tiny bubbles begin to appear around the edge of the liquid.

■ **Section.** A pulpy segment of citrus fruit with the membrane removed. The phrase also refers to the process of removing those segments (see "Sectioning Citrus Fruits" tip on page 15).

■ **Shred.** To push food across a fine or coarse shredding surface to make long, narrow strips. A food processor may be used.

■ **Sift.** To put one or more dry ingredients, especially flour or powdered sugar, through a sifter or sieve to remove lumps and incorporate air.

■ **Simmer.** To cook a food in liquid that is kept below the boiling point; a few bubbles will form slowly and burst before they reach the surface.

■ **Snip.** To cut food, often fresh herbs or dried fruit, with kitchen scissors into very small, uniform pieces, using short, quick strokes.

■ **Sponge.** A batterlike mixture of yeast, flour, and liquid used in some bread recipes. The mixture is set aside until it bubbles and becomes foamy, which can be several hours or overnight. During this time, the sponge develops a tangy flavor; the remaining ingredients are added to the sponge, and the dough is kneaded and baked as usual.

■ **Steam.** To cook a food in the vapor given off by boiling water.

■ **Vanilla bean.** The pod of an orchid plant that is dried and cured. During curing, the pod turns a dark chocolate color and shrivels to the size of a pencil.

■ **Weeping.** A condition in which liquid separates out of a solid food, such as jellies, custards, and meringues.

■ **Whip.** To beat a food lightly and rapidly using a wire whisk, rotary beater, or electric mixer to incorporate air into the mixture and increase its volume.

■ **Whisk.** A kitchen utensil made of a group of looped wires held together by a long handle. Whisks are used in baking for whipping ingredients such as eggs and cream to incorporate air into them.

■ **Zest.** The colored outer portion of a citrus fruit peel. It is rich in fruit oils and often used as a seasoning. To remove the zest, use a grater, a fruit zester, or a vegetable peeler; be careful to avoid the bitter white membrane beneath the peel.

old-fashioned
desserts

Peach Cobbler with Cinnamon-Swirl Biscuits,
recipe page 29

OLD-FASHIONED DESSERTS

BRANDIED APRICOT-PEAR DUMPLINGS

BEST-LOVED

Prep: 1 hour Bake: 40 minutes
Makes: 4 servings Oven: 400°F

　2 **tablespoons snipped dried apricots**
　2 **tablespoons cream cheese**
　4 **small pears (about 4 to 5 ounces each)**
　1 **recipe Single-Crust Pastry (see recipe, page 45) or ½ of a 15-ounce package folded refrigerated unbaked piecrust (1 crust)**
　4 **whole cloves (optional)**
　1 **slightly beaten egg white**
　1 **tablespoon water**
　1 **tablespoon sugar**
1¼ **cups pear or apricot nectar**
　¼ **cup dark-colored corn syrup**
　¼ **cup apricot brandy, brandy, or pear or apricot nectar**

1 **For filling,** in a small bowl combine apricots and cream cheese. Peel and core pears. Spoon some filling into the center of each pear.

2 **On a lightly floured surface flatten** pastry dough. (Or, unwrap refrigerated crust according to package directions.) Roll dough into a 13-inch circle. Trim to form a 12-inch square (leave trim pieces uncut). Using a fluted pastry wheel or long sharp knife, cut dough into twelve 12×¾-inch strips. Pat pears with paper towels.

3 **Using 1 of the pastry strips** and starting ½ inch above the base of a pear (do not cover bottom of pear), wrap pastry strip around pear. Moisten end of strip; seal to the end of a second pastry strip and continue wrapping. Seal to the end of a third pastry strip; finish wrapping pear, covering hole and filling. Moisten end to seal. Press gently, if necessary, to shape pastry around pear. Repeat for each pear.

4 **Cut leaf shapes** (similar to diamonds) from remaining pastry using a knife; mark veins on leaves. Attach leaves to tops of pears, moistening as necessary to attach. Top pears with whole cloves for stems. In a small bowl beat together egg white and water; brush onto pastry. Sprinkle with sugar.

5 **Using a wide spatula,** transfer pears to an ungreased 2-quart square baking dish. Stir together pear nectar, corn syrup, and brandy; pour around pears in dish. Bake, uncovered, in a 400°F oven for 40 to 45 minutes or until golden. Serve dumplings and sauce while warm.

Nutrition Facts per serving: 553 cal., 20 g total fat (6 g sat. fat), 8 mg chol., 187 mg sodium, 84 g carbo., 4 g fiber, 6 g pro. **Daily Values:** 6% vit. A, 9% vit. C, 3% calcium, 21% iron

Brandied Apricot-Pear Dumplings: Dress apricot-cream-stuffed pears in pastry wraps and bake until golden in a brandy-pear nectar sauce. This soul-soothing dessert is as impressive tasting as it looks.

PICKING FRUITS FOR BAKING

Q What kinds of apples and pears are best for baking?

A The best varieties for baking and filling are those that hold their shape and retain their flavor when baked. Apple varieties that work well for baking include Cortland, Golden Delicious, Granny Smith, Jonathan, McIntosh, Newtown Pippin, Rome Beauty, and Winesap. In the pear department, try Anjou, Bartlett, and Bosc, though most pear varieties work fine. Keep in mind that firmer pears hold their shape better than soft, very ripe ones, as do whole pears and apples left unpeeled or just partially peeled.

BEST-EVER BAKED APPLES

LOW-FAT

Prep: 15 minutes   Bake: 45 minutes
Makes: 4 servings   Oven: 350°F

To keep the apples from turning brown while you work, brush cut areas with lemon juice.

> 1 recipe desired filling: choose from Dried Fruit, Ginger-Almond, Orange-Macaroon, Peanut Butter, and Apple-Walnut (right)
> 4 large baking apples (7 ounces each)
> ⅓ cup apple juice, apple cider, or sweet white wine
> Sweetened whipped cream, vanilla yogurt, light cream, or frozen vanilla yogurt (optional)
> Ground nutmeg (optional)

1 Prepare desired filling; set aside. To core apples, use an apple corer or the rounded tip of a vegetable peeler. Push corer or peeler most of the way through the apple center, but do not cut through the other end; turn corer or peeler to loosen the upper part of the core. Remove and discard core. Enlarge hole slightly at top of the apple for filling.

2 Using a vegetable peeler or paring knife, remove the peel from the top half of each apple. If desired, use tines of a fork to score peeled apple.

3 Place apples in an ungreased 2-quart square baking dish. Spoon filling into center of each apple. Add apple juice to dish. Bake, covered, in a 350°F oven about 45 minutes or until fork-tender. Transfer apples to dessert dishes; spoon liquid in dish over apples. Sprinkle with nutmeg.

Nutrition Facts per serving (with Dried Fruit Filling):
215 cal., 1 g total fat (0 g sat. fat), 0 mg chol.,
8 mg sodium, 56 g carbo., 6 g fiber, 1 g pro.
Daily Values: 0% vit. A, 16% vit. C, 2% calcium, 7% iron

Dried Fruit Filling: Combine ⅔ cup raisins, currants, or mixed dried fruit bits; 2 tablespoons brown sugar; and ½ teaspoon ground cinnamon.

Ginger-Almond Filling: Stir together ¼ cup slivered almonds, 2 tablespoons apricot preserves, and 1 tablespoon chopped crystallized ginger.

Orange-Macaroon Filling: Toss ⅔ cup crumbled soft coconut macaroon cookies with 2 tablespoons orange marmalade.

Peanut Butter Filling: Stir together ⅓ cup coconut with ⅓ cup chunky peanut butter.

Apple-Walnut Filling: Stir together ⅓ cup apple butter with ¼ cup chopped walnuts.

Best-Ever Baked Apples:
Savor America's favorite fruit in one of America's most cherished recipes—baked apples. With this versatile recipe, choose a new filling every time you make it.

APPLE-CHERRY PANDOWDY

Prep: 30 minutes **Bake:** 50 minutes
Makes: 6 servings **Oven:** 350°F

Tart cherries add color and flavor to this traditional apple deep-dish dessert.

>   4 cups sliced, peeled cooking apples
> 1½ cups fresh or frozen unsweetened
>   pitted tart red cherries, thawed
>   ¾ cup sugar
>   3 tablespoons all-purpose flour
>   ¼ teaspoon ground nutmeg
>   Dash ground cloves
>   1 cup all-purpose flour
>   ¼ teaspoon salt
>   ¼ cup butter
>   1 egg yolk
>   3 tablespoons cold water
>   Whipped cream or vanilla ice
>   cream (optional)

1 For filling, in a mixing bowl combine apples, cherries, sugar, the 3 tablespoons flour, nutmeg, and cloves. Transfer fruit filling to an ungreased 2-quart rectangular baking dish.

2 For crust, in a medium bowl stir together the 1 cup flour and the salt. With a pastry blender, cut in the butter just until mixture resembles coarse crumbs; make a well in the center. Beat together egg yolk and cold water. Add to flour mixture all at once. Using a fork, stir just until the dough forms a ball.

3 On a lightly floured surface roll dough into a 12×8-inch rectangle; place on fruit filling in baking dish. Fold under edge of crust to fit dish; crimp to sides of dish. Cut a 3-inch slit in crust to allow steam to escape.

4 Bake in a 350°F oven about 50 minutes or until golden. Use a sharp knife to cut a lattice pattern in the crust. Cool on a wire rack for 30 minutes. If desired, serve with whipped cream or ice cream.

Nutrition Facts per serving: 323 cal., 9 g total fat (5 g sat. fat), 56 mg chol., 169 mg sodium, 59 g carbo., 2 g fiber, 3 g pro. **Daily Values:** 16% vit. A, 6% vit. C, 1% calcium, 9% iron

CHERRY-BLUEBERRY COBBLER SUPREME

Prep: 20 minutes **Bake:** 40 minutes
Makes: 12 servings **Oven:** 350°F

The batter starts out on the bottom and ends up on top of this unique cobbler.

>   2 cups fresh or frozen unsweetened
>   pitted tart red cherries
>   1 cup fresh or frozen unsweetened
>   blueberries
>   Cherry juice or water (about 2 cups)
>   1 cup all-purpose flour
>   1 cup whole wheat flour
>   2 teaspoons baking powder
>   ¼ teaspoon salt
>   ½ cup butter, softened
>   1 cup granulated sugar
>   ¾ cup milk
>   ½ to ¾ cup granulated sugar
>   Powdered sugar (optional)
>   Ice cream or light cream (optional)

1 Thaw fruit, if frozen; drain, reserving juice. Add enough cherry juice or water to fruit liquid to equal 2 cups. If using fresh fruit, measure 2 cups cherry juice or water. Set aside. Grease a 3-quart oval baking dish or 13×9×2-inch baking pan; set aside.

2 In a medium bowl combine flours, baking powder, and salt; set aside. In a large mixing bowl beat butter and the 1 cup sugar with an electric mixer until fluffy; add flour mixture alternately with milk. Beat until smooth. Spread batter evenly over the bottom of prepared dish or pan.

3 Sprinkle batter with cherries and blueberries. Sprinkle with remaining ½ to ¾ cup sugar, depending on sweetness of fruit. Pour the 2 cups of fruit juice or water mixture over fruit.

4 Bake in a 350°F oven for 40 to 45 minutes or until a wooden toothpick inserted in cake comes out clean. (Some of the fruit should sink toward bottom as the cake rises to top.) Cool about 45 minutes. If desired, sprinkle lightly with sifted powdered sugar; serve warm with ice cream.

Nutrition Facts per serving: 280 cal., 9 g total fat (5 g sat. fat), 22 mg chol., 195 mg sodium, 50 g carbo., 2 g fiber, 4 g pro. **Daily Values:** 11% vit. A, 8% vit. C, 8% calcium, 7% iron

WHAT'S IN A NAME?

Cobbler: A distant cousin of the deep-dish pie, cobbler gets its name from its biscuit topping, which resembles cobblestones. For a traditional cobbler, be sure the fruit filling is very hot when you drop the biscuit dough on it or the bottom of the topping might not cook properly.

Betty: Betties are topped with soft bread cubes, rather than dry cubes as in bread pudding. The bread is easier to cut if it's frozen; use a serrated knife and a sawing motion to cut the bread into ½-inch cubes.

Crisp: Crisps are topped with a crunchy oatmeal mixture. The topping stores well, so try mixing a double batch and put the extra batch in a freezer bag, seal, label, and freeze it for up to a month.

Pandowdy: A funny name for a delicious dish, this baked apple or fruit dessert has a pastrylike biscuit topping and is usually served with light cream or a sauce. Traditionally, the topping is broken up with a spoon and stirred into the fruit filling (the "dowdying" of the dish) before it is served.

PEACH COBBLER WITH CINNAMON-SWIRL BISCUITS

Prep: 30 minutes   Bake: 25 minutes
Makes: 6 servings   Oven: 375°F

Many cobbler recipes have a drop biscuit topping, but this one has biscuit slices filled with a nut-and-spice mixture (see photo, page 23).

     1 cup all-purpose flour
     1 tablespoon brown sugar
  1½ teaspoons baking powder
    ⅛ teaspoon baking soda
    ¼ teaspoon salt
    ¼ cup butter
    ⅓ cup milk
    ½ cup finely chopped walnuts
     3 tablespoons brown sugar
    ¼ teaspoon ground cinnamon
     1 tablespoon butter, melted
    ⅔ cup packed brown sugar
     4 teaspoons cornstarch
    ½ teaspoon finely shredded
        lemon peel
     6 cups sliced, peeled peaches or
        6 cups frozen unsweetened
        peach slices

1 **For biscuits,** in a medium bowl stir together flour, the 1 tablespoon brown sugar, the baking powder, baking soda, and ¼ teaspoon salt. With a pastry blender, cut in the ¼ cup butter until the mixture resembles coarse crumbs; make a well in the center. Add milk all at once. Using a fork, stir just until dough forms a ball.

2 **On a lightly floured surface knead** dough gently for 10 to 12 strokes. Roll or pat dough into a 12×6-inch rectangle. Combine walnuts, the 3 tablespoons brown sugar, and the cinnamon; brush dough with the melted butter and sprinkle with nut mixture. Roll into a spiral, starting from one of the short sides. Seal edge. Use a sharp knife to cut into six 1-inch slices; set aside.

3 **For peach filling,** in a large saucepan stir together the ⅔ cup brown sugar, the cornstarch, and lemon peel. Add peaches and ⅔ cup water. Cook and stir until bubbly. Carefully pour hot filling into an ungreased 2-quart rectangular baking dish. Arrange biscuit slices, cut side down, on hot filling. Bake in a 375°F oven about 25 minutes or until biscuit slices are golden.

Nutrition Facts per serving: 436 cal., 17 g total fat (3 g sat. fat), 13 mg chol., 315 mg sodium, 71 g carbo., 4 g fiber, 5 g pro. Daily Values: 19% vit. A, 19% vit. C, 12% calcium, 14% iron

Apple Cobbler: Substitute 6 cups sliced, peeled cooking apples for the peaches and add 1 teaspoon apple pie spice to the fruit filling.

Rhubarb Cobbler: Substitute 6 cups sliced rhubarb

BLACKBERRY COBBLER

Prep: 25 minutes   Bake: 20 minutes
Makes: 8 servings   Oven: 400°F

1½ cups all-purpose flour
 ¼ cup granulated sugar
 2 teaspoons baking powder
 ¼ teaspoon salt
 ¼ teaspoon ground cinnamon
 ⅛ teaspoon ground nutmeg
 ⅓ cup shortening
 ¾ cup packed brown sugar or
      granulated sugar
 4 teaspoons cornstarch
 5 cups fresh or frozen unsweetened
      blackberries
 ¾ cup water
 2 teaspoons finely shredded orange
      peel (optional)
 ½ teaspoon vanilla
 1 egg
 ½ cup milk
      Coarse sugar or granulated sugar
      Whipped cream or vanilla ice
      cream (optional)

1 **For topping,** in a large bowl combine flour, the ¼ cup granulated sugar, the baking powder, salt, cinnamon, and nutmeg. With a pastry blender, cut in shortening until mixture resembles coarse crumbs; make a well in the center. Set aside.

2 **For filling,** in a medium saucepan stir together the brown sugar and cornstarch. Stir in fresh or frozen blackberries, water, and orange peel (if using). Cook and stir until thickened and bubbly. Stir in vanilla. Keep filling hot.

3 **In a small bowl use** a fork to beat egg and milk together. Add egg mixture all at once to the flour mixture; stir just until moistened. Transfer hot filling to an ungreased 2-quart rectangular baking dish. Immediately drop topping into 8 mounds on the hot filling. Sprinkle topping with coarse or granulated sugar.

4 **Bake in a 400°F oven** for 20 to 25 minutes or until a wooden toothpick inserted into topping comes out clean. If desired, serve warm with whipped cream or ice cream.

Nutrition Facts per serving: 317 cal., 10 g total fat (3 g sat. fat), 28 mg chol., 179 mg sodium, 54 g carbo., 6 g fiber, 4 g pro. **Daily Values:** 3% vit. A, 31% vit. C, 12% calcium, 14% iron

STRAWBERRY-RHUBARB BETTY

Prep: 25 minutes   Bake: 25 minutes
Makes: 6 servings   Oven: 375°F

Use the larger measure of sugar with fruit that is extra tart and the smaller amount with fruit that is not quite so tart.

 3 cups sliced fresh or frozen
      unsweetened strawberries
 2 cups thinly sliced fresh or frozen
      unsweetened rhubarb
 ¾ to 1 cup sugar
 2 tablespoons all-purpose flour
 ¼ teaspoon salt
 4 cups soft bread cubes
      (about 5 slices)
 ¼ cup butter, melted

1 **Thaw strawberries and rhubarb,** if frozen. Do not drain. For filling, in a large bowl stir together sugar, flour, and salt. Add strawberries, rhubarb, and their juices; gently toss until coated.

2 **For topping,** place the bread cubes in a medium bowl. Drizzle with the melted butter; toss until mixed. Transfer half the buttered bread cubes to an ungreased 1½-quart casserole. Pour fruit mixture over bread cubes. Sprinkle the remaining bread cubes over the fruit filling.

3 **Bake in a 375°F oven** for 25 to 30 minutes or until fruit is tender and the bread-cube topping is golden. Serve warm.

Nutrition Facts per serving: 256 cal., 9 g total fat (5 g sat. fat), 20 mg chol., 272 mg sodium, 44 g carbo., 3 g fiber, 3 g pro. **Daily Values:** 7% vit. A, 75% vit. C, 6% calcium, 7% iron

Country Pear and Cherry Crisp: The topping stays extra-crunchy, and the best part is that it's a simple combination of granola and melted butter.

COUNTRY PEAR AND CHERRY CRISP

EASY

Prep: 20 minutes   Bake: 30 minutes
Makes: 6 servings   Oven: 375°F

1 16-ounce package frozen
   unsweetened pitted tart red
   cherries, thawed, or one
   16-ounce can pitted tart red
   cherries (water pack)
⅓ to ½ cup sugar
2 tablespoons all-purpose flour
1 teaspoon finely shredded orange
   peel
½ teaspoon ground cinnamon
3 to 4 medium pears (1 pound),
   peeled, cored, and thinly sliced
   (3 cups)
1½ cups granola

2 tablespoons butter, melted
   Vanilla ice cream (optional)

1 **If using canned cherries,** drain cherries, reserving ½ cup juice. In a large bowl combine frozen or canned cherries and reserved juice; add sugar and toss to coat. Let stand for 5 minutes.

2 **In a small bowl combine** flour, peel, and cinnamon; sprinkle over cherries. Toss to mix. Add pears; toss to mix. Transfer to an ungreased 2-quart square baking dish. Combine granola and butter; sprinkle over filling. Bake in a 375°F oven about 30 minutes or until pears are tender. If necessary, to prevent overbrowning, cover with foil the last 5 to 10 minutes. If desired, serve warm with ice cream.

Nutrition Facts per serving: 318 cal., 10 g total fat (4 g sat. fat), 5 mg chol., 94 mg sodium, 58 g carbo., 6 g fiber, 4 g pro. Daily Values: 10% vit. A, 10% vit. C, 3% calcium, 12% iron

---

IN CASE OF LEFTOVERS ...

Baked fruit desserts and bread puddings are good keepers because leftovers can taste nearly fresh baked if they're stored and reheated the right way.

On the slim chance you have any leftover dessert, transfer it to a smaller casserole or ovenproof dish; cover and store in the refrigerator for up to 2 days. (Be sure to refrigerate desserts that contain dairy products, such as bread pudding, right away.) To reheat, simply cover with a casserole lid or foil and bake in a 350°F oven until the dessert is warmed through.

TOOL BOX: COBBLERS AND CRISPS

True to their homey nature, cobblers and crisps bake well in either metal baking pans or casseroles of any kind: glass, pottery, or ceramic baking dishes. Remember these tips:

- Size is more important than shape. Always use the size dish called for in the recipe. The dish needs to be deep enough to allow for the fruit filling to bubble up during baking. It's best to place a baking sheet beneath the dish to catch any spills.
- If the fruit filling is acidic (pineapple, citrus fruits, and cranberries contain acid, for instance), the cobbler or crisp can be baked in a metal pan but shouldn't be stored in one because the acid can react with the metal. However, any leftovers can be stored in a glass baking dish.

A few helpful gadgets to keep on hand when preparing cobblers and crisps include:

- An apple corer for removing the core and seeds from apples and pears.
- A vegetable peeler for removing cores and peeling fruits.
- A pastry blender for easily cutting in cold butter for biscuit toppings and crumbly crisp toppings.

CHOOSE-A-FRUIT CRISP

Prep: 30 minutes   Bake: 30 minutes
Makes: 6 servings   Oven: 375°F

> 5 cups sliced, peeled apples, pears, peaches, or apricots; or frozen unsweetened peach slices
> 2 to 4 tablespoons granulated sugar
> ½ cup regular rolled oats
> ½ cup packed brown sugar
> ¼ cup all-purpose flour
> ¼ teaspoon ground nutmeg, ginger, or cinnamon
> ¼ cup butter
> ¼ cup chopped nuts or coconut
>   Vanilla ice cream or light cream (optional)

1 **For filling,** thaw fruit, if frozen. Do not drain. Place fruit in an ungreased 2-quart square baking dish. Stir in the granulated sugar.

2 **For topping,** in a mixing bowl combine oats; brown sugar; flour; and nutmeg. With a pastry blender, cut in butter until mixture resembles coarse crumbs. Stir in nuts. Sprinkle topping over filling.

3 **Bake in a 375°F oven** for 30 to 35 minutes (40 minutes for thawed fruit) or until fruit is tender and topping is golden. If desired, serve warm with ice cream.

Microwave directions: Prepare filling as at left, making sure you use a microwave-safe baking dish. Microwave filling, covered with vented plastic wrap, on 100% power (high) for 4 to 7 minutes or until fruit is tender, stirring twice. (Additional cooking time may be needed if using thawed fruit.) Prepare topping. Sprinkle over filling. Microwave, uncovered, on high for 2 to 3 minutes or until topping is heated, giving the dish a half-turn once.

Nutrition Facts per serving with apple filling: 275 cal.,
12 g total fat (5 g sat. fat), 20 mg chol.,
83 mg sodium, 43 g carbo., 3 g fiber, 3 g pro.
Daily Values: 7% vit. A, 7% vit. C, 2% calcium, 7% iron

Blueberry Crisp: Prepare as in recipe, except for filling, increase granulated sugar to ¼ cup and combine with 3 tablespoons all-purpose flour. Toss with 5 cups fresh or frozen* unsweetened blueberries.

Cherry Crisp: Prepare as in recipe, except for filling, increase granulated sugar to ½ cup and combine with 3 tablespoons all-purpose flour. Toss the sugar-flour mixture with 5 cups fresh or frozen* unsweetened pitted tart red cherries.

Rhubarb Crisp: Prepare as in recipe, except for filling, increase granulated sugar to ¾ cup and combine with 3 tablespoons all-purpose flour. Toss with 5 cups fresh or frozen* unsweetened sliced rhubarb.

*Note: If fruit is frozen, thaw but do not drain.

HAWAIIAN PINEAPPLE CRISP

Prep: 25 minutes   Bake: 45 minutes
Makes: 6 to 8 servings   Oven: 375°F

⅔ **cup granulated sugar**
1 **tablespoon cornstarch**
1 **teaspoon finely shredded lemon peel**
¾ **teaspoon ground cinnamon**
¼ **teaspoon ground nutmeg**
4 **medium baking apples, peeled, cored, and sliced (4 cups)**
1 **20-ounce can pineapple chunks, drained**
¾ **cup rolled oats**
¼ **cup all-purpose flour**
¼ **cup packed brown sugar**
¼ **cup butter**
¾ **cup chopped macadamia nuts (3.5-ounce jar) or almonds**

1 **In an ungreased 1½-quart casserole** stir together granulated sugar, cornstarch, lemon peel, cinnamon, and nutmeg. Add apples and pineapple; toss to coat.

2 **For topping,** in a medium bowl stir together oats, flour, and brown sugar. With a pastry blender, cut in butter until thoroughly combined (the mixture should be dry). Stir in nuts. Sprinkle nut topping over fruit mixture.

3 **Bake in a 375°F oven** for 30 minutes. Cover the casserole loosely with foil to prevent overbrowning. Bake about 15 minutes more or until apples are tender. Serve warm.

Nutrition Facts per serving: 459 cal., 22 g total fat (4 g sat. fat), 10 mg chol., 120 mg sodium, 69 g carbo., 4 g fiber, 3 g pro. **Daily Values:** 8% vit. A, 21% vit. C, 3% calcium, 9% iron

Hawaiian Pineapple Crisp: Weave a little island dreaming into dessert tonight. This pineapple-macadamia nut crisp, with its tropical flavors, redefines an old-fashioned treat.

Peach and Almond Crisp:
Several years ago this ginger-spiced fruit crisp made its debut in *Better Homes and Gardens*® magazine. It's been a real favorite ever since.

PEACH AND ALMOND CRISP

BEST-LOVED

Prep: 30 minutes   **Bake:** 30 minutes
Makes: 12 servings   **Oven:** 400°F

Select peaches that have a healthy golden yellow skin without tinges of green. The ripe fruit should yield slightly to gentle pressure.

>   8 cups sliced, peeled peaches or
>   nectarines or frozen
>   unsweetened peach slices
> ²/₃ cup packed brown sugar
> ½ cup rolled oats
> ½ cup toasted sliced almonds
> ¾ cup all-purpose flour
>   3 tablespoons granulated sugar
> ½ cup butter
> ⅓ cup granulated sugar
> ½ teaspoon ground cinnamon
> ¼ teaspoon ground nutmeg
> ⅛ teaspoon ground ginger
> ¼ cup peach nectar or orange juice
>   Vanilla ice cream (optional)

1 Thaw frozen peaches, if using. Do not drain. For topping, in a medium bowl stir together brown sugar, oats, almonds, ½ cup of the flour, and the 3 tablespoons granulated sugar. Using a pastry blender, cut in butter until the mixture resembles coarse crumbs.

2 For filling, in a large bowl stir together remaining flour, the ⅓ cup granulated sugar, the cinnamon, nutmeg, and ginger. Add the peach slices with their juices and peach nectar. Toss gently to coat. Transfer filling to an ungreased 3-quart rectangular baking dish. Sprinkle topping over the filling.

3 Bake in a 400°F oven for 30 to 35 minutes or until peach slices are tender and the topping is golden. If desired, serve warm or at room temperature with ice cream.

Nutrition Facts per serving: 258 cal., 11 g total fat (5 g sat. fat), 20 mg chol., 94 mg sodium, 40 g carbo., 3 g fiber, 3 g pro. **Daily Values:** 15% vit. A, 13% vit. C, 2% calcium, 6% iron

WHISKEY-SAUCED BREAD PUDDING

Prep: 30 minutes   **Bake:** 35 minutes
Makes: 8 or 9 servings   **Oven:** 325°F

Cubes of cinnamon-raisin bread sandwiched together with cream cheese give bread pudding a lovable update.

>   6 slices dry cinnamon-raisin bread
> ½ of an 8-ounce tub cream cheese
>   (about ½ cup)
>   4 beaten eggs
>   2 cups milk

⅓ **cup sugar**
1 teaspoon finely shredded lemon
peel (optional)
1 recipe Whiskey Sauce (see below)
or whipped cream

1 Generously spread 3 slices of the dry bread with cream cheese. Top with remaining bread slices. Cut bread "sandwiches" into cubes and place in an ungreased 2-quart square baking dish. In a bowl beat together eggs, milk, sugar, and lemon peel. Pour over bread cubes in dish.

2 Bake in a 325°F oven for 35 to 40 minutes or until center is nearly set. Cool slightly. Serve warm with Whiskey Sauce.

Whiskey Sauce: In a small saucepan melt ¼ cup butter. Stir in ½ cup sugar, 1 beaten egg yolk, and 2 tablespoons water. Cook, stirring constantly, over medium heat for 5 to 6 minutes or until sugar dissolves and mixture boils. Remove from heat. Stir in 1 tablespoon bourbon and 1 tablespoon lemon juice. Serve warm. Makes about ¾ cup.

Nutrition Facts per serving: 316 cal., 16 g total fat (7 g sat. fat), 161 mg chol., 234 mg sodium, 35 g carbo., 0 g fiber, 8 g pro. **Daily Values:** 24% vit. A, 2% vit. C, 9% calcium, 8% iron

ORANGE BREAD PUDDING WITH WARM MAPLE SAUCE *LOW-FAT*

Prep: 30 minutes   Bake: 55 minutes
Makes: 6 servings   Oven: 325°F

So much flavor, so little fat—this bread pudding seemingly has it all.

4 slices white or whole wheat bread
⅓ **cup raisins**
3 eggs
2 egg whites
1¾ **cups milk**
⅓ **cup orange marmalade**
¼ **cup sugar**
½ **teaspoon ground cinnamon**
½ **teaspoon vanilla**

1 recipe Maple Sauce (see below)
Orange slices, halved

1 Cut bread into 2-inch strips; spread strips in an ungreased 14×10×2-inch baking pan. Bake in a 325°F oven for 10 to 15 minutes or until dry, stirring twice. Transfer strips to an ungreased 8×1½-inch round baking pan. Sprinkle with raisins. Set aside.

2 In a medium bowl use a wire whisk, fork, or rotary beater to combine eggs, egg whites, milk, marmalade, sugar, cinnamon, and vanilla. Pour over bread and raisins in pan.

3 Bake in a 325°F oven about 55 minutes or until a knife inserted near the center comes out clean. Cool slightly on a wire rack. Serve warm with warm Maple Sauce and garnish with orange slices.

Maple Sauce: In a small saucepan combine 1 tablespoon cornstarch and ¼ teaspoon finely shredded orange peel. Stir in ¾ cup orange juice and ⅓ cup maple syrup. Cook and stir until thickened and bubbly; cook 2 minutes more. Remove from heat; stir in 1 teaspoon butter. Makes about 1 cup sauce.

Nutrition Facts per serving: 299 cal., 5 g total fat (2 g sat. fat), 113 mg chol., 187 mg sodium, 56 g carbo., 2 g fiber, 9 g pro. **Daily Values:** 10% vit. A, 39% vit. C, 12% calcium, 10% iron

Orange Bread Pudding with Warm Maple Sauce: Bread puddings have a long history, dating to the 1800s, as a common way to use up stale bread. Today we consider it a delicious treat.

LEMON-POPPY SEED STRAWBERRY SHORTCAKE

Prep: 35 minutes Bake: 15 minutes
Makes: 8 to 10 servings Oven: 450°F

   2 **cups all-purpose flour**
   2 **tablespoons granulated sugar**
   2 **tablespoons poppy seed**
   2 **teaspoons baking powder**
  ⅛ **teaspoon salt**
  ½ **cup butter**
  ¾ **cup buttermilk or sour milk**
     (see sour milk tip, page 208)
   1 **teaspoon finely shredded lemon peel**
   6 **cups sliced fresh strawberries**
  ¼ **cup granulated sugar (optional)**
  ⅔ **cup whipping cream**
   8 **ounces mascarpone cheese or one**
     8-ounce tub plain cream cheese
  ⅔ **cup sifted powdered sugar**
   1 **teaspoon finely shredded lemon peel**

1 **For shortcake,** in a medium mixing bowl combine flour, the 2 tablespoons granulated sugar, poppy seed, baking powder, and salt. With a pastry blender, cut in butter until mixture resembles coarse crumbs. Make a well in the center; add buttermilk or sour milk and the 1 teaspoon lemon peel all at once. Stir just until dough clings together.

2 **On a lightly floured surface knead** dough gently for 10 to 12 strokes. Pat dough into an 8-inch circle on an ungreased baking sheet. Bake

in a 450°F oven for 15 to 18 minutes or until golden. Cool on a wire rack for 10 to 15 minutes.

3 **In medium bowl stir** together strawberries and, if desired, ¼ cup granulated sugar; set aside.

4 **In a chilled bowl beat** cream until soft peaks form. Add cheese, powdered sugar, and 1 teaspoon lemon peel; beat until fluffy (mixture will thicken as it is beaten). Split shortcake into 2 layers. Place bottom layer on serving platter. Spoon half of the cheese mixture over bottom layer. Spoon some of the strawberries onto cheese layer. Add top cake layer. Repeat cheese and strawberry layers. Cut into wedges. Pass remaining strawberries. Serve at once.

Nutrition Facts per serving: 502 cal., 34 g total fat (15 g sat. fat), 79 mg chol., 279 mg sodium, 45 g carbo., 3 g fiber, 11 g pro. **Daily Values:** 20% vit. A, 107% vit. C, 14% calcium, 14% iron

---

STRAWBERRY TIPS

Although the peak season for strawberries is March through August, they're generally available in the supermarket year-round. When buying strawberries, select plump, fresh-looking berries with bright green caps, avoiding those that are bruised, wet, or mushy. Store strawberries in the refrigerator, loosely covered. Don't wash or remove the hulls from the fresh berries until you're ready to use them.

PECAN STRAWBERRY SHORTCAKE

BEST-LOVED

Prep: 35 minutes Bake: 10 minutes
Makes: 8 to 10 servings Oven: 450°F

   2 **cups all-purpose flour**
  ½ **cup finely ground pecans**
  ¼ **cup sugar**
   2 **teaspoons baking powder**
  ¼ **teaspoon salt**
  ½ **cup butter**
   1 **beaten egg**
  ⅔ **cup milk**
   1 **tablespoon finely shredded**
     orange peel
   1 **teaspoon vanilla**
   6 **cups sliced fresh strawberries**
  ¼ **cup sugar**
   1 **cup whipping cream**
   2 **tablespoons sugar**
  ½ **teaspoon vanilla**
     Whole strawberries (optional)
     Chopped pecans (optional)

1 **For shortcake,** in a large bowl combine flour, ground pecans, ¼ cup sugar, baking powder, and salt. Cut in butter until mixture resembles coarse crumbs. In small bowl combine egg, milk, 2 teaspoons of the peel, and 1 teaspoon vanilla; add all at once to flour mixture. Stir just until moistened.

Pecan Strawberry Shortcake: Count on the flaky, biscuitlike texture that you would expect from this American springtime classic, with a bonus of toasted nuts and orange peel in the shortcake.

2 **Drop dough** into 8 or 10 mounds on an ungreased baking sheet; flatten each mound with back of a spoon until about ¾ inch thick. Bake in a 450°F oven about 10 minutes or until golden. Cool shortcakes on wire rack about 10 minutes.

3 **Meanwhile, in a bowl stir** together strawberries, the second ¼ cup sugar, and the remaining 1 teaspoon orange peel; let stand about 20 minutes.

4 **In a chilled medium mixing bowl combine** cream, the 2 tablespoons sugar, and the ½ teaspoon vanilla. Beat on medium speed until soft peaks form.

5 **Using a sharp serrated knife,** cut shortcakes in half horizontally. Lift off top layers. Place bottom layers on dessert plates. Spoon half of the strawberry mixture and half of the whipped cream over bottom layers. Replace shortcake tops. Top with remaining strawberry mixture; spoon remaining

cream onto berries. If desired, garnish with whole strawberries and pecans. Serve at once.

Nutrition Facts per serving: 475 cal., 29 g total fat (11 g sat. fat), 84 mg chol., 294 mg sodium, 49 g carbo., 3 g fiber, 6 g pro. **Daily Values:** 27% vit. A, 108% vit. C, 13% calcium, 14% iron

For a large shortcake: Grease an 8×1½-inch round baking pan; set aside. Prepare shortcake dough as directed; spread in pan. Build up edges slightly. Bake in 450°F oven for 15 to 18 minutes or until top is golden and wooden toothpick inserted in center comes out clean (do not overbake). Cool in pan on rack 10 minutes; remove. Split into 2 layers. Place bottom layer on serving platter. Spoon half of the strawberry mixture over bottom layer; top with about half of the whipped cream. Add top. Add remaining strawberry mixture; spoon remaining cream onto berries. Garnish and serve as above.

PUDDING CAKE MAGIC

Mention pudding cake to nearly anyone, and undoubtedly they have memories of a grandmother, father, aunt, or uncle who loved it—maybe gilded with a little vanilla ice cream or whipped cream. Popular in the 1930s, this simple, homey dessert belies the magic that happens when pudding cake batter is put in the oven: The cake rises to the top of the pan, leaving a creamy pudding on the bottom. There's no need for frosting, and one of the best features of this nostalgic two-layer wonder is it's fairly easy to make so it's right in step with modern times.

BROWNIE PUDDING CAKE

EASY

Prep: 15 minutes   Bake: 30 minutes
Makes: 4 servings   Oven: 350°F

This cake makes its own chocolaty sauce.

  ½ **cup all-purpose flour**
  ¼ **cup sugar**
  3 **tablespoons unsweetened cocoa powder**
  ¾ **teaspoon baking powder**
  ¼ **cup milk**
  1 **tablespoon cooking oil**
  ½ **teaspoon vanilla**
  ¼ **cup chopped walnuts or pecans**
  ⅓ **cup sugar**
  ¾ **cup boiling water**

1 **In a medium bowl stir** together flour, the ¼ cup sugar, 1 tablespoon of the cocoa powder, and the baking powder. Add milk, oil, and vanilla. Stir until smooth. Stir in nuts. Transfer batter to an ungreased 1-quart casserole.

2 **In a small bowl stir** together ⅓ cup sugar and the remaining 2 tablespoons cocoa powder. Gradually stir in the boiling water. Pour the mixture evenly over batter in casserole.

3 **Bake in a 350°F oven** about 30 minutes or until a wooden toothpick inserted near the center of cake comes out clean. Serve warm.

Nutrition Facts per serving: 270 cal., 9 g total fat (1 g sat. fat), 1 mg chol., 78 mg sodium, 44 g carbo., 1 g fiber, 4 g pro. **Daily Values:** 1% vit. A, 11% calcium, 9% iron

Mocha Pudding Cake: Prepare as directed at left, except add 2 teaspoons instant coffee crystals with the boiling water.

LEMON PUDDING CAKE

Prep: 20 minutes   Bake: 40 minutes
Makes: 4 servings   Oven: 350°F

The egg whites that are folded in give the cake a light texture. Be sure to spoon some of the tasty pudding over the cake layer when serving.

  ½ **cup sugar**
  3 **tablespoons all-purpose flour**
  1 **teaspoon finely shredded lemon peel**
  3 **tablespoons lemon juice**
  2 **tablespoons butter, melted**
  2 **slightly beaten egg yolks**
  1 **cup milk**
  2 **egg whites**

1 **In a medium bowl stir** together sugar and flour. Stir in lemon peel, lemon juice, and melted butter. Combine egg yolks and milk. Add to flour mixture; stir just until combined.

2 **In a mixing bowl beat** egg whites until stiff peaks form (tips stand straight). Gently fold egg whites into lemon batter. Transfer batter to an ungreased 1-quart casserole. Place the casserole in a large pan on an oven rack. Pour hot water into the large pan around the casserole to a depth of 1 inch.

3 **Bake in a 350°F oven** about 40 minutes or until golden and top springs back when lightly touched near the center. Serve warm.

Nutrition Facts per serving: 237 cal., 9 g total fat (5 g sat. fat), 126 mg chol., 120 mg sodium, 33 g carbo., 0 g fiber, 6 g pro. Daily Values: 25% vit. A, 10% vit. C, 7% calcium, 4% iron

PEANUT BUTTER AND HOT FUDGE PUDDING CAKE

Prep: 15 minutes   Bake: 30 minutes
Makes: 4 servings   Oven: 400°F

Brownie pudding cake takes on an irresistible partner—peanut butter. Together these flavors make this fudgy dessert a winner with kids.

½ **cup all-purpose flour**
¼ **cup sugar**
¾ **teaspoon baking powder**
⅓ **cup milk**
1 **tablespoon cooking oil**
½ **teaspoon vanilla**
¼ **cup peanut butter**

½ **cup sugar**
3 **tablespoons unsweetened cocoa powder**
1 **cup boiling water**
   Vanilla ice cream
   Fudge ice-cream topping (optional)
⅓ **cup chopped peanuts**

1 **In a medium bowl stir** together flour, the ¼ cup sugar, and the baking powder. Add milk, oil, and vanilla. Stir until smooth. Stir in peanut butter. Transfer batter to an ungreased 1½-quart casserole.

2 **In the same bowl stir** together the ½ cup sugar and the cocoa powder. Gradually stir in the boiling water. Pour the mixture evenly over batter in casserole.

3 **Bake in a 400°F oven** about 30 minutes or until a wooden toothpick inserted near the center of cake comes out clean. Serve warm with vanilla ice cream. If desired, top with fudge ice-cream topping. Sprinkle with chopped peanuts.

Nutrition Facts per serving: 421 cal., 18 g total fat (3 g sat. fat), 1 mg chol., 211 mg sodium, 57 g carbo., 2 g fiber, 10 g pro. Daily Values: 1% vit. A, 0% vit. C, 12% calcium, 12% iron

Peanut Butter and Hot Fudge Pudding Cake: Top the warm pudding cake with a scoop of vanilla ice cream and a drizzle of fudge topping. Your family will love the sprinkling of peanuts that gives this dessert tin-roof sundae appeal.

BAKED RICE PUDDING

Prep: 15 minutes   Bake: 50 minutes
Makes: 8 servings   Oven: 325°F

Surprise! You thought you were overindulging when actually rice pudding is fairly low in fat.

    4 beaten eggs
    2 cups milk, half-and-half, or
         light cream
   ½ cup sugar
    1 teaspoon vanilla
 1½ cups cooked rice, cooled*
   ½ to ¾ cup raisins
   ⅛ teaspoon ground nutmeg
   ⅛ teaspoon ground cinnamon

1 **In ungreased 2-quart casserole** combine eggs, milk, sugar, vanilla, and ¼ teaspoon salt. Beat until combined but not foamy. Stir in cooked rice and raisins. Place casserole in a 13×9×2-inch baking dish on an oven rack. Pour boiling water into baking dish around the casserole to a depth of 1 inch.

2 **Bake in a 325°F oven** for 30 minutes. Stir well; sprinkle with nutmeg and cinnamon. Bake for 20 to 30 minutes more or until a knife inserted near the center comes out clean. Serve warm or cold. To serve cold, cover and chill pudding for up to 3 days.

Nutrition Facts per serving: 184 cal., 4 g total fat (2 g sat. fat), 111 mg chol., 130 mg sodium, 31 g carbo., 0 g fiber, 6 g pro. **Daily Values:** 8% vit. A, 1% vit. C, 7% calcium, 6% iron

*Note: Leftover rice works well in rice pudding.

COOKING RICE

When a recipe calls for cooked rice, keep in mind these proportions: 1 cup of rice (cooked in 2 cups of water) yields about 3 cups cooked rice. Follow package directions, or here's a general guide: Measure water into a saucepan; bring to a full boil. Slowly add rice and return to boiling. Cover; simmer for time specified on package or until rice is tender and most of the water is absorbed. Remove from heat and let stand, covered, about 5 minutes.

CINNAMON ROLLS

Prep: 45 minutes   Rise: 1 hour
Chill: 2 to 24 hours   Stand: 30 minutes
Bake: 20 minutes   Makes: 24 rolls   Oven: 375°F

 4¾ to 5¼ cups all-purpose flour
    1 package active dry yeast
    1 cup milk
   ⅓ cup butter
   ⅓ cup granulated sugar
   ½ teaspoon salt
    3 eggs
    1 recipe Brown Sugar Filling
         (see page 41)
   ½ cup golden raisins (optional)
   ½ cup chopped pecans (optional)
    1 tablespoon half-and-half or
         light cream
    1 recipe Vanilla Glaze (see page 41)

1 **In a large mixing** bowl combine 2¼ cups of the flour and the yeast. In a saucepan heat and stir milk, butter, granulated sugar, and salt just until warm (120°F to 130°F) and butter almost melts. Add milk mixture to flour mixture along with eggs. Beat with electric mixer on low speed 30 seconds, scraping bowl. Beat on high speed 3 minutes. Stir in as much of the remaining flour as you can.

2 **Turn dough** out onto a lightly floured surface. Knead in enough of the remaining flour to make a moderately soft dough that is smooth and elastic (3 to 5 minutes total). Shape into a ball. Place in a greased bowl, turning once. Cover; let rise in a warm place until double (about 1 hour).

3 **Punch dough** down. Turn out onto a lightly floured surface. Divide in half. Cover; let rest for 10 minutes. Lightly grease two 9×1½-inch round baking pans or 2 baking sheets. Roll each half of dough into a 12×8-inch rectangle. Sprinkle Brown Sugar Filling over dough rectangles. If desired, sprinkle with raisins and pecans. Roll each rectangle into a spiral, starting from a long side. Seal seams. Slice each roll into 12 pieces. Place, cut sides down, in prepared pans or on prepared baking sheets.

4 **Cover dough** loosely with clear plastic wrap, leaving room for rolls to rise. Refrigerate for 2 to 24 hours. Uncover; let stand at room temperature

Maple-Nut Rolls: One of the most wonderful features of this recipe is that you can shape the rolls the night before you plan to enjoy them. When you awaken in the morning, just pop the rolls in the oven and serve them warm.

30 minutes. (Or, to bake rolls right away, don't chill dough. Instead, cover loosely; let dough rise in warm place until nearly double, about 30 minutes.)

5 Break any surface bubbles with a greased toothpick. Brush dough with half-and-half. Bake in 375°F oven for 20 to 25 minutes or until light brown (if necessary, cover rolls loosely with foil for the last 5 to 10 minutes of baking to prevent overbrowning). Remove from oven. Brush again with half-and-half. Cool for 1 minute. Carefully invert rolls onto wire rack. Cool slightly. Invert again onto a serving platter. Drizzle with Vanilla Glaze. Serve warm.

Brown Sugar Filling: In a medium bowl stir together ¾ cup packed brown sugar, ¼ cup all-purpose flour, and 1 tablespoon ground cinnamon. Cut in ⅓ cup butter until crumbly.

Vanilla Glaze: In small bowl stir together 1¼ cups sifted powdered sugar, 1 teaspoon light-colored corn syrup, and ½ teaspoon vanilla. Stir in enough half-and-half or light cream (1 to 2 tablespoons) to make drizzling consistency.

Nutrition Facts per roll: 203 cal., 6 g total fat (4 g sat. fat), 42 mg chol., 120 mg sodium, 33 g carbo., 1 g fiber, 4 g pro. **Daily Values:** 8% vit. A, 0% vit. C, 2% calcium, 10% iron

Apple-Cinnamon Rolls: Prepare as at left, except substitute 1 cup finely chopped, peeled apple for the raisins and nuts.

Chocolate-Cinnamon Rolls: Prepare as at left, except substitute 1 cup semisweet chocolate pieces for the raisins and nuts.

Old-Fashioned Cinnamon Rolls: Prepare as at left, except omit Brown Sugar Filling. Brush dough rectangles with 3 tablespoons melted butter. Combine ⅔ cup granulated sugar and 2 teaspoons ground cinnamon; sprinkle over rectangles. Continue as at left.

Maple-Nut Rolls: Prepare as at left, except omit the Brown Sugar Filling and Vanilla Glaze. Mix ¾ cup packed brown sugar, ¼ cup all-purpose flour, and 1 tablespoon apple pie spice. Using a pastry blender, cut in ¼ cup butter until crumbly. Stir in 1 cup finely snipped dried apricots. Sprinkle over rectangles; top with ½ cup chopped toasted pecans. Continue as at left. Drizzle rolls with 1 recipe Maple Glaze (see below).

Maple Glaze: Heat 3 tablespoons butter over medium-low heat 7 to 10 minutes or until light brown; remove from heat. Stir in 1½ cups sifted powdered sugar and ¼ cup maple or maple-flavored syrup. If needed, stir in milk to make drizzling consistency.

BAKED CUSTARDS

Prep: 20 minutes **Bake:** 30 minutes
Makes: 4 servings **Oven:** 325°F

Bake this time-honored, smooth-as-silk dessert in individual cups or in one large dish.

    3 beaten eggs
1½ cups milk
 ⅓ cup sugar
    1 teaspoon vanilla
       Ground nutmeg or cinnamon
       (optional)

1 **In a medium bowl combine** eggs, milk, sugar, and vanilla. Beat until well combined but not foamy. Place four ungreased 6-ounce custard cups or one 3½-cup soufflé dish in a 2-quart square baking dish.

2 **Pour egg mixture** into custard cups or soufflé dish. If desired, sprinkle with nutmeg or cinnamon. Place baking dish on oven rack. Pour boiling water into the baking dish around custard cups or soufflé dish to a depth of about 1 inch (see top photo, right).

3 **Bake in a 325°F oven** for 30 to 45 minutes for custard cups (50 to 60 minutes for soufflé dish) or until a knife inserted near the centers or center comes out clean (see bottom photo, right). Remove cups or dish from water. Cool slightly on wire rack before serving. Or, cool completely; cover and chill.

4 **To unmold individual custards,** loosen edges with a knife, slipping point of knife down sides to let in air. Invert a dessert plate over each custard; turn custard cup and plate over together.

Nutrition Facts per serving: 170 cal., 6 g total fat (2 g sat. fat), 167 mg chol., 93 mg sodium, 22 g carbo., 0 g fiber, 8 g pro. **Daily Values:** 12% vit. A, 1% vit. C, 10% calcium, 3% iron

Carefully pour boiling water into the baking dish around custard cups, making sure no water gets into the custard mixture. Add water to a depth of 1 inch.

Insert tip of a knife into the center of each custard to test for doneness. The knife will come out clean when the custard is done. If any clings to knife, bake a little longer and test again.

Microwave directions: In a 4-cup microwave-safe measure microwave milk, sugar, and vanilla, uncovered, on 100% power (high) for 2½ to 5 minutes or until steaming but not boiling, stirring once or twice. Stir milk mixture into beaten eggs. Pour into the custard cups. Place cups in the baking dish. (Do not use the soufflé dish version.) Pour boiling water into the baking dish around the custard cups to a depth of about 1 inch (about 2½ cups). Microwave, uncovered, on high for 3 minutes, giving dish a quarter-turn every minute. Rotate custard cups. Microwave for 1 to 3 minutes more or until edges are set but centers still quiver. (After the first minute, check for doneness every 15 seconds, turning cups as necessary.) Remove each cup from dish when it is done.

pies and tarts

Tarte Tatin, recipe page 64

PIES AND TARTS

PASTRY FOR SINGLE-CRUST PIE

Prep: 10 minutes   Makes: 8 servings

1¼ cups all-purpose flour
¼ teaspoon salt
⅓ cup shortening
4 or 5 tablespoons cold water

1 **In a medium bowl** stir together flour and salt. Using a pastry blender, cut in shortening until pieces are pea-size.

2 **Sprinkle 1 tablespoon** of the water over part of the mixture; gently toss with a fork. Push moistened dough to the side of the bowl. Repeat, using 1 tablespoon of the water at a time, until all the dough is moistened. Form dough into a ball.

3 **On a lightly** floured surface, use your hands to slightly flatten dough. Roll dough from center to edge into a 12-inch circle.

4 **To transfer pastry,** wrap it around rolling pin. Unroll pastry into 9-inch pie plate. Ease pastry into pie plate, being careful not to stretch pastry.

5 **Trim pastry** to ½ inch beyond edge of pie plate (see photo, top right). Fold under extra pastry. Crimp edge as desired. Do not prick pastry. Fill and bake as directed in individual recipes.

Nutrition Facts per serving: 141 cal., 9 g total fat (2 g sat. fat), 0 mg chol., 67 mg sodium, 14 g carbo., 0 g fiber, 2 g pro. **Daily Values:** 5% iron

Food processor directions: Prepare as above, except place steel blade in food processor bowl. Add flour, salt, and shortening. Cover and process with on/off turns until most of mixture resembles cornmeal, but with a few larger pieces. With processor running, add 3 tablespoons water through feed tube. Stop processor when all water is added; scrape down sides. Process with 2 on/off turns (mixture may not all be moistened). Remove from bowl; shape into a ball.

Baked Pastry Shell: Prepare as above, except generously prick bottom and side of pastry in pie plate with a fork. Prick all around where bottom and side meet. Line pastry with a double thickness of foil (see bottom photo, right). Bake in a 450°F oven for 8 minutes. Remove foil. Bake for 5 to 6 minutes more or until golden. Cool on wire rack.

Trim pastry to ½ inch beyond the edge of the pie plate. Fold the extra pastry under, even with the plate's rim, to build up the edge.

To prevent pastry from shrinking during baking, line it with a double thickness of regular foil or one layer of heavy-duty foil.

OIL PASTRY

Prep: 15 minutes   Makes: 8 servings

2¼ cups all-purpose flour
¼ teaspoon salt
½ cup cooking oil
⅓ cup cold milk

1 **In a large bowl** combine flour and salt. Pour oil and milk into a measuring cup (do not stir); add all at once to flour mixture. Stir lightly with a fork. Form into 2 balls; flatten each slightly with your hands.

2 **Cut waxed paper** into four 12-inch squares. Place each ball of dough between 2 squares of paper. Roll each ball of dough into a circle to edges of paper. (Dampen work surface with a little water to prevent paper from slipping.)

3 **Peel off top** papers and fit dough, paper side up, into 9-inch pie plates. (Or, reserve one portion for use as a top crust.) Remove paper. Continue as directed for Pastry for Single-Crust or Double-Crust Pie (see left and page 46).

Nutrition Facts per serving: 243 cal., 14 g total fat (2 g sat. fat), 1 mg chol., 72 mg sodium, 25 g carbo., 1 g fiber, 4 g pro. **Daily Values:** 1% calcium, 10% iron

PASTRY FOR DOUBLE-CRUST PIE

Prep: 15 minutes   Makes: 8 servings

  2 **cups all-purpose flour**
  ½ **teaspoon salt**
  ⅔ **cup shortening**
  6 or 7 **tablespoons cold water**

1 In a large bowl stir together flour and salt. Using a pastry blender, cut in shortening until pieces are pea-size.

2 Sprinkle 1 tablespoon of the water over part of the mixture; gently toss with a fork. Push moistened dough to side of bowl. Repeat, using 1 tablespoon water at a time, until all the dough is moistened. Divide in half. Form each half into ball.

3 On a lightly floured surface, use your hands to slightly flatten 1 ball of dough. Roll from the center to the edge into a 12-inch circle.

4 To transfer pastry, wrap it around the rolling pin. Unroll into a 9-inch pie plate. Ease pastry into pie plate, being careful not to stretch pastry. Transfer filling to pastry-lined pie plate. Trim pastry even with rim of pie plate.

5 Roll remaining dough into a 12-inch circle. Cut slits to allow steam to escape. Place remaining pastry on filling; trim ½ inch beyond edge of plate. Fold top pastry under bottom pastry. Crimp edge as desired. Bake as directed in individual recipes.

Nutrition Facts per serving: 256 cal., 17 g total fat (4 g sat. fat), 0 mg chol., 134 mg sodium, 22 g carbo., 1 g fiber, 3 g pro. **Daily Values:** 8% iron

Pastry for Lattice-Top Pie: Prepare as above, except trim bottom pastry to ½ inch beyond edge of pie plate. Fill pastry-lined pie plate with desired filling. Roll out remaining pastry and cut into ½-inch-wide strips. Weave strips over filling. Press ends of strips into crust rim. Fold bottom pastry over strips; seal and crimp edge as desired. (For a quick lattice, roll out top pastry. Use a mini cookie or canapé cutter to make cutouts an equal distance apart from pastry center to edge. Place pastry on filling; seal and crimp edge.) Bake as directed in individual recipes.

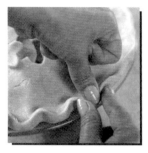

For a fluted edge, place your thumb against the inside of the pastry; press dough around your thumb with your other hand's thumb and index finger.

For a petal edge, flute the pastry as directed in photo above. Press the tines of a fork lightly into the center of each flute.

APPLE-CRANBERRY DEEP-DISH PIE

Prep: 50 minutes   Bake: 50 minutes
Makes: 8 servings   Oven: 375°F

  ¼ **cup sugar**
  3 **tablespoons all-purpose flour**
  1 **teaspoon apple pie spice or**
     ¼ **teaspoon ground nutmeg**
  1 **teaspoon finely shredded orange peel**
1½ **cups canned whole cranberry sauce**
  7 **cups thinly sliced, peeled cooking apples (about 2¼ pounds)**
  1 **recipe Pastry for Single-Crust Pie (see page 45)**
  1 **egg yolk**
  1 **tablespoon water**
  1 **tablespoon sugar**
     Vanilla ice cream (optional)

1 In a large bowl combine the ¼ cup sugar, the flour, spice, and orange peel. Stir in cranberry sauce. Add apples. Gently toss to coat. Transfer to a

FOOLPROOF PASTRY

You can make perfect pastry every time with these few pointers:

- Measure your ingredients accurately. Too much flour makes for tough pastry; too much shortening makes it crumble; and too much water makes it tough.
- Stir together the flour and salt, then cut in the shortening until the mixture resembles small peas.
- Add water gradually to the mixture, then gently toss it together just until it's evenly moistened.
- Flour the rolling surface just enough to keep the dough from sticking.
- Roll the pastry to an even thickness. Try not to stretch it as you're transferring it to the pie plate.
- Use a glass pie plate or dull metal pie pan so the pastry browns evenly.
- If you're making a double-crust pie, trim the edge of the bottom pastry after you pour in the filling so it doesn't pull the pastry down into the pie plate.
- Patch any cracks with a pastry scrap before adding the filling. Moisten the underside of the scrap with a little water so it stays in place.
- Check that your oven temperature is accurate. If it is too low, the bottom crust will be soggy.
- To prevent pastry edges from overbrowning, tear off a 12-inch square of foil. Fold it in quarters and cut a quarter circle off the folded corner (about 3 inches from the tip). Unfold the foil and place it on the pie, slightly molding the foil over the edge.
- After baking, cool your pie on a wire rack. Allowing the air to circulate under the pie prevents the crust from becoming soggy.

10-inch deep-dish pie plate or a 1½-quart casserole.

2 Prepare pastry. On a lightly floured surface, flatten pastry dough. Roll dough from center to edge into a 14-inch circle. Using cookie cutters, cut desired shapes from pastry, rerolling and cutting trimmings as necessary. Arrange cutouts on apple mixture so just the edges overlap (see photo, below).

3 In small bowl stir together egg yolk and water; brush onto pastry cutouts. Sprinkle with the 1 tablespoon sugar. To prevent overbrowning, cover edge of pie with foil. Place on baking sheet. Bake in a 375°F oven for 25 minutes. Remove foil. Bake for 25 to 30 minutes more or until top is golden and apples are tender. Cool slightly on a wire rack; serve warm. If desired, serve with vanilla ice cream.

Nutrition Facts per serving: 347 cal., 10 g total fat (2 g sat. fat), 27 mg chol., 85 mg sodium, 65 g carbo., 5 g fiber, 3 g pro. **Daily Values:** 4% vit. A, 4% vit. C, 1% calcium, 10% iron

Apple-Cranberry Deep-Dish Pie: For comfort food at its best, spoon this two-fruit pastry combo into dessert dishes and top it off with some big scoops of vanilla ice cream.

APPLE PIE

Prep: 50 minutes Bake: 50 minutes
Makes: 8 servings Oven: 375°F

   **1 recipe Pastry for Double-Crust Pie
     (see page 46)**
   **6 cups thinly sliced, peeled cooking
     apples (about 2¼ pounds)**
   1 tablespoon lemon juice (optional)
  ¾ cup sugar
   2 tablespoons all-purpose flour
  ½ teaspoon ground cinnamon
  ⅛ teaspoon ground nutmeg
  **½ cup raisins or chopped walnuts
     (optional)**

1 Prepare and roll out pastry. Line a 9-inch pie plate with half of the pastry; set aside.

2 If desired, sprinkle apples with lemon juice. In a large bowl stir together sugar, flour, cinnamon, and nutmeg. Add apple slices and, if desired, raisins or walnuts. Gently toss to coat.

3 Transfer apple mixture to the pastry-lined pie plate. Trim pastry to edge of pie plate. Cut slits in remaining pastry; place on filling and seal. Crimp edge as desired.

4 To prevent overbrowning, cover edge of pie with foil. Bake in 375°F oven for 25 minutes. Remove foil. Bake for 25 to 30 minutes more or until top is golden. Cool completely on a wire rack.

Nutrition Facts per serving: 380 cal., 18 g total fat (4 g sat. fat), 0 mg chol., 135 mg sodium, 54 g carbo., 3 g fiber, 3 g pro. 11% iron

---

AMERICAN PIE

Baseball and hot dogs are as American as, well, you know the rest. Apple pie may be America's favorite, but its origins date back to 14th-century England when apple filling was substituted in traditional meat pies.

The Pilgrims brought apples to America and served apple pie for breakfast (a tradition that should definitely be resurrected). In colonial America, apple pie was served with—not after—the main course at lunch or dinner.

NO-PEEL APPLE PIE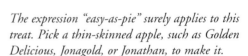

Prep: 35 minutes Bake: 1 hour
Makes: 8 servings Oven: 375°F

The expression "easy-as-pie" surely applies to this treat. Pick a thin-skinned apple, such as Golden Delicious, Jonagold, or Jonathan, to make it.

   **1 15-ounce package (2 crusts) folded
     refrigerated unbaked piecrust**
   6 large cooking apples
  ½ cup water
   2 tablespoons lemon juice
  ½ cup granulated sugar
   2 tablespoons all-purpose flour
 1½ teaspoons apple pie spice
    Whipping cream or milk
    Coarse and/or granulated sugar

1 Let piecrust stand according to package directions. Line a 9-inch pie plate with half of the pastry; set aside.

2 For filling, core and slice unpeeled apples (you should have 8 cups). In a large bowl combine apples with water and lemon juice. Gently toss to coat. In another large bowl stir together the ½ cup sugar, flour, and spice. Drain apples well; add to sugar mixture. Gently toss to coat.

3 Spoon the apple mixture into the pastry-lined pie plate. Trim pastry to edge of pie plate. Moisten edge with water. Cut out desired shapes from center of remaining crust; set shapes aside. Center top crust on filling and seal. Crimp edge as desired. Brush the top crust with whipping cream. If desired, top with reserved pastry cutouts; brush cutouts with cream. Sprinkle the pie with coarse and/or granulated sugar.

4 To prevent overbrowning, cover the edge of pie with foil. Bake in a 375°F oven for 30 minutes. Remove foil. Bake about 30 minutes more or until the top is golden. Cool slightly on a wire rack; serve warm.

Nutrition Facts per serving: 373 cal., 16 g total fat (1 g sat. fat), 18 mg chol., 211 mg sodium, 58 g carbo., 3 g fiber, 2 g pro. **Daily Values:** 1% vit. A, 13% vit. C, 1% calcium, 3% iron

No-Peel Apple Pie: This juicy pie works perfectly, and without using a paring knife. Ready-made refrigerated piecrust saves time, too.

APPLE-CRANBERRY STREUSEL PIE

Prep: 40 minutes   Bake: 55 minutes
Makes: 8 servings   Oven: 375°F

1 recipe Baked Pastry Shell,
      unpricked (see page 45)
½ cup dried cranberries or dried tart
      cherries
6 large cooking apples, peeled,
      cored, and sliced (6 cups)
⅔ cup granulated sugar
3 tablespoons all-purpose flour
1 teaspoon apple pie spice
1 teaspoon finely shredded lemon peel
¼ teaspoon salt
⅓ cup half-and-half or light cream
⅓ cup all-purpose flour
⅓ cup toasted finely chopped pecans
      or walnuts (see tip, page 181)
⅓ cup packed brown sugar
¼ teaspoon ground nutmeg
3 tablespoons butter

1 **Prepare Baked Pastry Shell** as directed, except do not prick the pastry.

2 **For filling,** pour boiling water over cranberries. Let stand for 5 minutes; drain. Mix cranberries and apples; place in the Baked Pastry Shell. Combine granulated sugar, the 3 tablespoons flour, spice, lemon peel, and salt. Stir in half-and-half. Pour over fruit.

3 **For topping,** combine the ⅓ cup flour, the nuts, brown sugar, and nutmeg. Using a pastry blender, cut in butter until the pieces are pea-size. Sprinkle over filling.

4 **To prevent** overbrowning, cover edge of pie with foil. Bake in a 375°F oven for 45 minutes. Remove foil. Bake for 10 to 15 minutes more or until topping is golden and fruit is tender. Cool for 45 minutes on a wire rack; serve warm. (Or, cool completely on wire rack.) Store any leftover pie, covered, in the refrigerator.

Nutrition Facts per serving: 415 cal., 18 g total fat
(6 g sat. fat), 15 mg chol., 185 mg sodium,
64 g carbo., 3 g fiber, 4 g pro. Daily Values: 5% vit. A,
8% vit. C, 3% calcium, 12% iron

Apple-Cranberry Streusel Pie: A whisper of cream gives the filling of this streusel-crowned creation a touch of richness. Dried cranberries provide lively bursts of flavor.

THE APPLE OF YOUR PIE

The sweet and crisp Red Delicious has won the affection of the lunchbox set, but bake it in a pie and it turns to mush. Unlike the old adage about the rose, "an apple is an apple is an apple" doesn't hold true. When you bake a pie, you need to choose an apple variety that can stand up to the heat. Try one of these to find your heart's delight:

- **Rome Beauty:** Called the Queen of Bakers, cooking accentuates the rich but mellow flavor of this medium-tart, deep red apple.
- **Golden Delicious:** The way this sweet apple keeps its shape when cooked makes it a natural in pies.
- **Granny Smith:** For the tart-and-tangy lovers

out there, this bright green fruit has found legions of fans.
- **Cortland:** A balanced apple, the Cortland is slightly sweet, slightly tart.
- **Newtown Pippin:** Benjamin Franklin and Thomas Jefferson sang the praises of this green-gold fruit. Its highly perfumed flesh is crisp and juicy and has a sweet-tart flavor.
- **Stayman:** This winter apple has a rich, mildly tart taste.
- **Winesap:** As suggested by its name, this delicious all-purpose apple has a tangy, winelike taste.
- **York Imperial:** A good apple for those who like their fruit a little bit tart, but not too much.

MIXED BERRY PIE

Prep: 30 minutes   Bake: 45 minutes
Makes: 8 servings   Oven: 375°F

Showcase the summer's best berries in this cream-of-the-crop pie.

1 **recipe Pastry for Double-Crust Pie (see page 46)**
1 **cup sugar**
3 **tablespoons cornstarch**
1 **teaspoon finely shredded orange peel**
½ **teaspoon ground cinnamon**
¼ **teaspoon ground nutmeg**
⅛ **teaspoon ground ginger**
2 **cups sliced fresh strawberries**
2 **cups fresh blackberries or raspberries**
1 **cup fresh blueberries**
  Milk
  Sugar

1 **Prepare and roll** out pastry. Line a 9-inch pie plate with half of the pastry; set aside.

2 **In a large** bowl combine the 1 cup sugar, the cornstarch, orange peel, cinnamon, nutmeg, and ginger. Add strawberries, blackberries and blueberries. Gently toss to coat. Transfer berry mixture to the pastry-lined pie plate. Trim pastry to the edge of the pie plate. Cut slits in remaining pastry; place on filling and seal. Crimp edge as desired. Brush top crust with milk and sprinkle with sugar.

3 **To prevent** overbrowning, cover edge of pie with foil. Bake in a 375°F oven for 25 minutes. Remove foil. Bake for 20 to 25 minutes more or until top is golden and filling is bubbly. Cool completely on a wire rack.

Nutrition Facts per serving: 411 cal., 18 g total fat (4 g sat. fat), 0 mg chol., 137 mg sodium, 61 g carbo., 4 g fiber, 4 g pro. **Daily Values:** 1% vit. A, 52% vit. C, 2% calcium, 12% iron

BLUEBERRY PIE

Prep: 30 minutes   **Bake:** 45 minutes
Makes: 8 servings   **Oven:** 375°F

Bring a smile to blueberry-stained lips by baking this timeless pie any time of year with berries fresh-from-the-patch or from the freezer.

> 1 **recipe Pastry for Double-Crust Pie**
>   **(see page 46)**
> ¾ **cup sugar**
> ⅓ **cup all-purpose flour**
> 2 **teaspoons finely shredded lemon**
>   **peel**
> 1 **tablespoon lemon juice**
> 5 **cups fresh or frozen blueberries**
>   **Milk (optional)**
>   **Sugar (optional)**

1 Prepare and roll out pastry. Line a 9-inch pie plate with half of the pastry; set aside.

2 In a large bowl stir together the ¾ cup sugar, the flour, lemon peel, and lemon juice. Add blueberries. Gently toss to coat. (If using frozen fruit, let mixture stand for 15 to 30 minutes or until fruit is partially thawed, but still icy.)

3 Transfer berry mixture to pastry-lined pie plate. Trim pastry to edge of pie plate. Cut slits in remaining pastry; place on filling and seal. Crimp edge as desired. If desired, brush top with milk and sprinkle with sugar.

4 To prevent overbrowning, cover edge of the pie with foil. Bake in a 375°F oven for 25 minutes for fresh fruit (50 minutes for frozen fruit). Remove

foil. Bake for 20 to 25 minutes more for fresh fruit (20 to 30 minutes more for frozen fruit) or until top is golden. Cool completely on a wire rack.

Nutrition Facts per serving: 397 cal., 18 g total fat (4 g sat. fat), 0 mg chol., 140 mg sodium, 57 g carbo., 3 g fiber, 4 g pro. **Daily Values:** 22% vit. C, 1% calcium, 11% iron

RASPBERRY PIE

Prep: 25 minutes   **Bake:** 50 minutes
Makes: 8 servings   **Oven:** 375°F

Be sure to stir the tender raspberries with a light hand to avoid crushing them.

> 1 **recipe Pastry for Double-Crust Pie**
>   **(see page 46)**
> ½ to ¾ **cup sugar**
> 3 **tablespoons all-purpose flour**
> 5 **cups fresh or frozen unsweetened**
>   **red raspberries**

1 Prepare and roll out pastry. Line a 9-inch pie plate with half of the pastry; set aside.

2 In a large mixing bowl stir together sugar and flour. Add raspberries. Gently toss to coat. (If using frozen fruit, let mixture stand for 15 to 30 minutes or until fruit is partially thawed, but still icy.)

3 Transfer berry mixture to the pastry-lined pie plate. Trim pastry to edge of pie plate. Cut slits in remaining pastry; place on filling and seal. Crimp edge as desired.

BLUEBERRY LORE

Blueberries—and picking them in the wild—have an undeniable romance about them. In Northern Europe, families trek into the woods in late summer, to jealously guarded locations, in search of wild blueberries they take home and eat with sugar and cream or turn into compotes, cold soups, preserves, and tarts.

Blueberries have a history on this side of the Atlantic, too. When the pilgrims arrived here they found Native Americans gathering blueberries in the wild and using them—both fresh and dried—in dishes both sweet and savory. By the mid-19th century, blueberries were being cultivated on a large scale in the woods of the northern states.

THE PROPER PLATE

If you want your pie perfectly shaped and as nicely browned and flaky on the bottom crust as it is on the top (and who wouldn't?), you need to choose the pie plate you use with some forethought. Here are the qualities to look for:

- **Surface:** Always use a standard glass or dull metal pie plate. Shiny metal pie pans—which work fine for crumb-crust pies—can cause a bottom pastry crust to turn out soggy.

- **Size:** Although they may be pretty to look at, ceramic or pottery pie plates aren't necessarily standard size (a standard-size plate holds about 3¾ cups liquid). You can simply adjust the amount of filling and baking time.

- **When Using Foil:** Disposable foil pans are usually smaller than standard pie plates; deep-dish foil pie pans are closer to standard size.

---

4 To prevent overbrowning, cover edge of the pie with foil. Bake in a 375°F oven for 25 minutes for fresh fruit (50 minutes for frozen fruit). Remove foil. Bake for 25 to 30 minutes more for fresh fruit (about 30 minutes more for frozen fruit) or until top is golden. Cool completely on a wire rack.

Nutrition Facts per serving: 351 cal., 18 g total fat (4 g sat. fat), 0 mg chol., 134 mg sodium, 45 g carbo., 4 g fiber, 4 g pro. **Daily Values:** 1% vit. A, 32% vit. C, 1% calcium, 12% iron

STRAWBERRY PIE

Prep: 40 minutes   Chill: 2 hours
Makes: 8 servings

A glaze which uses pureed berries makes the whole berries in this beautiful pie glisten and shine—and adds fresh berry flavor, too.

   **8 cups fresh strawberries (2 quarts)
     Water**
   ⅔ cup granulated sugar
   2 tablespoons cornstarch
   **1 recipe Baked Pastry Shell
       (see page 45)**
   1 cup whipping cream
   2 tablespoons sifted powdered sugar
   **2 tablespoons amaretto or
       ¼ teaspoon almond extract**

1 Remove stems from strawberries. In food processor/blender container process 1 cup of the berries and ⅔ cup water until smooth. Sieve, if desired. Add water to make 1½ cups mixture.

2 In a medium saucepan combine granulated sugar and cornstarch. Stir in berry mixture. Cook and stir over medium heat until mixture is thickened and bubbly. Reduce heat. Cook and stir for 2 minutes more. Remove from heat. Cool 10 minutes without stirring.

3 Spread about ¼ cup of the berry mixture over bottom of Baked Pastry Shell. Arrange half of the remaining berries in pastry shell, stem ends down, cutting larger berries in half lengthwise, if necessary. Spoon half of the remaining berry mixture over berries, being careful to cover all of the fruit. Repeat layers. Chill in the refrigerator 2 hours or until set.

4 To serve, in a small mixing bowl beat whipping cream and powdered sugar until stiff peaks form. Beat in amaretto or almond extract. Serve with pie.

Nutrition Facts per serving: 382 cal., 20 g total fat (9 g sat. fat), 41 mg chol., 81 mg sodium, 47 g carbo., 3 g fiber, 3 g pro. **Daily Values:** 13% vit. A, 141% vit. C, 3% calcium, 9% iron

Cherry-Pear Pie: An afternoon coffee break with a slice of homemade pie is an old-time ritual worth resurrecting—especially if you're serving this delicious double-fruit creation.

CHERRY-PEAR PIE

Prep: 40 minutes   Bake: 55 minutes
Makes: 8 servings   Oven: 375°F

The surprise ingredient in this pie is a subtle hint of rosemary that enhances the fresh fruit flavors of the ripe pears and red cherries.

  ⅔ **cup granulated sugar**
  3 **tablespoons cornstarch**
  ¼ **teaspoon ground nutmeg**
  ¼ **teaspoon dried rosemary, crushed (optional)**
  4 **cups thinly sliced, peeled pears**
  3 **cups frozen pitted tart red cherries**
  1 **recipe Pastry for Double-Crust Pie (see page 46)**
  1 **beaten egg white**
  1 **tablespoon water**
    Coarse sugar
    Vanilla ice cream (optional)

1 **In a large** bowl stir together the ¾ cup granulated sugar, the cornstarch, nutmeg, and, if desired, rosemary. Add pears and cherries. Gently toss to coat. Let mixture stand at room temperature for 20 minutes.

2 **Meanwhile,** prepare and roll out pastry. Line a 9-inch pie plate with half of the pastry; set aside.

3 **Transfer fruit** mixture to the pastry-lined pie plate. Trim pastry to edge of pie plate. Using a miniature cookie cutter, cut out hearts from the center of the remaining pastry; set cutouts aside. Place pastry on filling and seal. Crimp edge as desired. Combine egg white and water; brush onto pastry. Top with heart cutouts. Brush again. Sprinkle with coarse sugar.

4 **To prevent** overbrowning, cover edge of pie with foil. Bake in a 375° oven for 25 minutes. Remove foil. Bake for 30 to 35 minutes more or until the top is golden. Cool slightly on a wire rack; serve warm. (Or, cool completely on wire rack.) If desired, serve with ice cream.

Nutrition Facts per serving: 418 cal., 18 g total fat (4 g sat. fat), 0 mg chol., 143 mg sodium, 62 g carbo., 4 g fiber, 4 g pro. **Daily Values:** 7% vit. A, 15% vit. C, 1% calcium, 11% iron

CHERRY PIE

Prep: 50 minutes Bake: 50 minutes
Makes: 8 servings Oven: 375°F

Celebrate the Fourth of July with a cherry pie. Montmorency, Early Richmond, and English Morello cherries are good pie choices.

1¼ to 1½ cups sugar
2 tablespoons quick-cooking tapioca
5 cups fresh or frozen unsweetened pitted tart red cherries
¼ teaspoon almond extract
1 recipe Pastry for Double-Crust Pie (see page 46)

1 **In a large** bowl stir together sugar and tapioca. Add cherries and almond extract. Gently toss to coat. Let mixture stand about 15 minutes or until a syrup forms, stirring occasionally. (If using frozen fruit, let mixture stand about 1 hour.)

2 **Meanwhile,** prepare and roll out pastry. Line a 9-inch pie plate with half of the pastry; set aside.

3 **Stir cherry** mixture. Transfer cherry mixture to pastry-lined pie plate. Trim pastry to edge of pie plate. Cut slits in remaining pastry; place on filling and seal. Crimp edge as desired.

4 **To prevent** overbrowning, cover edge of the pie with foil. Bake in a 375°F oven for 25 minutes for fresh fruit (50 minutes for frozen fruit). Remove foil. Bake for 25 to 35 minutes more for fresh fruit (about 30 minutes more for frozen fruit) or until top is golden. Cool completely on a wire rack.

Lattice Cherry Pie: Prepare as above, except substitute 1 recipe Pastry for Lattice-Top Pie (see page 46) for Pastry for Double-Crust Pie.

Nutrition Facts per serving: 417 cal., 18 g total fat (4 g sat. fat), 0 mg chol., 135 mg sodium, 63 g carbo., 2 g fiber, 4 g pro. **Daily Values:** 6% vit. A, 2% vit. C, 1% calcium, 11% iron

---

FRUIT PIES 101

A sweet fruit filling paired with a plain pastry makes for a delicious pie. No matter the fruit used, here are a few tips for making each one of your creations a winning combination:

■ Be sure to use either a double-crust or lattice-top as the recipe specifies. It won't work to substitute one for the other because some fillings require the venting of the lattice; others, such as apples, benefit from steaming under a top crust.

■ You can use either fresh or frozen fruit in your pie. Be sure to mix frozen fruit with the sugar-flour mixture; let it thaw for 15 to 30 minutes—until the fruit is partially thawed but still icy—before transferring it to a pastry-lined plate. Pies made with frozen fruit will take a little longer to bake. Before the foil is removed, bake a pie made with frozen fruit in a 375° oven about 50 minutes (rather than 25). Remove the foil and continue baking until the pie is done (usually 20 to 30 minutes longer).

■ Make several cuts in the top of a double-crust pie before baking to allow the steam to escape and prevent excessive bubbling.

■ For an attractive glazed crust, brush the top crust with milk, then sprinkle with granulated sugar before baking.

■ Place a pizza pan or baking sheet under a double-crust fruit pie when you put it in the oven to catch any filling that bubbles over.

■ Fruit pies need to bubble in the center to be properly cooked—otherwise, the thickener (flour, cornstarch, or tapioca) won't be clear. To see if the pie is done, make a small hole in the top crust and spoon out some of the juice. If the juice is clear, the pie is done. If it's cloudy, bake the pie a little longer.

■ To serve the pie at its flavorful best—and so the pieces don't fall apart when you cut it—let a pie cool for 3 to 4 hours before slicing.

Banana Streusel Pie:
A banana lover's delight!
This macadamia-nut
streusel is a touch of
pure decadence.

BANANA STREUSEL PIE

Prep: 35 minutes   **Bake:** 40 minutes
Makes: 8 servings   **Oven:** 450°/375°F

*When you buy bananas to make this pie, select
ones that are firm but not green.*

  1 recipe Pastry for Single-Crust Pie
     (see page 45)
  4 cups sliced ripe bananas
     (about 5 medium)
 ²/₃ cup unsweetened pineapple juice
 ¼ cup granulated sugar
1½ teaspoons finely shredded lemon
     peel
 ½ teaspoon ground cinnamon
  1 teaspoon cornstarch
 ½ cup all-purpose flour
 ½ cup packed brown sugar
 ⅓ cup chopped macadamia nuts
     or almonds
  1 teaspoon ground cinnamon
 ¼ cup butter

1 **Prepare and** roll out pastry. Line a 9-inch pie
plate with the pastry. Trim and crimp edge as
desired. Line pastry with a double thickness of foil
(see photo, page 45). Bake in a 450°F oven for
8 minutes. Remove foil. Bake 4 to 5 minutes more
or until pastry is set and dry. Cool in pie plate on a
wire rack. Reduce oven temperature to 375°F.

2 **Meanwhile,** in a bowl gently toss together
bananas and pineapple juice. Drain, reserving
juices. Gently toss bananas with granulated sugar,
lemon peel, and the ½ teaspoon cinnamon. Spoon
banana mixture into partially baked pastry shell. In
saucepan stir together the reserved juice and
cornstarch. Cook and stir over medium heat until
thickened and bubbly. Pour over banana mixture.

3 **For topping,** combine the flour, brown sugar,
nuts, and the 1 teaspoon cinnamon. Using a
pastry blender, cut in butter until mixture resembles
coarse crumbs. Sprinkle over banana mixture.

4 **To prevent** overbrowning, cover edge of pie with
foil. Bake in the 375°F oven for 40 minutes or
until topping is golden and edge is bubbly. Cool
completely on a wire rack.

Nutrition Facts per serving: 402 cal., 19 g total fat
(6 g sat. fat), 15 mg chol., 130 mg sodium,
57 g carbo., 2 g fiber, 4 g pro. **Daily Values:** 5% vit. A,
15% vit. C, 2% calcium, 13% iron

THE ALLURE OF LARD

Marketers may have coined the phrase "butter is better," but for many grandmothers and other experienced pie-bakers, nothing beats lard, a kind of pork fat.

In the late 18th and early 19th centuries, pie was a workhorse food—folks grabbed a hearty slice of it to hold in their hands and eat as they went about their morning chores. The crust had to be substantial—that's why most old-fashioned crust recipes called for lard. Lard makes a dense, flaky crust, but is commonly replaced by shortening today.

PECAN PIE

Prep: 25 minutes   Bake: 45 minutes
Makes: 8 servings   Oven: 350°F

  1 **recipe Pastry for Single-Crust Pie**
     (see page 45)
  3 **slightly beaten eggs**
  1 **cup corn syrup**
  ⅔ **cup sugar**
  ⅓ **cup butter, melted**
  1 **teaspoon vanilla**
  1¼ **cups pecan halves or chopped**
       macadamia nuts

1 **Prepare and roll** out pastry. Line a 9-inch pie plate with the pastry. Trim and crimp edge as desired; set aside.

2 **For filling,** in a bowl combine eggs, corn syrup, sugar, butter, and vanilla. Stir in pecans. Place pastry-lined pie plate on oven rack. Carefully pour filling into pastry shell.

3 **To prevent** overbrowning, cover edge of pie with foil. Bake in a 350°F oven 25 minutes. Remove foil. Bake 20 to 25 minutes more or until a knife inserted near center comes out clean. Cool for 1 to 2 hours on a wire rack. Refrigerate within 2 hours.

Nutrition Facts per serving: 541 cal., 30 g total fat (8 g sat. fat), 100 mg chol., 197 mg sodium, 67 g carbo., 2 g fiber, 6 g pro. **Daily Values:** 10% vit. A, 2% calcium, 11% iron

RHUBARB PIE

Prep: 25 minutes   Bake: 45 minutes
Makes: 8 servings   Oven: 375°F

To prepare fresh rhubarb, wash it well, trim off the dry ends of the stalks, and slice.

  1 **recipe Pastry for Single-Crust Pie***
     (see page 45)
  1 **recipe Crumb Topping**
  ¾ **cup granulated sugar**
  ¼ **cup all-purpose flour**
  ½ **teaspoon ground cinnamon**
       (optional)
  4 **cups fresh or frozen unsweetened**
       sliced rhubarb

1 **Prepare and roll** out pastry. Line a 9-inch pie plate with the pastry. Trim and crimp edge as desired; set aside. Prepare Crumb Topping; set aside.

2 **In a large** bowl stir together granulated sugar, flour, and, if desired, cinnamon. Add rhubarb. Gently toss to coat. (If using frozen rhubarb, let mixture stand for 15 to 30 minutes or until fruit is partially thawed, but still icy.)

3 **Transfer rhubarb** to the pastry-lined pie plate. Sprinkle Crumb Topping over filling.

4 **To prevent** overbrowning, cover edge of the pie with foil. Bake in a 375°F oven for 25 minutes for fresh fruit (50 minutes for frozen fruit). Remove foil. Bake for 20 to 25 minutes more for fresh fruit (20 to 30 minutes more for frozen fruit) or until topping is golden. Cool completely on a wire rack.

Crumb Topping: In a small bowl, stir together ½ cup all-purpose flour and ½ cup packed brown sugar. Using a pastry blender, cut in 3 tablespoons butter until mixture resembles coarse crumbs.

*Note: A double-crust pastry works equally well for this pie. Simply prepare the Pastry for Double-Crust Pie (see page 46), omit the Crumb Topping, and bake as directed in step 4.

Nutrition Facts per serving: 345 cal., 13 g total fat (5 g sat. fat), 12 mg chol., 117 mg sodium, 54 g carbo., 2 g fiber, 4 g pro. **Daily Values:** 4% vit. A, 8% vit. C, 5% calcium, 11% iron

PUMPKIN PIE

Prep: 25 minutes **Bake:** 50 minutes
Makes: 8 servings **Oven:** 375°F

Instead of measuring three different spices, you can use 1½ teaspoons of pumpkin pie spice.

 1 **recipe Pastry for Single-Crust Pie (see page 45)**
 1 **16-ounce can pumpkin**
 ⅔ **cup sugar**
 1 **teaspoon ground cinnamon**
 ½ **teaspoon ground ginger**
 ½ **teaspoon ground nutmeg**
 3 **slightly beaten eggs**
 1 **5-ounce can (⅔ cup) evaporated milk**
 ½ **cup milk**

1 **Prepare and roll** out pastry. Line a 9-inch pie plate with the pastry. Trim and crimp edge as desired; set aside.

2 **For filling,** in a mixing bowl combine pumpkin, sugar, cinnamon, ginger, and nutmeg. Add eggs. Beat lightly with a rotary beater or fork just until combined. Gradually stir in evaporated milk and milk; mix well.

3 **Place the** pastry-lined pie plate on the oven rack. Carefully pour filling into pastry shell.

4 **To prevent** overbrowning, cover edge of the pie with foil. Bake in a 375°F oven for 25 minutes.

Remove foil. Bake about 25 minutes more or until a knife inserted near the center comes out clean. Cool for 1 to 2 hours on a wire rack. Refrigerate within 2 hours; cover for longer storage.

Nutrition Facts per serving: 286 cal., 13 g total fat (4 g sat. fat), 86 mg chol., 120 mg sodium, 38 g carbo., 2 g fiber, 7 g pro. **Daily Values:** 130% vit. A, 9% vit. C, 7% calcium, 13% iron

PUMPKIN-CREAM CHEESE PIE

BEST-LOVED

Prep: 20 minutes **Bake:** 1 hour
Makes: 8 servings **Oven:** 350°F

 1 **recipe Pastry for Single-Crust Pie (see page 45)**
 1 **8-ounce package cream cheese, softened**
 ¼ **cup granulated sugar**
 ½ **teaspoon vanilla**
 1 **slightly beaten egg**
 1¼ **cups canned pumpkin**
 1 **cup evaporated milk**
 2 **beaten eggs**
 ¼ **cup granulated sugar**
 ¼ **cup packed brown sugar**
 1 **teaspoon ground cinnamon**
 ¼ **teaspoon salt**
 ¼ **teaspoon ground nutmeg**
 ½ **cup chopped pecans**

THE GREAT PUMPKIN

Canned pumpkin is definitely convenient, but if time allows, here's how you can make your own pumpkin puree:

Choose a medium (about 6 pounds) pie pumpkin (pumpkins that make happy jack-o'-lanterns don't make the best pie). Cut the pumpkin into 5-inch-square pieces. Remove the seeds and fibrous strings. Arrange the pieces in a single layer, skin side up, in a large shallow baking pan. Cover with foil. Bake in a 375°F oven for 1 to 1½ hours or until tender. Scoop the pulp from the rind. Working with part of the pulp at a time, place pulp in a food processor/blender container. Cover and blend or process until smooth. Place pumpkin in a 100-pecent-cotton cheesecloth-lined strainer and press out any liquid. Makes about 2 cups pumpkin puree.

Pumpkin-Cream Cheese Pie: This special pie—with its rich creamy base, spicy pumpkin layer, and nutty topping—catapults the Thanksgiving standard into pumpkin-pie paradise. Top it off with whipped cream and nutmeg.

2 tablespoons all-purpose flour
2 tablespoons brown sugar
1 tablespoon butter, softened

1 **Prepare and roll** out pastry. Line a 9-inch pie plate with the pastry. Trim and crimp edge as desired; set aside.

2 **In small** bowl beat cream cheese, ¼ cup granulated sugar, the vanilla, and the 1 slightly beaten egg with electric mixer on low to medium speed until smooth. Chill in refrigerator for 30 minutes. Spoon into pastry-lined pie plate.

3 **In a medium bowl** combine pumpkin, evaporated milk, the 2 eggs, ¼ cup granulated sugar, ¼ cup brown sugar, cinnamon, salt, and nutmeg. Carefully pour over cream-cheese mixture.

4 **To prevent** overbrowning, cover edge of the pie with foil. Bake in a 350°F oven for 25 minutes. Remove foil. Bake for 25 minutes more.

5 **Meanwhile,** combine the pecans, flour, the 2 tablespoons brown sugar, and butter. Sprinkle over the pie. Bake for 10 to 15 minutes more or until a knife inserted near the center comes out clean. Cool for 1 to 2 hours on a wire rack. Refrigerate within 2 hours; cover for longer storage.

Nutrition Facts per serving: *477 cal., 29 g total fat (11 g sat. fat), 122 mg chol., 295 mg sodium, 46 g carbo., 2 g fiber, 10 g pro.* **Daily Values:** *103% vit. A, 4% vit. C, 12% calcium, 17% iron*

SWEET POTATO PIE

Prep: 1 hour   Bake: 50 minutes
Makes: 8 servings   Oven: 375°F

     1 pound sweet potatoes
    ¼ cup butter, cut up
     1 recipe Cornmeal Pastry
    ½ cup packed brown sugar
     1 tablespoon finely shredded orange
        peel
     1 teaspoon ground cinnamon
    ½ teaspoon ground nutmeg
    ½ teaspoon ground ginger
     3 slightly beaten eggs
     1 cup half-and-half or light cream
     1 recipe Hazelnut Streusel Topping

1 **Peel sweet potatoes.** Cut off woody portions and ends. Cut into quarters. In a covered saucepan cook sweet potatoes in enough boiling salted water to cover for 25 to 35 minutes or until tender. Drain sweet potatoes; mash. (You should have 1½ cups mashed sweet potatoes.) Add butter to hot sweet potatoes, stirring until melted.

2 **Meanwhile,** prepare Cornmeal Pastry. Roll dough into a 12-inch circle. Ease pastry into a 9-inch pie plate, being careful not to stretch pastry. Trim pastry to ½ inch beyond edge of plate. Fold under the extra pastry. Crimp the edge high. Do not prick the pastry.

3 **For filling,** stir brown sugar, orange peel, cinnamon, nutmeg, and ginger into sweet potato mixture. Stir in eggs and half-and-half. Place pastry shell on oven rack. Carefully pour filling into pastry-lined pie plate.

4 **To prevent** overbrowning, cover edge of the pie with foil. Bake in a 375°F oven for 30 minutes. Remove foil. Sprinkle with Hazelnut Streusel Topping. Bake for 20 to 25 minutes more or until a knife inserted near the center comes out clean. Cool for 1 to 2 hours on a wire rack. Refrigerate within 2 hours; cover for longer storage.

Cornmeal Pastry: In a medium bowl stir together ¾ cup all-purpose flour, ½ cup yellow cornmeal, 1 tablespoon granulated sugar, and ¼ teaspoon salt. Using a pastry blender, cut in ⅓ cup shortening until pieces are pea-size. Sprinkle

3 to 5 tablespoons cold water, 1 tablespoon at a time, over mixture, tossing with a fork after each addition until all is moistened. Form into a ball.

Hazelnut Streusel Topping: Mix ¼ cup all-purpose flour, ¼ cup packed brown sugar, ⅛ teaspoon ground cinnamon, and ⅛ teaspoon ground nutmeg. Cut in 2 tablespoons butter until mixture resembles coarse crumbs. Stir in ¼ cup chopped toasted hazelnuts or almonds (see tip, page 181).

Nutrition Facts per serving: 457 cal., 25 g total fat (10 g sat. fat), 114 mg chol., 216 mg sodium, 53 g carbo., 3 g fiber, 7 g pro. **Daily Values:** 114% vit. A, 20% vit. C, 7% calcium, 14% iron

MERINGUE FOR PIE

Prep: 20 minutes   Stand: 30 minutes
Makes: 8 servings

     3 egg whites
    ½ teaspoon vanilla
    ¼ teaspoon cream of tartar
     6 tablespoons sugar

1 **Allow egg whites** to stand at room temperature for 30 minutes. In a large mixing bowl combine egg whites, vanilla, and cream of tartar. Beat with an electric mixer on medium speed about 1 minute or until soft peaks form (tips curl).

2 **Gradually add** sugar, 1 tablespoon at a time, beating on high speed about 4 minutes more or until mixture forms stiff, glossy peaks (tips stand straight) and sugar dissolves.

3 **Immediately** spread meringue over warm pie filling, carefully sealing meringue to edge of pastry to prevent shrinkage. Bake as directed in individual recipes.

Nutrition Facts per serving: 44 cal., 0 g total fat, 0 mg chol., 21 mg sodium, 10 g carbo., 0 g fiber, 1 g pro.

Four-Egg-White Meringue: Prepare as above, except use 4 egg whites, 1 teaspoon vanilla, ½ teaspoon cream of tartar, and ½ cup sugar. Beat about 5 minutes or until stiff, glossy peaks form.

CROWNING GLORY

A golden, textured, melt-in-your-mouth meringue is a regal topping for any cream pie. To ensure that your meringue is the crown jewel of your pie, heed these suggestions:

- Let egg whites stand at room temperature for 30 minutes, and use a clean bowl.
- Add sugar gradually as soon as soft peaks form (the tips bend over slightly).
- After adding the sugar, continue beating the egg whites until stiff peaks form, the sugar is dissolved, and whites feel completely smooth beneath your fingers. Underbeaten whites may cause your meringue to shrink as it bakes.

- Spread meringue over the hot filling, sealing it well by pushing it into the edge of the pastry.
- To store a meringue-topped cream pie, first let it cool 1 hour, then refrigerate. Chill it for 3 to 6 hours before serving—there's no need to cover it unless you're going to store it longer.
- If you need to cover a meringue-capped pie, insert wooden toothpicks halfway between the centers and edges of the pie and drape loosely with clear plastic wrap.
- An easy way to cut a meringue-topped cream pie is to dip the knife in water (don't dry it off) before cutting each slice of pie. This prevents the meringue from clinging to the knife.

VANILLA CREAM PIE

Prep: 1 hour   **Bake:** 25 minutes   **Cool:** 1 hour
Chill: 3 to 6 hours   **Makes:** 8 servings
Oven: 325°F

If you wish, skip the meringue and crown the chilled pie with whipped cream instead.

　　1 **recipe Baked Pastry Shell**
　　　　(see page 45)
　　4 **eggs**
　　¾ **cup sugar**
　　¼ **cup cornstarch or ½ cup**
　　　　all-purpose flour
　　3 **cups milk**
　　1 **tablespoon butter**
　1½ **teaspoons vanilla**
　　1 **recipe Four-Egg-White Meringue**
　　　　(see page 60)

1 **Prepare** Baked Pastry Shell; set aside. Separate egg yolks from whites; set the egg whites aside for meringue.

2 **For filling,** in a medium saucepan combine sugar and cornstarch or flour. Gradually stir in milk. Cook and stir over medium-high heat until thickened and bubbly. Cook and stir for 2 minutes more. Remove from heat. Slightly beat egg yolks with a rotary beater or fork. Gradually stir about

1 cup of the hot filling into yolks. Pour egg yolk mixture into hot filling in saucepan. Bring to gentle boil. Cook and stir for 2 minutes more. Remove from heat. Stir in butter and vanilla. Keep filling warm while preparing meringue.

3 **Pour warm** filling into pastry shell. Spread meringue over warm filling; seal to edge. Bake in a 325°F oven for 25 to 30 minutes or until lightly browned. Cool for 1 hour on a wire rack. Chill in the refrigerator for 3 to 6 hours before serving.

Nutrition Facts per serving: 377 cal., 14 g total fat (4 g sat. fat), 113 mg chol., 161 mg sodium, 54 g carbo., 1 g fiber, 8 g pro. **Daily Values:** 23% vit. A, 1% vit. C, 10% calcium, 8% iron

Coconut Cream Pie: Prepare as above, except stir in 1 cup flaked coconut with butter and vanilla.

Banana Cream Pie: Prepare as above, except before adding filling, arrange 3 medium bananas, sliced (about 2¼ cups), over bottom of pastry shell.

Dark Chocolate Cream Pie: Prepare as above, except increase the sugar to 1 cup. Stir in 3 ounces unsweetened chocolate, cut up, with the milk.

Milk Chocolate Cream Pie: Prepare as above, except stir in 3 ounces semisweet chocolate, cut up, with the milk.

KEY LIME PIE

Prep: 35 minutes   **Bake:** 45 minutes
Cool and Chill: 4 to 7 hours
Makes: 8 servings   **Oven:** 325°/350F°

Tiny Key limes grow only in Florida and the Caribbean, but Persian limes grow in many places and are available in most markets.

  1 recipe Pastry for Single-Crust Pie
      (see page 45)
  3 eggs
  1 14-ounce can (1¼ cups) sweetened
      condensed milk
  ½ to ¾ teaspoon finely shredded Key
      lime peel or 1½ teaspoons finely
      shredded Persian lime peel
  ½ cup water
  ⅓ cup lime juice (8 to 10 Key limes
      or 2 to 3 Persian limes)
      Several drops green food coloring
      (optional)
  1 recipe Meringue for Pie (page 60)

1 **Prepare and roll** out pastry. Line a 9-inch pie plate with pastry. Trim and crimp edge as desired; set aside.

2 **Separate** egg yolks from whites; set whites aside for meringue. For filling, in a medium bowl beat egg yolks with a rotary beater or fork. Gradually stir in sweetened condensed milk and lime peel. Add water, lime juice, and, if desired, food coloring. Mix well (mixture will thicken).

3 **Spoon** thickened filling into pastry-lined pie plate. Bake in a 325°F oven for 30 minutes.

4 **Meanwhile,** prepare meringue. Remove pie from oven. Increase the oven temperature to 350°F. Spread meringue over hot filling; seal to edge. Bake in the 350°F oven for 15 minutes. Cool for 1 hour on a wire rack. Chill in the refrigerator for 3 to 6 hours before serving; cover for longer storage.

Nutrition Facts per serving: 370 cal., 15 g total fat (6 g sat. fat), 97 mg chol., 157 mg sodium, 51 g carbo., 0 g fiber, 8 g pro. **Daily Values:** 8% vit. A, 7% vit. C, 13% calcium, 8% iron

DOUBLE-COCONUT CREAM PIE

Prep: 1 hour   **Bake:** 15 minutes
Cool and Chill: 4 to 7 hours
Makes: 8 servings   **Oven:** 350°F

Cream of coconut boosts the nutty flavor of the coconut in this dreamy pie.

  1 recipe Baked Pastry Shell
      (see page 45)
  3 beaten eggs
  ⅓ cup sugar
  ¼ cup cornstarch
  ¼ teaspoon salt
  2 cups milk
  1 8-ounce can (¾ cup) cream
      of coconut
  2 tablespoons butter
  1 cup coconut
  2 teaspoons vanilla
  1 recipe Meringue for Pie
      (see page 60)
  2 tablespoons coconut

1 **Prepare** Baked Pastry Shell. Separate egg yolks from egg whites; set whites aside for meringue.

2 **For filling,** in a medium saucepan combine sugar, cornstarch, and salt. Gradually stir in milk and cream of coconut. Cook and stir over medium heat until thickened and bubbly. Cook and stir 2 minutes more. Remove from heat. Slightly beat egg yolks with a rotary beater or fork. Gradually stir about 1 cup of the hot filling into egg yolks. Pour egg yolk mixture into hot filling in saucepan. Bring to a gentle boil. Cook and stir 2 minutes more. Remove from heat. Stir in butter until melted. Stir in the 1 cup coconut and vanilla. Keep filling warm while preparing meringue.

3 **Pour warm** filling into pastry shell. Spread meringue over warm filling; seal to edge. Sprinkle with the 2 tablespoons coconut. Bake in a 350°F oven for 15 minutes. Cool for 1 hour on a wire rack. Chill in refrigerator for 3 to 6 hours before serving; cover for longer storage.

Nutrition Facts per serving: 565 cal., 38 g total fat (13 g sat. fat), 92 mg chol., 229 mg sodium, 50 g carbo., 1 g fiber, 7 g pro. **Daily Values:** 18% vit. A, 0% vit. C, 7% calcium, 10% iron

Lemon Meringue Pie:
Cool, creamy, and with the refreshing taste of lemon in every bite, here's the perfect pie for catching up with the neighbors over coffee on a summer evening.

LEMON MERINGUE PIE

Prep: 45 minutes   Bake: 15 minutes
Cool and Chill: 4 to 7 hours
Makes: 8 servings   Oven: 350°F

  1 recipe **Baked Pastry Shell**
     (see recipe page 45)
  3 eggs
1½ cups sugar
  3 tablespoons all-purpose flour
  3 tablespoons cornstarch
1½ cups water
  2 tablespoons butter
  1 to 2 teaspoons finely shredded
     lemon peel
 ⅓ cup lemon juice
  1 recipe **Meringue for Pie**
     (see recipe page 60)

1 Prepare Baked Pastry Shell; set aside. Separate egg yolks from the egg whites; set whites aside for meringue.

2 For filling, in a medium saucepan combine the sugar, flour, cornstarch, and dash salt. Gradually stir in the water. Cook and stir over medium-high heat until thickened and bubbly. Reduce heat. Cook and stir 2 minutes more. Remove from heat. Slightly beat egg yolks with a rotary beater or fork. Gradually stir about 1 cup of the hot filling into yolks. Pour egg yolk mixture into hot filling in saucepan. Bring to a gentle boil. Cook and stir 2 minutes more. Remove from heat. Stir in butter and lemon peel. Gently stir in lemon juice. Keep filling warm while preparing meringue.

3 Pour warm filling into pastry shell. Spread meringue over warm filling; seal to edge. Bake in a 350°F oven for 15 minutes. Cool for 1 hour on wire rack. Chill in refrigerator for 3 to 6 hours before serving; cover for longer storage.

Nutrition Facts per serving: 395 cal., 14 g total fat (6 g sat. fat), 96 mg chol., 139 mg sodium, 65 g carbo., 1 g fiber, 5 g pro. **Daily Values:** 14% vit. A, 8% vit. C, 1% calcium, 8% iron

---

TROUBLESHOOTING PASTRY

If your pastry didn't turn out perfectly, look for one of the following problems (and its solution, too!):

If your pastry is crumbly and hard to roll:
- Add more water, 1 teaspoon at a time.
- Toss the flour mixture and water together just a little more, or until evenly moistened.

If your pastry is tough:
- Use a pastry blender to cut in the shortening or lard until well mixed and all of the mixture resembles small peas.
- Use less water to moisten the flour mixture.
- Toss the flour mixture and water together only until all of the flour mixture is moistened.

- Use less flour when rolling out your pastry.

If your crust shrinks excessively:
- Mix in the water only until evenly moistened.
- Let pastry rest for 5 minutes if it is hard to roll.
- Don't stretch pastry when transferring it.

If the bottom crust is soggy:
- Use a dull metal or glass pie plate rather than a shiny metal pan.
- Patch any cracks in the pastry with a pastry scrap before adding the filling.
- Make sure your oven temperature is accurate. If the temperature is too low, the bottom crust won't bake properly.

TARTE TATIN

Prep: 45 minutes   **Bake:** 30 minutes
Makes: 8 servings   **Oven:** 375°F

This French upside-down apple tart, baked in an ovenproof skillet, bears the name of the Tatin sisters, who first served it in their restaurant in the early 1900s (see photo, page 43).

⅔ **cup granulated sugar**
½ **cup butter**
2 **pounds (about 6) tart cooking apples, peeled, cored, and quartered**
1 **recipe Egg Tart Pastry**
1 **recipe Sweetened Whipped Cream (optional)**
  Orange peel curls (optional)

1 **In a** 10-inch ovenproof skillet combine granulated sugar and butter. Cook over medium heat, stirring occasionally, until boiling. Cook, without stirring, over medium-low heat for 9 to 10 minutes more or until mixture just begins to turn brown. (Mixture may appear separated.) Remove from heat.

2 **Arrange the apples,** cored sides up, in a single layer on top of the sugar mixture, overlapping them if necessary. Cover and cook over low heat about 10 minutes or until apples are tender.

3 **On a lightly** floured surface, use your hands to slightly flatten Egg Tart Pastry dough. Roll dough from center to edge, forming a 10-inch circle. Cut slits in the pastry. Wrap pastry around rolling pin. Unroll pastry over the apples in the skillet, being careful not to stretch the pastry.

4 **Bake in a** 375°F oven about 30 minutes or until the pastry is golden. Cool dessert in skillet for 5 minutes on a wire rack. Invert onto a large serving plate. Lift off the skillet. Serve warm. If desired, serve with Sweetened Whipped Cream and garnish with orange peel curls.

Egg Tart Pastry: In a medium bowl stir together 2 cups all-purpose flour and ¼ cup granulated sugar. Cut in ⅔ cup butter until pieces are pea-size. Using a fork, stir in 1 slightly beaten egg until all dough is moistened. Form into a ball.

Nutrition Facts per serving: 502 cal., 28 g total fat (17 g sat. fat), 72 mg chol., 323 mg sodium, 61 g carbo., 3 g fiber, 4 g pro. **Daily Values:** 34% vit. A, 0% vit. C, 1% calcium, 11% iron

Sweetened Whipped Cream: Chill a medium mixing bowl and the beaters of an electric mixer in the refrigerator. In the chilled bowl combine ½ cup whipping cream, 1 tablespoon sifted powdered sugar, and ¼ teaspoon vanilla. Beat with the chilled beaters on low speed until soft peaks form. Makes 1 cup.

PIE SAFE

Whether you're making a pie or tart ahead of time, or storing a few extra pieces, here are a few golden rules of pastry storage:

- Fruit pies may stand at room temperature for 24 hours. Cover and refrigerate for longer storage.
- Custard and cream pies should be served as soon as they are cool, or covered lightly with plastic wrap and refrigerated for up to 2 days. Don't freeze cream or custard pies.
- To freeze unbaked fruit pies, treat any light-colored fruit with an ascorbic-acid color keeper. Assemble the pie in a metal or freezer-to-oven pie plate. Place it in a freezer bag; seal, label,

and freeze. Frozen pies should be used within 2 to 4 months. To bake a frozen pie, unwrap it and cover with foil. Bake in a 450°F oven for 15 minutes; reduce the temperature to 375°F and bake another 15 minutes. Uncover and continue baking for 55 to 60 minutes more or until crust is golden and filling is bubbly.

- To freeze baked fruit pies, bake and cool the pie completely. Place it in a freezer bag, seal, label, and freeze for up to 8 months. To use it, thaw, covered, at room temperature. If desired, reheat it by baking it, covered, in a 325°F oven until warm.

FRENCH SILK PIE

Prep: 35 minutes **Chill:** 5 to 24 hours
Makes: 10 servings

For the chocoholic, this pie is pure bliss. Make it pretty with Double-Chocolate Whipped Cream.

> **1 recipe Baked Pastry Shell
>   (see page 45)**
> **1 6-ounce package (1 cup) semisweet
>   chocolate pieces**
> **¾ cup sugar**
> **¾ cup butter**
> **1 teaspoon vanilla**
> **¾ cup refrigerated or frozen egg
>   product, thawed**
> **1 recipe Double-Chocolate Whipped
>   Cream (optional)**

1 Prepare the Baked Pastry Shell. Heat chocolate pieces over low heat until melted. Cool.

To pipe large swirls on pie, hold pastry bag at 45° angle above center of pie. Squeeze bag gently while guiding the tip to edge to make a swirl. Stop pressure, then lift tip. Repeat.

2 For filling, in a large mixing bowl beat sugar and butter with an electric mixer on medium speed about 4 minutes or until fluffy. Stir in chocolate and vanilla. Gradually add egg product, beating on high speed until light and fluffy (scrape bowl constantly).

3 Transfer filling to pastry shell. Cover and chill in the refrigerator for 5 to 24 hours. If desired, top with Double-Chocolate Whipped Cream.

Nutrition Facts per serving: 392 cal., 26 g total fat (5 g sat. fat), 18 mg chol., 225 mg sodium, 38 g carbo., 0 g fiber, 5 g pro. **Daily Values:** 17% vit. A, 3% calcium, 9% iron

Double-Chocolate Whipped Cream: For semisweet chocolate portion, in a heavy, small saucepan combine ¼ cup whipping cream and 3 ounces chopped semisweet chocolate. Heat over low heat, stirring constantly, until the chocolate begins to melt. Immediately remove from the heat and stir until smooth. Cool. In a small mixing bowl beat ¾ cup whipping cream with an electric mixer on low speed until soft peaks form. Add the cooled chocolate mixture. Continue beating on low speed just until stiff peaks form; set aside.

For white chocolate portion, repeat as above, except substitute 3 ounces white chocolate or white baking bar for the semisweet chocolate.

Fit pastry bag with large star tip. Spoon the semisweet chocolate portion down 1 side of bag and the white chocolate portion down the other side; close bag. Pipe swirls on pie (see photo, left).

SOUR CREAM, RAISIN, AND PEAR PIE

Prep: 40 minutes **Bake:** 40 minutes
Makes: 8 servings **Oven:** 375°F

Wrapped in Cinnamon Pastry and beneath a layer of fresh pears lies the traditional sour cream-raisin pie. If you like a traditional topping, try the meringue version (see below right).

1 recipe Cinnamon Pastry
¾ cup light raisins
3 beaten egg yolks
1½ cups sour cream
1 cup granulated sugar
½ cup milk
3 tablespoons all-purpose flour
1 teaspoon ground cinnamon
¼ teaspoon ground nutmeg
⅛ teaspoon ground cloves
  Milk
  Granulated sugar
1½ cups water
⅔ cup packed brown sugar
2 tablespoons dark-colored corn syrup
1 tablespoon lemon juice
2 small pears, peeled and thinly sliced (2 cups)
1 tablespoon cold water
1 teaspoon cornstarch
  Pomegranate seeds (optional)

1 Prepare pastry. On a lightly floured surface, roll pastry to a 12-inch circle. Line a 9-inch pie plate with pastry. Trim to ¼ inch beyond edge of pie plate. Fold under extra pastry.

2 To decorate pastry edge with a leaf pattern, use a small, sharp knife to cut pastry scraps into small leaf shapes, about 1 inch long. Use the back side of the knife to score a vein down the middle of each leaf. Brush pastry edge with water. Gently press leaves along pastry edge, overlapping leaves. Do not prick pastry. Set aside.

3 In a small bowl pour enough hot water over raisins to cover. Let stand for 5 minutes; drain well.

4 In a medium bowl stir together raisins, egg yolks, sour cream, the 1 cup granulated sugar, the ½ cup milk, the flour, cinnamon, nutmeg, and cloves. Pour the raisin mixture into pastry-lined pie plate. Brush pastry edge with additional milk and sprinkle with additional granulated sugar.

5 To prevent overbrowning, cover the edge of the pie with foil. Bake in a 375°F oven for 20 minutes. Remove foil. Bake for 20 to 25 minutes more or until pie appears nearly set in center when gently shaken. Cool pie for 1 hour on a wire rack.

6 Meanwhile, in a large saucepan, combine the 1½ cups water, the brown sugar, corn syrup, and lemon juice; bring to boiling. Stir in pears. Reduce heat. Simmer, covered, about 5 minutes or until pears are tender. Drain pears, reserving ⅓ cup of the poaching liquid. Let pears cool slightly.

7 Combine the 1 tablespoon water and the cornstarch; stir into reserved poaching liquid. Cook and stir until thickened and bubbly. Cook and stir 1 minute. Remove from heat; cool slightly.

8 Arrange pear slices in a circle on cooled sour-cream filling, overlapping pears slightly. Brush with the thickened poaching mixture. Cool for 1 to 2 hours on a wire rack. Refrigerate within 2 hours; cover for longer storage. If desired, garnish with pomegranate seeds.

Cinnamon Pastry: In a bowl stir together 1¼ cups all-purpose flour, ½ teaspoon ground cinnamon, and ¼ teaspoon salt. Cut in ⅓ cup shortening until pieces are pea-size. Sprinkle 1 tablespoon cold water over part of the mixture; gently toss with a fork. Push moistened dough to side of bowl. Repeat with 3 to 4 tablespoons additional cold water, using 1 tablespoon water at a time, until all the dough is moistened. Form the dough into a ball.

Nutrition Facts per serving: 519 cal., 20 g total fat (9 g sat. fat), 100 mg chol., 113 mg sodium, 82 g carbo., 2 g fiber, 6 g pro. **Daily Values:** 23% vit. A, 6% vit. C, 9% calcium, 15% iron

Meringue-Topped Sour Cream-Raisin Pie: Prepare as above, except omit pear topping. Prepare 1 recipe Meringue for Pie (see page 60). Spread meringue over warm filling; seal to edge. Bake in a 350°F oven 15 minutes. Cool 1 hour on a wire rack. Chill 3 to 6 hours before serving; cover for longer storage.

Sour Cream, Raisin, and Pear Pie: If you love sour cream-raisin pie, try this pear-topped version with a cinnamon crust.

Mixed Fruit Tart with Amaretto Creme: Ideal for warm-weather get-togethers, this appealing almond tart boasts an array of fresh melon, grapes, tiny champagne grapes, strawberries, raspberries, and peaches.

MIXED FRUIT TART WITH AMARETTO CREME

Prep: 45 minutes **Bake:** 12 minutes
Makes: 8 servings **Oven:** 450°F

Use your 9-inch springform pan for this luscious almond and fruit tart.

  1 **recipe Pastry for Single-Crust Pie**
      (see page 45)
    Milk
  1 **tablespoon granulated sugar**
  1 **8-ounce package cream cheese,**
      softened
  1 **3-ounce package cream cheese,**
      softened
  ½ **cup amaretto***
  3 **tablespoons brown sugar**

½ **cup finely chopped almonds, toasted**
    (see tip, page 181)
  3 **to 4 cups chilled assorted fresh fruit**
  1 **tablespoon granulated sugar**

1 **Prepare pastry.** On a lightly floured surface, roll piecrust to an 11-inch circle. Wrap piecrust around rolling pin. Unroll into a 9-inch springform pan. Ease piecrust into pan. Press piecrust evenly

Line the piecrust shell in the springform pan with a double thickness of heavy foil. This prevents the piecrust from puffing while baking.

onto the bottom and 1 inch up the sides of the pan. If desired, flute edge of piecrust. Generously prick bottom and side. Line with a double thickness of foil (see photo, page 68).

2 **Bake in a** 450°F oven for 5 minutes. Remove the foil. Brush the edge of the piecrust with milk. Sprinkle piecrust with 1 tablespoon granulated sugar. Bake for 7 to 9 minutes more or until piecrust is golden. Cool completely in pan on a wire rack.

3 **In a small** mixing bowl beat the cream cheese, amaretto, and brown sugar with an electric mixer on medium speed until smooth. Stir in the almonds. Spread the almond mixture evenly over the cooled piecrust. Serve immediately or chill in the refrigerator for up to 4 hours.

4 **To serve,** top almond mixture with desired fruits. Remove side of pan. If desired, remove bottom of pan. Sprinkle the fruit with 1 tablespoon granulated sugar.

*Note: If desired, substitute ¼ cup milk and ¼ teaspoon almond extract for the amaretto.

Nutrition Facts per serving: 398 cal., 26 g total fat (9 g sat. fat), 51 mg chol., 226 mg sodium, 35 g carbo., 2 g fiber, 6 g pro. **Daily Values:** 35% vit. A, 14% vit. C, 8% calcium, 7% iron

BROWN BUTTER TART

Prep: 40 minutes   Bake: 35 minutes
Makes: 12 to 16 servings   Oven: 350°F

A generous spoonful of honeyed fresh fruit brings out the best in each wedge of buttery tart.

　1 **recipe Sweet Tart Pastry**
　3 **eggs**
1¼ **cups sugar**
　½ **cup all-purpose flour**
　1 **vanilla bean, split lengthwise,**
　　　or 1 teaspoon vanilla
　¾ **cup butter**
　⅓ **cup orange juice**
　2 **tablespoons honey**
　1 **tablespoon orange liqueur**
　3 **cups assorted mixed berries or**
　　　assorted cut-up fresh fruit

1 **On a lightly** floured surface, use your hands to slightly flatten Sweet Tart Pastry dough. Roll dough from center to edge into a 12-inch circle. Wrap pastry around rolling pin. Unroll into an ungreased 10-inch tart pan with a removable bottom. Ease pastry into tart pan, being careful not to stretch pastry. Press pastry into the fluted sides of tart pan. Trim edge; set aside.

2 **In a large** bowl use a rotary beater or a wire whisk to beat eggs just until mixed. Stir in sugar, flour, and, if using, liquid vanilla; set aside.

3 **In a heavy,** medium saucepan combine the butter and, if using, vanilla bean. Cook over medium-high heat until the butter turns the color of light brown sugar. Remove from heat. Remove and discard vanilla bean. Slowly add the browned butter to the egg mixture, stirring until mixed. Pour into the pastry-lined tart pan.

4 **Bake in a** 350°F oven about 35 minutes or until the top is crisp and golden. Cool 1 to 2 hours in pan on a wire rack. Refrigerate within 2 hours; cover for longer storage.

5 **In a medium mixing bowl** stir together the orange juice, honey, and orange liqueur. Stir in the fruit. Let fruit mixture stand up to 1 hour.

6 **To serve,** remove sides of the tart pan. Cut tart into wedges. Place wedges on dessert plates. Using a slotted spoon, spoon some of the fruit mixture beside each wedge of tart.

Sweet Tart Pastry: In a medium mixing bowl stir together 1¼ cups all-purpose flour and ¼ cup sugar. Using a pastry blender, cut in ½ cup cold butter until pieces are pea-size. In a small bowl stir together 2 beaten egg yolks and 1 tablespoon water. Gradually stir egg yolk mixture into mixture. Using your fingers, gently knead dough just until a ball forms. If necessary, cover with plastic wrap and chill in refrigerator for 30 to 60 minutes or until dough is easy to handle.

Nutrition Facts per serving: 387 cal., 21 g total fat (12 g sat. fat), 140 mg chol., 212 mg sodium, 46 g carbo., 2 g fiber, 4 g pro. **Daily Values:** 25% vit. A, 24% vit. C, 2% calcium, 8% iron

COUNTRY CHERRY AND APRICOT TART

Prep: 40 minutes   Bake: 45 minutes
Makes: 8 servings   Oven: 375°F

¾ **cup granulated sugar**
3 **tablespoons cornstarch**
¾ **cup apricot nectar**
3 **tablespoons cherry brandy, apricot brandy, or orange juice**
2 **tablespoons butter**
3 **cups sliced fresh apricots**
2 **cups pitted fresh sweet cherries**
1 **recipe Tart Pastry (see page 74)**
  Milk
  Powdered sugar

1 **For filling,** in a medium saucepan combine granulated sugar and cornstarch. Stir in nectar. Cook and stir over medium heat until thickened

Using your fingers, fold the pastry border up and over the apricot-cherry filling, pleating the pastry to fit.

and bubbly. Cook and stir 2 minutes more. Remove from heat. Stir in the brandy and butter. Stir in apricots and cherries; set aside.

2 **For pastry,** on a lightly floured surface, use your hands to slightly flatten Tart Pastry dough. Roll dough from center to the edge into a 14-inch circle. Wrap pastry around rolling pin. Unroll into a 10-inch pie plate or quiche dish. Ease pastry into the plate or dish, being careful not to stretch pastry. Trim pastry to 1½ inches beyond the edge.

Country Cherry and Apricot Tart: The "country" in this beautiful tart featuring plump cherries and ripe apricots comes from the rustic form of its classic flaky pastry.

3 Pour filling into the pastry-lined pie plate. Fold the pastry border up and over the filling (see photo, page 70). Lightly brush pastry with milk.

4 Bake in a 375°F oven for 45 to 50 minutes or until pastry is golden. Cool completely in pan on wire rack. Before serving, sift powdered sugar over pastry edges.

Nutrition Facts per serving: 350 cal., 16 g total fat (4 g sat. fat), 0 mg chol., 102 mg sodium, 47 g carbo., 2 g fiber, 3 g pro. **Daily Values:** 18% vit. A, 9% vit. C, 2% calcium, 8% iron

FRESH BLUEBERRY TART

Prep: 30 minutes   Bake: 15 minutes
Chill: 1 hour   Makes: 10 servings   Oven: 375°F

Glazed blueberries crown lemony cream cheese in a beautifully speckled Poppy-Seed Pastry.

  1 recipe Poppy-Seed Pastry
  1 8-ounce package cream cheese, softened
  ½ cup marshmallow creme
  ½ teaspoon finely shredded lemon peel
  3 cups fresh blueberries
  ¼ cup grape jelly
    Lemon peel curls (optional)

1 Grease a 10- to 11-inch tart pan with a removable bottom (use vegetable shortening, not nonstick spray coating). On lightly floured surface, use your hands to slightly flatten Poppy-Seed Pastry dough. Roll dough from center to edge into a circle 2 inches larger than tart pan. Wrap pastry around rolling pin. Unroll into prepared tart pan. Ease pastry into pan, being careful not to stretch pastry. Press pastry into fluted side of tart pan. Trim edges. Prick pastry. Line pastry in pan with a double thickness of foil (see photo, page 45).

2 Bake in a 375°F oven for 10 minutes. Remove foil. Bake for 5 to 10 minutes more or until golden. Cool completely in pan on a wire rack.

3 For filling, in a medium mixing bowl beat cream cheese with an electric mixer on medium speed until light. Fold in marshmallow creme and lemon peel. Spread filling in the cooled pastry shell. Arrange blueberries on filling. In a small saucepan heat and stir jelly over medium heat until jelly is melted. Brush jelly over berries. Chill in the refrigerator for 1 hour or until jelly is set.

4 To serve, remove side of the tart pan. If desired, garnish with lemon peel curls. Cover and refrigerate any leftovers.

Poppy-Seed Pastry: In a medium bowl stir together 1¼ cups all-purpose flour and ¼ cup sugar. Using a pastry blender, cut in ½ cup cold butter until pieces are pea-size. In a small mixing bowl combine 2 beaten egg yolks, 1 tablespoon water, and 1 teaspoon poppy seed. Gradually stir egg yolk mixture into flour mixture. (Dough will not be completely moistened.) Using your fingers, gently knead the dough just until a ball forms. If necessary, cover dough with plastic wrap and chill for 30 to 60 minutes or until dough is easy to handle.

Nutrition Facts per serving: 320 cal., 19 g total fat (8 g sat. fat), 80 mg chol., 162 sodium, 35 g carbo., 2 g fiber, 4 g pro. **Daily Values:** 25% vit. A, 10% vit. C, 37% calcium, 8% iron

Mango Cream Tart: Treat family and friends to a taste of the tropics with this magnificent mango dessert. Garnishing with fresh raspberries or other fresh fruit makes the tart as eye-catching as it is delicious.

MANGO CREAM TART

Prep: 40 minutes **Bake:** 13 minutes
Chill: 4 hours **Makes:** 8 servings **Oven:** 450°F

You can use fresh mangoes or refrigerated mango slices (found in your supermarket produce section) to make this creamy tart.

> 1 recipe Pastry for Single-Crust Pie
>   (see page 45)
> 1 cup sugar
> ¼ cup cornstarch
> ¼ teaspoon salt
> 2½ cups sliced ripe mango
>   (about 1½ mangoes)
> 1½ cups plain yogurt or dairy sour
>   cream
> 3 egg yolks
> 1 tablespoon lime juice
>   Fresh fruit (optional)

1 Prepare pastry. Roll dough into 13-inch circle. Ease pastry into an ungreased 11-inch tart pan with a removable bottom. Press pastry into pan; trim edges. Prick bottom and sides of pastry. Line with a double thickness of foil (see photo, page 45). Bake in a 450°F oven for 8 minutes. Remove foil. Bake 5 to 6 minutes more or until lightly browned. Cool completely in pan on a wire rack.

2 For filling, in a heavy, medium saucepan stir together sugar, cornstarch, and salt. Place mango in food processor/blender container. Cover; process until smooth (should have 1½ cups). Stir mango and yogurt into sugar mixture. Cook and stir over medium heat until thickened and bubbly. Cook and stir 2 minutes more. Remove from heat. Slightly beat egg yolks. Gradually, stir about 1 cup of the hot filling into egg yolks. Pour egg yolk mixture into hot filling in saucepan. Bring to gentle boil. Cook and stir for 2 minutes more. Remove from heat. Stir in lime juice.

3 Pour warm filling into pastry shell. Cool for 1 hour on wire rack. Chill in refrigerator for at least 4 hours before serving; cover for longer storage. If desired, garnish with fresh fruit.

Nutrition Facts per serving: 327 cal., 11 g total fat (3 g sat. fat), 83 mg chol., 168 mg sodium, 52 g carbo., 1 g fiber, 5 g pro. **Daily Values:** 28% vit. A, 19% vit. C, 7% calcium, 7% iron

LINZER TORTE

Prep: 50 minutes **Bake:** 35 minutes **Chill:** 1 hour
Makes: 8 servings **Oven:** 325°F

> ⅔ cup butter
> ⅔ cup granulated sugar
> 1 egg
> 2 hard-cooked egg yolks, sieved
> 1 tablespoon kirsch (cherry brandy)
>   or water
> 1 teaspoon finely shredded lemon peel
> ½ teaspoon ground cinnamon
> ¼ teaspoon ground cloves
> 1½ cups all-purpose flour
> 1¼ cups ground almonds or hazelnuts

1 12-ounce jar seedless red
  raspberry jam
  Powdered sugar

1 **In a medium** mixing bowl beat the butter with an electric mixer on medium to high speed about 30 seconds or until softened. Add the granulated sugar, whole egg, hard-cooked egg yolks, kirsch or water, lemon peel, cinnamon, and cloves. Beat until thoroughly combined, scraping side of bowl occasionally. Stir in the flour and almonds. Form dough into a ball. Wrap dough in plastic wrap; chill in the refrigerator for 1 hour.

2 **On a lightly** floured surface, use your hands to slightly flatten two-thirds of the dough. (Refrigerate remaining dough until ready to use.) Roll dough from the center to edge into an 11-inch circle. Wrap pastry around rolling pin. Unroll onto an ungreased 10-inch tart pan with removable bottom or into 10-inch springform pan. Ease pastry into pan, pressing dough about ½ inch up the side. Spread the raspberry jam over the bottom of pastry in pan.

3 **Roll the** remaining pastry to form a 10×6-inch rectangle. Cut six 1-inch-wide strips. Carefully weave strips on top of jam to make a lattice. Press ends of strips into rim of bottom crust, trimming ends as necessary.

4 **Bake in a** 325°F oven for 35 to 40 minutes or until crust is golden. Cool completely in pan on wire rack. To serve, remove side of pan. Sift powdered sugar over torte.

Nutrition Facts per serving: 558 cal., 29 g total fat (6 g sat. fat), 100 mg chol., 158 mg sodium, 70 g carbo., 3 g fiber, 8 g pro. **Daily Values:** 24% vit. A, 6% calcium, 16% iron

PEACHES-AND-CREAM TART

EASY

Prep: 25 minutes   Bake: 15 minutes
Makes: 10 to 12 servings   Oven: 350°F

9 soft coconut macaroon cookies,
  crumbled (2 cups)
1 cup (4 ounces) ground pecans*
3 tablespoons butter or margarine
½ cup whipping cream

1 8-ounce package cream cheese,
  softened
⅓ cup sugar
2 teaspoons dark rum or orange
  juice
1 teaspoon vanilla
¼ teaspoon almond extract
2 to 4 medium peaches, peeled, pitted,
  and thinly sliced (1½ to 3 cups)
2 tablespoons lemon juice
½ cup fresh raspberries
¼ cup apricot preserves
2 teaspoons honey

1 **For crust,** in a large bowl stir together macaroon crumbs, pecans, and butter. Press mixture onto bottom and up sides of a 10- to 11-inch tart pan with a removable bottom, or into a 12-inch pizza pan. Bake in a 350°F oven until golden, allowing 15 to 18 minutes for tart pan and 12 to 15 minutes for pizza pan. Cool on a wire rack.

2 **For filling,** chill a medium mixing bowl and beaters of an electric mixer. In the chilled bowl beat whipping cream with a mixer on medium speed until soft peaks form; set aside.

3 **In a small** mixing bowl beat cream cheese and sugar with an electric mixer on medium speed until fluffy. Add rum vanilla, and almond extract; beat until smooth. Gently fold in whipped cream. Turn mixture into cooled crust; spread evenly. Cover and chill for 2 to 4 hours.

4 **Before serving,** toss peach slices with lemon juice. Place peaches and raspberries over filling.

5 **For glaze,** in small saucepan combine preserves and honey; heat and stir just until melted. Snip any large pieces of fruit in the glaze. Strain glaze, if desired. Carefully brush or spoon the glaze over the fruit.

6 **To serve,** remove sides of pan (if using tart pan). Transfer tart to serving platter. Cut into wedges.

*Note: To grind pecans, process or blend the nuts, ½ cup at a time, in your food processor or blender. Cover and process or blend until very finely chopped. Be careful not to overprocess or the nuts will form a paste.

Nutrition Facts per serving: 388 cal., 28 g total fat (11 g sat. fat), 51 mg chol., 115 mg sodium, 33 g carbo., 2 g fiber, 4 g pro. **Daily Values:** 19% vit. A, 8% vit. C, 3% calcium, 5% iron

WARM PEACH AND NUTMEG TART

Prep: 1 hour   Bake: 30 minutes
Makes: 8 servings   Oven: 400°F

Peach season is fleeting but sweet. Showcase summer's best in this irresistible tart.

    1 recipe Tart Pastry
    1 beaten egg
      Sugar
  ⅔ cup sugar
    3 tablespoons all-purpose flour
1½ teaspoons finely shredded orange
      peel
  ¼ teaspoon ground nutmeg
    4 cups sliced, peeled peaches
      (7 to 8 medium)
    1 recipe Orange Whipped Cream
      Coarsely shredded orange peel

1 **For the crust,** on a lightly floured surface, roll three-fourths of the Tart Pastry into a 13×10-inch rectangle. (Refrigerate remaining pastry until ready to use.) Ease pastry into an ungreased 11×8×1-inch rectangular tart pan with a removable bottom. (Or, roll pastry into a 12-inch circle. Ease pastry into a 10-inch round tart pan with a removable bottom.) Use your fingers to trim pastry from pan edge or roll a rolling pin across the pan edge to remove excess pastry; reserve trimmings. Line pastry with a double thickness of foil (see photo, page 68); set aside.

Use the dull edge of a table knife to make decorative marks, such as veins in leaves and indents in peaches, in the pastry shapes.

2 **On a lightly** floured surface, roll remaining pastry and any pastry trimmings to ⅛-inch thickness. Using a small knife, cookie cutters, or your hands, cut or shape pastry into desired shapes, such as a bunch of grapes, peaches, cherries, branches, and leaves. Transfer shapes to an ungreased baking sheet. Make decorative marks in pastry shapes (see photo, below left). Brush with beaten egg; sprinkle with a little sugar.

3 **Bake crust** and pastry shapes in a 400°F oven for 10 to 12 minutes or until pastry shapes are golden (if sizes of pastry shapes vary, smaller shapes may brown more quickly). Transfer pastry shapes to a wire rack. Carefully remove foil from crust; place crust in the pan on a wire rack.

4 **For filling,** in a large mixing bowl stir together the ⅔ cup sugar, the flour, the 1½ teaspoons orange peel, and the nutmeg. Add peaches; toss gently to coat. Spoon mixture into pastry.

5 **Bake in a** 400°F oven for 30 to 40 minutes or until pastry is golden. Cool slightly on a wire rack.

6 **Top tart** with pastry shapes. Serve warm, or cover and store at room temperature for up to 1 day. For longer storage, cover and chill in the refrigerator for up to 3 days.

7 **To serve,** transfer Orange Whipped Cream to a serving bowl; top with coarsely shredded orange peel. Serve with tart.

Tart Pastry: In a medium mixing bowl combine 1½ cups all-purpose flour and ¼ teaspoon salt. Using a pastry blender, cut in ½ cup shortening until pieces are pea-size. Sprinkle 1 tablespoon cold water over part of the mixture; gently toss with a fork. Push the moistened dough to side of bowl. Repeat with 3 to 4 tablespoons additional cold water, using 1 tablespoon water at a time, until all the dough is moistened. Form dough into a ball.

Orange Whipped Cream: Chill a medium mixing bowl and the beaters of an electric mixer in refrigerator. In chilled bowl beat ½ cup whipping cream, 1 tablespoon sugar, and ½ teaspoon finely shredded orange peel with electric mixer on medium-high speed just until soft peaks form.

Nutrition Facts per serving: 348 cal., 19 g total fat (7 g sat. fat), 47 mg chol., 81 mg sodium, 42 g carbo., 2 g fiber, 4 g pro. **Daily Values:** 15% vit. A

Warm Peach and Nutmeg Tart: Pure and simple in its flavors, this peach of a tart—embellished with exquisite pastry shapes— is absolutely beautiful.

Raspberry-Lemon Tartlets: Sharing is nice, but having your own tart isn't too bad, either. During the height of raspberry season, top these diminutive desserts with a combination of red, yellow, and black raspberries.

RASPBERRY-LEMON TARTLETS

Prep: 1 hour   Bake: 16 minutes
Chill: 1 hour   Makes: 8 servings   Oven: 375°F

½ cup sugar
1 tablespoon cornstarch
1½ teaspoons finely shredded lemon peel
3 tablespoons lemon juice
3 beaten egg yolks
¼ cup unsalted butter
   Nonstick spray coating
1 recipe Poppy-Seed Pastry
   (see page 71)
¼ cup apple jelly
2 to 2½ cups fresh raspberries

Use your fingers to press the Poppy-Seed Pastry onto the bottom and up the sides of each tart pan.

1 **For lemon** curd filling, in a small saucepan stir together sugar and cornstarch. Stir in the lemon peel, lemon juice, and 3 tablespoons water. Cook and stir over medium heat until thickened and bubbly.

2 **Gradually stir** half of the hot filling into yolks. Pour yolk mixture into hot filling in saucepan. Bring to gentle boil. Cook and stir for 2 minutes more. Remove from heat. Stir in butter. Cover surface with plastic wrap. Chill in refrigerator at least 1 hour or for up to 48 hours.

3 **Spray nonstick** coating onto four 4- to 4¼-inch tart pans with removable bottoms. Divide Poppy-Seed Pastry into 4 equal portions. Press 1 portion of pastry onto bottom and up the sides of each tart pan. Generously prick bottom and sides of pastry in each tart pan. Line pastry shells with a double thickness of foil (see photo, page 68).

4 **Bake in a** 375°F oven for 7 minutes. Remove foil. Bake for 9 to 10 minutes more or until golden. Cool completely in pan on a wire rack.

5 **Heat and** stir jelly and 2 teaspoons water until melted; cool slightly. Spread filling into pastry shells. Top with berries; brush gently with jelly. Cover and chill in refrigerator for up to 4 hours.

Nutrition Facts per serving: 374 cal., 21 g total fat (12 g sat. fat), 179 mg chol., 124 mg sodium, 45 g carbo., 2 g fiber, 4 g pro. **Daily Values:** 36% vit. A, 18% vit. C, 3% calcium, 10% iron

pastries

Mocha-Filled Cream Horns, recipe page 85

PASTRIES

QUICK-METHOD CROISSANT DOUGH

Prep: 1 hour   Chill: 5 hours

This method doesn't require the frequent attention that the classic recipe demands. Use the dough for plain or filled croissants, or try one of the other pastries (see pages 80, 81, 96).

1½ cups cold butter
4½ cups all-purpose flour
1 package active dry yeast
1¼ cups milk
¼ cup sugar
¼ teaspoon salt
1 egg
¼ to ½ cup all-purpose flour

1 **Cut butter** into ½-inch slices. In a medium bowl stir slices into 3 cups of the flour until slices are coated and separated (see top photo, right). Chill butter mixture while preparing the dough.

2 **For dough,** in a large mixing bowl combine remaining 1½ cups flour and the yeast; set aside. In a medium saucepan heat and stir milk, sugar, and salt just until warm (120°F to 130°F). Add to flour-yeast mixture. Add egg. Beat with an electric mixer on low to medium speed 30 seconds, scraping sides of bowl. Beat on high speed 3 minutes.

3 **Using a wooden spoon,** stir chilled flour-butter mixture into dough until flour is moistened (butter will remain in large pieces).

4 **Sprinkle a pastry cloth** or surface with ¼ cup of the remaining flour. Turn dough out onto surface. With floured hands, gently knead dough for 8 strokes. Using a well-floured rolling pin, roll dough into a 21×12-inch rectangle (if necessary, sprinkle surface of dough with enough remaining flour to prevent sticking) (see middle photo, right). Fold dough crosswise into thirds to form a

Completely coat the butter pieces with flour. The butter will make layers in the baked dough, producing flaky croissants.

Roll out dough on a well-floured surface or pastry cloth using a floured rolling pin. After the first rolling, the dough will be bumpy from the pieces of butter.

Fold the rolled out dough crosswise into thirds. Repeat the rolling and folding steps. The folding helps to make flaky croissants.

7×12-inch rectangle. Loosely wrap in plastic wrap; chill 1 to 1½ hours in refrigerator or 20 to 30 minutes in freezer or until firm but not excessively stiff.

5 **On a well-floured surface roll** dough into a 21×12-inch rectangle. Fold dough crosswise into thirds again (see bottom photo, above) and give dough a quarter-turn. Then roll, fold, and turn twice more, flouring surface as needed (it is not necessary to chill dough between each rolling). Place dough in a plastic bag. Seal bag, leaving room for dough to expand. Chill dough for 4 to 24 hours. Use as directed in recipes on pages 80, 81, and 96.

FREEZING DOUGH FOR FUTURE TREATS

Croissant and puff pastry doughs can be frozen for future pastry making, shifting some of the preparation time to another day. To freeze, wrap the dough portions tightly in foil or place in freezer bags. Label with contents and date; freeze up to 3 months. Thaw in the refrigerator overnight.

Baked Croissants: Enjoy a morning cup of java coffeehouse-style—with a buttery, homemade croissant and jelly. Or, opt for a filled variety, choosing from the fillings offered on page 81.

BAKED CROISSANTS

Prep: 20 minutes plus dough   Rise: 1 hour
Bake: 15 minutes   Makes: 16   Oven: 375°F

1 recipe Quick-Method Croissant Dough (see recipe, page 79)
1 egg
1 tablespoon water or milk

1 Prepare and chill Quick-Method Croissant Dough as directed. Cut dough crosswise into 4 portions. Wrap and return 3 portions to refrigerator until ready to use.

2 To shape croissants, on a lightly floured surface, roll 1 portion of dough into a 16×8-inch rectangle. Cut rectangle crosswise in half to form 2 squares. Cut each square diagonally in half to form 2 triangles. (You will have 4 triangles from each rectangle.) Loosely roll up each triangle from an 8-inch side, rolling toward opposite point.

3 Repeat cutting and shaping with remaining 3 portions. Place croissants, points down, 4 inches apart on ungreased baking sheets. Curve ends. Cover and let rise in a warm place until double (about 1 hour).

4 Beat egg and the water using a fork. Lightly brush croissants with egg mixture. Bake in a 375°F oven for 15 minutes or until golden. Remove from baking sheets. Cool slightly on wire racks. Serve warm or cool.

Nutrition Facts per croissant: 308 cal., 18 g total fat (11 g sat. fat), 74 mg chol., 225 mg sodium, 30 g carbo., 1 g fiber, 5 g pro. **Daily Values:** 18% vit. A, 3% calcium, 12% iron

FILLED CROISSANTS

Prep: 30 minutes plus dough   Rise: 1 hour
Bake: 15 minutes   Makes: 16   Oven: 375°F

1 recipe Quick-Method Croissant Dough (see page 79)
1 recipe Blueberry Filling, Cheese Filling, Almond Filling, or Dilled Ham Filling (see page 81)
1 egg
1 tablespoon water

1 Prepare and chill Quick-Method Croissant Dough as directed. Prepare desired filling. Cut dough crosswise into 4 portions. Wrap and return 3 portions to refrigerator until ready to use.

2 On a lightly floured surface roll 1 portion of dough into a 16×8-inch rectangle. Cut rectangle into four 8×4-inch rectangles. Spoon filling onto center of each smaller rectangle. In a small mixing bowl beat egg and water using a fork. Brush edges of dough with egg mixture. Fold short sides of the rectangles over the filling to overlap in center, forming bundles. Pinch edges together to seal. Place 4 inches apart, seam sides down, on ungreased baking sheets. Repeat with remaining 3 portions.

3 Cover and let rise until nearly double (about 1 hour). Brush again with egg mixture. Bake in a 375°F oven about 15 minutes or until golden. Remove from baking sheets. Cool on wire racks.

Nutrition Facts per croissant with blueberry filling: 343 cal., 19 g total fat (11 g sat. fat), 87 mg chol., 231 mg sodium, 39 g carbo., 1 g fiber, 6 g pro. **Daily Values:** 18% vit. A, 2% vit. C, 3% calcium, 13% iron

Blueberry Filling: Using ½ cup blueberry preserves and 1 cup fresh or frozen blueberries, spoon 2 teaspoons of the preserves in the center of each rectangle. Add 3 or 4 blueberries.

Cheese Filling: In a bowl beat together one 8-ounce package cream cheese, softened; ¼ cup sugar; and 2 teaspoons finely shredded orange peel. Spoon 1 tablespoon in the center of each rectangle.

Almond Filling: In a bowl stir together 1 egg white, one 8-ounce can almond paste*, ½ cup granulated sugar, and ½ cup packed brown sugar. Spoon 1 tablespoon in center of each rectangle.

Dilled Ham Filling: In a bowl combine one 8-ounce package cream cheese, softened; ⅓ cup finely chopped cooked ham; 2 tablespoons sliced green onion; and ½ teaspoon dried dillweed. Spoon 1 tablespoon in center of each rectangle.

*Note: For best results, use an almond paste made without syrup or liquid glucose.

CHEESE AND LEMON DANISH

Prep: 50 minutes plus dough   **Rise:** 30 minutes
Bake: 18 minutes   **Makes:** 20   **Oven:** 375°F

Traditionally made from a buttery yeast-bread dough with a sweet filling, Danishes have long been a favorite of their namesake country.

   1 recipe Quick-Method Croissant
      Dough (see recipe, page 79)
   1 8-ounce package cream cheese,
      softened

⅓ cup sugar
1 tablespoon all-purpose flour
1 tablespoon dairy sour cream
1 egg yolk
1 teaspoon butter
1 teaspoon finely shredded lemon peel
½ teaspoon vanilla
1 egg
1 tablespoon water

1 **Prepare and chill** Quick-Method Croissant Dough as directed.

2 **For filling,** in a medium mixing bowl beat cream cheese, sugar, flour, sour cream, egg yolk, butter, lemon peel, and vanilla with an electric mixer on medium speed for 3 minutes or until well mixed. Set aside.

3 **To shape pastries,** on a lightly floured surface roll the chilled dough into a 20×12-inch rectangle. Cut rectangle into twenty 12×1-inch strips. Twist ends of each strip in opposite directions 3 or 4 times. Place 1 twisted strip on an ungreased baking sheet; form it into a wide U-shape. Then coil 1 end of the strip to the center to form a snail shape. Coil the opposite end of the U-shape strip to the center so the 2 coils nearly touch. Repeat with remaining strips, placing them 4 inches apart on baking sheets. Spoon 1 teaspoon of the filling onto the center of each coil (2 teaspoons per roll). Cover and let rise until nearly double (30 to 45 minutes).

4 **In a small bowl beat** egg and water using a fork. Lightly brush dough portions of pastries with egg mixture. Bake in a 375°F oven for 18 to 20 minutes or until golden. Remove from baking sheets. Cool slightly on wire racks.

Nutrition Facts per pastry: 305 cal., 19 g total fat (12 g sat. fat), 83 mg chol., 217 mg sodium, 28 g carbo., 1 g fiber, 5 g pro. **Daily Values:** 21% vit. A, 3% calcium, 10% iron

TOOL BOX: PASTRIES

As for any project, the right tools for pastry-making will help your pastry turn out right every time. Consider these:
- **Rolling pin:** A good, all-purpose wooden rolling pin that fits your hands comfortably.
- **Pastry cloth:** A cloth for rolling dough thin.
- **Pastry bag:** A reusable pastry bag with decorative tips for piping pastry dough.
- **Pastry brush:** A fine-bristled pastry brush for brushing on butter, milk, and egg glazes.

SOUR CREAM DANISH DOUGH

Prep: 25 minutes Chill: 1 hour

This dough is flaky and rich, like the croissant dough recipe, but it's substantially quicker to make and requires less chilling time.

 2 cups all-purpose flour
 ¼ teaspoon salt
 1 cup cold butter, cut up
 ½ cup dairy sour cream
 1 to 2 tablespoons cold water

1 **In a medium bowl stir** together flour and salt. Add butter. Using a pastry blender, cut cold butter into flour until mixture resembles coarse meal, leaving some pieces of butter the size of small peas.

2 **In a small bowl stir** together the sour cream and 1 tablespoon of the water. Add to the flour mixture and stir with a fork until the mixture starts to clump together. Add the remaining water, if necessary, to moisten. Form into a ball. Shape the dough into a rectangle. Place between 2 pieces of waxed paper or plastic wrap. Roll to 18×9-inch rectangle.

3 **Peel off the top sheet** of waxed paper or plastic wrap. Turn the dough over onto a lightly floured surface and peel off remaining paper or wrap. Fold the dough crosswise into thirds, forming a 6×9-inch rectangle. Fold dough in thirds again, forming a thick piece about 3×6 inches. Wrap dough and chill in the refrigerator 1 hour or until firm. (Dough may be chilled up to 24 hours; let stand at room temperature until easily rolled.) For longer storage, wrap in heavy foil. Seal, label, and freeze up to 3 months. Thaw the dough, covered, in the refrigerator overnight before using. Use the dough as directed in Sunrise Apple Tartlets (see recipe, right) and Apricot -Almond Breakfast Pastries (see recipe, page 83).

SUNRISE APPLE TARTLETS

Prep: 30 minutes plus dough Bake: 25 minutes
Makes: 4 Oven: 400°F

Don't be surprised if these pastries pop open a bit during baking, unveiling the buttery apple filling.

 ½ recipe Sour Cream Danish Dough
    (see recipe, left)
 ⅓ cup sugar
 1 teaspoon cornstarch
 3 large baking apples, peeled, cored,
    and sliced ⅛ inch thick
    (about 4 cups)
 2 tablespoons butter
 1 tablespoon lemon juice

1 **Prepare and chill** the Sour Cream Danish Dough as directed. Line a baking sheet with parchment paper or foil; set aside.

2 **For filling,** in a large skillet stir together sugar and cornstarch. Add apple slices, butter, and lemon juice. Cook over medium heat about 8 minutes or until apples are tender, stirring occasionally. Place in bowl to cool completely.

3 **On a lightly floured surface roll** dough to a 12-inch square and cut into four 6-inch squares. Place pastry squares on prepared baking sheet.

4 **Divide apple mixture** among the pastry squares, spooning about ½ cup in the center of each square. Fold corners up over the apple mixture to center of tarts (they should just meet).

5 **Bake in a 400°F oven** about 25 minutes or until golden brown. Remove tartlets from baking sheet. Cool slightly on wire rack. Serve warm.

Nutrition Facts per tartlet: 518 cal., 32 g total fat (20 g sat. fat), 83 mg chol., 365 mg sodium, 57 g carbo., 3 g fiber, 4 g pro. **Daily Values:** 30% vit. A, 13% vit. C, 3% calcium, 10% iron

APRICOT-ALMOND BREAKFAST PASTRIES

BEST-LOVED

Prep: 50 minutes plus dough   Bake: 25 minutes
Makes: 8   Oven: 375°F

Prepare both the dough and almond filling a day ahead and store them in the refrigerator.

> 1 recipe Sour Cream Danish Dough
> (see recipe, page 82)
> 1 cup sliced almonds
> 3 tablespoons sugar
> 3 tablespoons honey
> 1 egg
> 1 tablespoon water
> 1 8-ounce package cream cheese,
> softened
> ½ cup snipped dried apricots
> ½ cup apricot preserves
> 4 teaspoons sugar
> ¼ cup sliced almonds

1 **Prepare and chill** the Sour Cream Danish Dough as directed.

2 **For filling,** in a food processor bowl combine the almonds, the 3 tablespoons sugar, and the honey. Cover and process until the almonds are ground and the mixture begins to form a ball. (If mixture seems dry, add 1 teaspoon water.) Divide into 8 equal portions and roll each on lightly floured surface to a 3½-inch circle. Cover and set aside.

3 **On a lightly floured surface roll** the dough about ⅛ inch thick. Cut eight 4½-inch circles. Cut the pastry scraps into ½-inch-wide strips. Beat egg and water using a fork; use to brush top edges of pastry circles. Arrange the pastry strips around the top edge of each pastry circle, trimming as needed. Place pastry circles on an ungreased baking sheet. Place almond circle in center of each pastry circle.

4 **Place the softened cream cheese** in a small plastic food storage bag. Snip off one corner of the bag and pipe cream cheese in dots over almond mixture. In a small bowl combine dried apricots and preserves. Spoon over the cream cheese. Brush the pastry-strip edges of the circles with egg mixture and sprinkle lightly with the 4 teaspoons sugar. Sprinkle the preserves with almonds.

5 **Bake in a 375°F oven** about 25 minutes or until golden. Remove from baking sheets; cool on wire rack. Serve warm or at room temperature.

Nutrition Facts per pastry: 689 cal., 47 g total fat (24 g sat. fat), 126 mg chol., 406 mg sodium, 60 g carbo., 3 g fiber, 11 g pro. **Daily Values:** 43% vit. A, 1% vit. C, 9% calcium, 21% iron

Apricot-Almond Breakfast Pastries: Treat your overnight company to the best bed and breakfast pastries in town. Filled with a homemade almond-paste layer, cream cheese dollops, and apricot glaze, these a.m. delights are incredibly memorable.

QUICK-METHOD PUFF PASTRY DOUGH

Prep: 40 minutes   Chill: 40 minutes

Save preparation steps with this shortcut method by tossing the butter with the flour instead of making a rolled-out butter layer.

> 4 cups all-purpose flour
> 1 teaspoon salt
> 2 cups cold butter (1 pound)
> 1¼ cups ice water

1 **In a large mixing bowl stir** together flour and salt. Cut the cold butter into ½-inch slices (not cubes). Add butter slices to the flour mixture and toss until slices are coated and separated.

2 **Pour ice water** over flour mixture. Using a spoon, quickly mix (butter will remain in large pieces and flour will not be completely moistened).

3 **Turn the dough out** onto a lightly floured pastry cloth. Knead dough 10 times by pressing and pushing dough together to form a rough-looking ball, lifting the pastry cloth if necessary to press dough together. Shape dough into a rectangle (dough still will have some dry-looking areas). Make corners as square as possible. Slightly flatten dough.

4 **Working on a well-floured pastry cloth,** roll the dough into a 15×12-inch rectangle. Fold dough crosswise into thirds to form a 5×12-inch rectangle. Give dough a quarter turn; fold crosswise into thirds to form a 4×5-inch rectangle.

5 **Repeat the rolling** and folding process once more, forming a 4×5-inch rectangle. Wrap the dough with plastic wrap. Chill dough in the refrigerator for 20 minutes. Repeat rolling and folding process 2 more times. Chill dough in the refrigerator for 20 minutes more before using.

6 **Using a sharp knife,** cut the dough in half crosswise into 2 equal portions. To store the dough, wrap each portion in plastic wrap and refrigerate until ready to use or for up to 3 days. For longer storage, wrap each dough portion in heavy foil. Seal, label, and freeze up to 3 months. Thaw the dough, covered, in the refrigerator about 24 hours before using. Use the dough as directed in recipes on pages 84 to 86.

BANANA CREAM NAPOLEONS

Prep: 40 minutes plus dough
Bake: 18 minutes   Makes: 8   Oven: 425°F

Some believe that pastries similar to these are named after the French emperor Napoleon Bonaparte. Others think that Napoleons got their name from an elaborately decorated cake called a napolitain. So what are the similarities between the cake and the pastries? Both are rectangles and are made of many layers glossed with a rich cream filling.

> 1 portion Quick-Method Puff Pastry Dough (see recipe, left) or ½ of a 17¼-ounce package (1 sheet) frozen puff pastry, thawed
> 1 recipe Cream Filling (see page 85)
> 1 cup sifted powdered sugar
> 1 to 2 tablespoons milk
> 2 ripe medium bananas or 1 cup fresh raspberries or strawberries
> 2 tablespoons orange juice
> 1 ounce semisweet chocolate, chopped, melted, and cooled

1 **Prepare and chill** Quick-Method Puff Pastry Dough. Line a baking sheet with parchment paper or plain brown paper; set aside.

2 **On a lightly floured surface roll** the Quick-Method pastry into a 9×8-inch rectangle. Using a sharp knife, cut off ½ inch on all 4 sides to make an 8×7-inch rectangle. (Or, if using purchased puff pastry, unfold the thawed sheet and trim to an 8×7-inch rectangle.) Cut the pastry rectangle into eight 3½×2-inch rectangles. Transfer pastry rectangles to the prepared baking sheet. Using the tines of a fork, prick pastry rectangles.

3 **Bake in a 425°F oven** for 18 to 23 minutes or until golden. Carefully remove pastry rectangles and cool on a wire rack.

4 **Meanwhile, prepare Cream Filling;** set aside to chill in the refrigerator. For glaze, in a bowl combine powdered sugar and 1 tablespoon of the milk. If necessary, stir in enough additional milk until glaze is of spreading consistency; set aside. Thinly slice the bananas or strawberries (if using). Sprinkle with orange juice.

5 To assemble, use the tines of a fork to separate each pastry rectangle horizontally into 3 layers. Spread about 1 tablespoon of Cream Filling on each bottom layer. Arrange about half of the fruit on filling. Top with middle pastry layers; spread each with another 1 tablespoon Cream Filling and top with remaining fruit. Finally, top with remaining pastry layers. Spoon glaze over each pastry, spreading as necessary to glaze tops. Drizzle with the melted chocolate. Serve immediately or cover and keep at room temperature up to 30 minutes.

Cream Filling: In a heavy saucepan stir together ¼ cup sugar, 2 tablespoons all-purpose flour, and ⅛ teaspoon salt. Gradually stir in 1 cup half-and-half or light cream. Cook and stir over medium heat until thickened and bubbly. Cook and stir for 1 minute more. Gradually stir about half of the hot mixture into 2 beaten egg yolks. Return all of the yolk mixture to the saucepan. Bring to a gentle boil; reduce heat. Cook and stir for 2 minutes. Remove from heat and stir in ½ teaspoon finely shredded orange peel or lemon peel and ½ teaspoon vanilla. Transfer to a bowl. Cover surface with plastic wrap. Chill until serving time (do not stir).

Nutrition Facts per pastry: 487 cal., 29 g total fat (18 g sat. fat), 127 mg chol., 418 mg sodium, 53 g carbo., 2 g fiber, 6 g pro. **Daily Values:** 33% vit. A, 8% vit. C, 4% calcium, 12% iron

MOCHA-FILLED CREAM HORNS

Prep: 40 minutes plus dough   Bake: 15 minutes
Chill: 2 hours   Makes: 12   Oven: 425°F

Fill sugared puff pastry tubes with a chocolate-coffee cream filling (see photo, page 77).

> 1 **portion Quick-Method Puff Pastry Dough (see page 84) or one 17¼-ounce package (2 sheets) frozen puff pastry, thawed**
> 1 **egg white**
> 1 **tablespoon water**
> 1 **tablespoon sugar**
> 1 **recipe Mocha Pastry Cream**

1 Prepare and chill Quick-Method Puff Pastry Dough. Line a baking sheet with parchment paper or plain brown paper.

2 On a lightly floured surface roll the puff pastry dough into a 16×12-inch rectangle. Using a sharp knife, cut pastry lengthwise into twelve 16×1-inch strips. (If using purchased pastry, unfold and roll each sheet into a 12×10-inch rectangle. Cut each sheet into twelve 10×1-inch strips. Press 2 strips of purchased pastry together at ends to make a long strip; repeat with remaining strips.)

3 Wrap each strip of dough around a well-greased cream horn mold or ¾-inch-wide cannoli tube. Overlap layers slightly and press gently. Place 1 inch apart on the prepared baking sheet. In a small bowl beat egg white and water using a fork; use to brush over pastry. Sprinkle with the sugar.

4 Bake in a 425°F oven for 15 to 20 minutes or until golden for Quick-Method pastry (12 to 15 minutes for purchased pastry). Transfer to a wire rack. While still warm, slightly twist the molds and remove from pastry horns. Cool on a wire rack.

5 Prepare Mocha Pastry Cream; chill. Spoon cream mixture into a pastry bag fitted with a large star tip (about 1-inch opening). Pipe cream into each horn. If desired, chill up to 1 hour.

Mocha Pastry Cream: In a heavy saucepan stir together ½ cup sugar, ¼ cup all-purpose flour, and ¼ teaspoon salt. Gradually stir in 1½ cups half-and-half or light cream; 4 ounces semisweet chocolate, chopped; and 1 tablespoon instant coffee crystals. Cook and stir over medium heat until thickened and bubbly. Cook and stir 1 minute more. Gradually stir about half of the hot mixture into 4 beaten egg yolks. Return all of the yolk mixture to the saucepan. Bring to a gentle boil; reduce heat. Cook and stir for 2 minutes. Remove from heat; stir in 1 teaspoon vanilla. Transfer to a bowl. Cover surface with plastic wrap. Cool slightly. Chill 2 to 3 hours or until cold (do not stir). In a chilled small mixing bowl beat ½ cup whipping cream until soft peaks form. Gradually fold whipped cream into cooled pastry cream; chill well before using.

Nutrition Facts per cream horn: 433 cal., 30 g total fat (16 g sat. fat), 142 mg chol., 273 mg sodium, 37 g carbo., 1 g fiber, 6 g pro. **Daily Values:** 35% vit. A, 5% calcium, 11% iron

CINNAMON PALMIERS

Prep: 30 minutes plus dough **Bake:** 15 minutes
Makes: about 60 **Oven:** 375°F

When time is too short to make puff pastry dough, use the directions for purchased.

>   1 portion Quick-Method Puff Pastry
>   Dough (see recipe, page 84) or
>   one 17¼-ounce package (2
>   sheets) frozen puff pastry,
>   thawed
> ½ cup sugar
>   1 teaspoon ground cinnamon

1 **Prepare and chill** Quick-Method Puff Pastry Dough or unfold thawed puff pastry. Line baking sheets with parchment paper; set aside.

2 **If using Quick-Method Puff Pastry,** cut the portion of dough crosswise in half. Cover and return 1 piece of the dough to the refrigerator. On a lightly floured surface roll the remaining piece of dough or 1 sheet of the purchased pastry into a 14×10-inch rectangle.

3 **Sprinkle the rectangle** with a mixture of ¼ cup of the sugar and ½ teaspoon of the cinnamon. Lightly press sugar into the dough. Roll up 2 short sides, spiral style, to meet in center.

Use a thin, sharp knife to cut the filled and shaped puff pastry dough.

4 **Cut the pastry roll crosswise** into about ¼-inch slices (see photo, above). If the roll is too soft to slice easily, chill the rolled dough for a few minutes. Place the slices 2 inches apart on the prepared baking sheets.

5 **Bake in a 375°F oven** for 15 to 18 minutes or until golden and crisp. Remove from baking sheet and cool on a wire rack. Repeat with remaining piece of dough or sheet of purchased pastry and remaining cinnamon and sugar.

Nutrition Facts per pastry: 49 cal., 3 g total fat (1 g sat. fat), 4 mg chol., 46 mg sodium, 5 g carbo., 0 g fiber, 0 g pro. **Daily Values:** 3% vit. A, 0% calcium, 1% iron

---

RASPBERRY DANISH

EASY

Prep: 15 minutes **Bake:** 15 minutes
Makes: 12 **Oven:** 400°F

In 30 minutes from start to finish, you can have fresh, showy pastries to serve for dessert or as a breakfast treat. These pastries are at their best when baked and served on the same day.

> ½ of a 17¼-ounce package (1 sheet)
>   frozen puff pastry, thawed
> ⅓ cup seedless raspberry preserves
>   Pressurized whipped dessert
>   topping
>   Chopped pistachio nuts or almonds

1 **On a lightly floured surface,** unfold the thawed puff pastry sheet. If necessary, use a rolling pin to flatten and smooth the pastry.

PUFF PASTRY PERFECTION

Heed these tips to assure flaky, tender puff pastry every time:

- Use only butter; don't try substituting margarine for the butter.

- Be sure to use *ice* water when making the puff pastry dough.

- Keep pastry dough in the refrigerator until you're ready to roll it out. That way, the butter won't soften and melt into the dough when you roll it.

- Be sure pastries are fully baked. They'll look golden when done.

2 Cut the pastry into 12 equal strips. Coil each strip, wrapping loosely, into a circle or spiral. Moisten the outside end of each strip with a little water and secure it to the pastry to prevent pastry from uncoiling during baking. Place pastries on an ungreased baking sheet.

3 Bake in a 400°F oven about 15 minutes or until golden. Cool on a wire rack. To serve, in a small saucepan heat preserves until melted, stirring often; drizzle over baked pastries. Let the preserves cool slightly. Top with whipped topping. Sprinkle pastries with chopped nuts. Serve immediately.

Nutrition Facts per pastry: 142 cal., 9 g total fat (0 g sat. fat), 0 mg chol., 81 mg sodium, 15 g carbo., 0 g fiber, 1 g pro. Daily Values: 1% vit. A, 1% iron

DUTCH LETTERS BEST-LOVED

Prep: 1 hour   Chill: 40 minutes
Bake: 20 minutes   Makes: 20   Oven: 375°F

To shortcut preparations, substitute two 17¼-ounce packages (4 sheets) frozen puff pastry instead of preparing dough. Roll each unfolded sheet into a 12½×10-inch rectangle. Cut, fill, and shape. Bake for 15 to 20 minutes.

4½ cups all-purpose flour
1 teaspoon salt
2 cups cold butter (1 pound)
1 beaten egg
1 cup ice water
1 egg white
1 8-ounce can almond paste*
½ cup granulated sugar
½ cup packed brown sugar
   Granulated sugar

1 In a large bowl stir together flour and salt. Cut cold butter into ½-inch slices (not cubes). Add butter slices to flour mixture and toss until slices are coated and are separated.

2 In a small bowl stir together egg and ice water. Add all at once to flour mixture. Using a spoon, quickly mix (butter will remain in large pieces and flour will not be completely moistened).

3 Turn the dough out onto a lightly floured pastry cloth. Knead the dough 10 times by pressing and pushing dough together to form a rough-looking ball, lifting pastry cloth if necessary to press the dough together. Shape the dough into a rectangle (dough still will have some dry-looking areas). Make corners as square as possible. Slightly flatten dough. Working on a well-floured pastry cloth, roll dough into a 15×10-inch rectangle. Fold 2 short sides to meet in center; fold in half like a book to form 4 layers each measuring 7½×5 inches.

4 Repeat the rolling and folding process once more. Wrap dough with plastic wrap. Chill dough for 20 minutes in refrigerator. Repeat rolling and folding process 2 more times. Chill dough for 20 minutes before using.

5 For filling, in a bowl stir together egg white, almond paste, ½ cup granulated sugar, and the brown sugar. Set aside.

6 Using a sharp knife, cut dough crosswise into 4 equal parts. Wrap 3 portions in plastic wrap and return to the refrigerator. On a well-floured surface, roll 1 portion into a 12½×10-inch rectangle. Cut rectangle into five 10×2½-inch strips.

7 Shape a slightly rounded tablespoon of filling into a 9-inch rope and place it down the center third of one strip. Roll up the strip lengthwise. Brush edge and ends with water; pinch to seal. Place, seam side down, on an ungreased baking sheet, shaping strip into a letter (traditionally the letter "S"). Brush with water and sprinkle with additional granulated sugar. Repeat with remaining dough strips and filling. Repeat with remaining 3 dough portions and filling. Bake in a 375°F oven for 20 to 25 minutes or until golden. Remove from baking sheet; cool on racks.

***Note:** For best results, use an almond paste made without syrup or liquid glucose.

Nutrition Facts per pastry: 362 cal., 23 g total fat (5 g sat. fat), 35 mg chol., 285 mg sodium, 36 g carbo., 1 g fiber, 5 g pro. Daily Values: 18% vit. A, 3% calcium, 11% iron

---

LET'S TALK ABOUT CHOUX

Amerca was introduced to cream puffs, or *choux* (pronounced "shoe") *à la creme pâtissiere*, when San Francisco was evolving from a frontier town into a cosmopolitan city. A citizen named François Pioche decided the city's cuisine should reflect its new elegance and sophistication, so he arranged for several French chefs to come to San Francisco. The rest, as they say, is history.

CREAM PUFF (CHOUX) PASTRY

Prep: 30 minutes   **Bake:** 30 minutes
Makes: 12   **Oven:** 400°F

Cream puffs are so versatile! Fill regular-size puffs with savory salads for a main dish and stuff miniature ones for appetizers. Or, add pudding, ice cream, or whipped cream and serve as a spectacular dessert for any meal.

  1 **cup water**
  ½ **cup butter**
  ⅛ **teaspoon salt**
  1 **cup all-purpose flour**
  4 **eggs**

1 **In a medium saucepan combine** water, butter, and salt. Bring to boiling. Add flour all at once, stirring vigorously. Cook and stir until mixture forms a ball (see top photo, right). Remove from heat. Cool 10 minutes. Add eggs, one at a time, beating well with a wooden spoon after each. Bake as directed below.

Baked Cream Puffs: Drop Cream Puff Pastry dough by heaping tablespoons into 12 mounds 3 inches apart onto a greased baking sheet (see middle photo, right). Bake in a 400°F oven for 30 to 35 minutes or until golden. Remove from baking sheet; cool on a wire rack. Cut off the tops of each puff; remove any soft dough from inside (see bottom photo, right). Fill each with ¼ cup whipped cream, pudding, ice cream, or as desired. Replace cream puff tops. If desired, sift powdered sugar over tops of the filled puffs.

After adding flour to the water and butter, stir vigorously until the mixture forms a ball that does not separate. Remove the pan from the heat before adding eggs.

Drop cream puff pastry using 2 spoons. For evenly shaped puffs, if possible, avoid going back to add more dough to the mounds.

After baking and cooling puffs, cut off the top fourth of each puff and remove any soft dough inside, using a fork or a spoon.

Nutrition Facts per cream puff (with whipped cream): 229 cal., 20 g total fat (12 g sat. fat), 132 mg chol., 132 mg sodium, 8 g carbo., 0 g fiber, 4 g pro.
Daily Values: 23% vit. A, 0% vit. C, 2% calcium, 4% iron

Chocolate Cream Puff Pastry: Prepare Cream Puff Pastry as directed, except in a small bowl combine flour with 3 tablespoons unsweetened cocoa powder and 2 tablespoons granulated sugar. Add flour mixture all at once to boiling water-butter mixture. Continue as directed.

DOUBLE-CHOCOLATE CREAM PUFFS

Prep: 20 minutes plus pastry   Bake: 30 minutes
Chill: 2 hours   Makes: 12   Oven: 400°F

If you really love chocolate, here's a dessert idea. Serve chocolate cream puffs filled with a creamy rich and chocolate filling.

1 recipe Chocolate Cream Puff
    Pastry (see recipe, page 88)
⅔ cup granulated sugar
⅓ cup all-purpose flour
⅛ teaspoon salt
1½ cups milk
1 ounce unsweetened chocolate,
    chopped
2 slightly beaten egg yolks
⅓ cup butter, softened
1 teaspoon vanilla
    Powdered sugar

1 Grease a baking sheet; set aside. Prepare Chocolate Cream Puff Pastry as directed. Drop dough by heaping tablespoons into 12 mounds about 3 inches apart onto the prepared baking sheet. Bake in a 400°F oven about 30 minutes or until firm. Remove puffs from baking sheet; cool the puffs on a wire rack.

2 For chocolate filling, in a heavy medium saucepan stir together granulated sugar, flour, and salt. Gradually stir in milk. Add chopped chocolate. Cook and stir over medium heat until thickened and bubbly. Reduce heat. Cook and stir for 2 minutes more. Remove from heat. Gradually stir about 1 cup of the hot filling into the beaten egg yolks. Return egg yolk mixture to saucepan. Bring to a gentle boil. Cook and stir for 2 minutes more. Remove from heat. Cover surface of filling with plastic wrap. Refrigerate about 2 hours or until cold.

3 In a medium bowl beat butter until creamy. Continue beating and gradually add chilled filling, beating until the mixture is light and creamy. Beat in vanilla.

4 To assemble, cut off the top fourth of each puff. Remove any soft dough from inside. Spoon a scant ¼ cup chocolate filling into each puff. Replace tops of the puffs. If desired, chill for up to 2 hours. Before serving, sift powdered sugar over the tops.

Nutrition Facts per cream puff: 279 cal., 17 g total fat
(10 g sat. fat), 143 mg chol., 234 mg sodium,
27 g carbo., 1 g fiber, 6 g pro. **Daily Values:**
22% vit. A, 6% calcium, 8% iron

Chocolate-Filled Cream Puffs: Prepare Double Chocolate Cream Puffs as directed, except substitute Cream Puff Pastry for the Chocolate Cream Puff Pastry. Bake, cool, and fill with chocolate filling.

CREAM PUFFS 101

The perfect cream puff is crisp, tender, and, well, puffy. If your cream puffs or éclairs fall short of your expectations, try again with these hints in mind:

■ Use large eggs; add them one at a time.
■ Be sure to measure the water carefully.
■ Add the flour as soon as the butter is melted and the water boils so that the water doesn't boil away in the saucepan.

■ Set a timer so the pastry dough cools for 10 minutes—then beat in the first egg.
■ Be sure the puffs are golden brown, firm, and dry before you remove them from the oven.
■ For mini appetizer puffs, drop dough by rounded teaspoons. Bake at 400°F about 18 minutes.
■ Fill the shells just before serving, or fill and chill the puffs up to 2 hours to keep the bottoms from getting soggy.

STORING CREAM PUFFS

Cream puff shells can be made ahead and won't lose their crisp freshness if you store them properly.

- For short-term storage, let the cream puffs cool completely; place the unfilled puffs in a plastic bag so they won't dry out. Store in the refrigerator for up to 24 hours.
- For long-term storage, place cooled, unfilled shells in an airtight container; seal, label, and freeze for up to 2 months. To thaw the shells, let them stand at room temperature about 15 minutes.
- For savory appetizers that you want to serve warm, make the puffs ahead, chill or freeze, and reheat them at the last minute. To warm for serving, transfer the chilled or frozen puffs to an ungreased baking sheet. Heat in a 350° oven for 5 to 10 minutes until warm.

STRAWBERRY-FILLED ALMOND PUFFS

Prep: 20 minutes plus pastry **Bake:** 25 minutes
Makes: 12 **Oven:** 400°F

Almond paste gives the cream puffs a nutty flavor while the amaretto or almond extract flavors the whipped cream.

> 1 recipe Cream Puff Pastry
>   (see page 88)
> ½ cup almond paste* (about ½ of an
>   8-ounce can)
> 1 cup whipping cream
> 2 tablespoons sifted powdered sugar
> 2 tablespoons amaretto or
>   ¼ teaspoon almond extract
> ½ cup dairy sour cream
> 3 cups strawberries, sliced
>   Powdered sugar

1 Grease a baking sheet; set aside. Prepare Cream Puff Pastry as directed except heat almond paste with butter and water. Drop dough by heaping tablespoons into 12 mounds 3 inches apart onto the prepared baking sheet. Bake in a 400°F oven for 25 to 30 minutes or until golden and firm. Remove puffs from baking sheet; cool on wire rack.

2 For filling, in a medium mixing bowl combine whipping cream, 2 tablespoons powdered sugar, and amaretto. Beat just until stiff peaks form. Fold in sour cream. Cover and refrigerate.

3 To assemble, cut off the top fourth of each puff. Remove any soft dough from inside. Spoon a heaping tablespoon of whipped cream filling into each puff. Top with about ¼ cup strawberries. Replace tops of the puffs. If desired, cover and chill for up to 2 hours. Before serving, sift powdered sugar over the tops.

*Note: For best results, use an almond paste made without syrup or liquid glucose.

Nutrition Facts per cream puff: 285 cal., 21 g total fat (11 g sat. fat), 123 mg chol., 158 mg sodium, 18 g carbo., 1 g fiber, 5 g pro. **Daily Values:** 21% vit. A, 35% vit. C, 5% calcium, 7% iron

Peach-Filled Almond Puffs: Prepare Strawberry-Filled Almond Puffs as directed, except substitute sliced fresh peaches for the strawberries.

CANNOLI-STYLE ÉCLAIRS

Prep: 20 minutes   Bake: 35 minutes
Makes: 12   Oven: 400°F

  1 recipe Cream Puff Pastry
      (see recipe, page 88)
1½ cups ricotta cheese
  ½ cup sugar
  2 teaspoons amaretto (optional)
  1 teaspoon vanilla
  ⅔ cup miniature semisweet chocolate
      pieces
  1 cup whipping cream
  1 tablespoon shortening
  1 teaspoon light-colored corn syrup
      Chopped pistachio nuts

1 **Grease a baking sheet;** set aside. Prepare Cream Puff Pastry as directed, except spoon batter into a pastry bag fitted with a large plain round tip (½- to 1-inch opening).

2 **Slowly pipe strips** of batter onto prepared baking sheet 3 inches apart, making each éclair about 4 inches long, 1 inch wide, and ¾ inch high. Bake in a 400°F oven for 35 to 40 minutes or until golden brown and puffy. Remove from baking sheet and cool on a wire rack.

3 **For filling,** in a bowl stir together ricotta cheese, sugar, amaretto (if desired), and vanilla. Stir in ⅓ cup of the chocolate pieces. Cover and chill the filling.

4 **Up to 1 hour** before serving beat the whipping cream until soft peaks form (tips curl). Fold into ricotta mixture. Cut off top of each éclair. Remove any soft dough from inside. Fill éclairs with ricotta filling. Replace tops.

5 **In a small saucepan** melt remaining chocolate pieces, shortening, and corn syrup over low heat. Drizzle over éclairs and sprinkle with nuts. Chill up to 2 hours.

Nutrition Facts per éclair: 334 cal., 24 g total fat
(12 g sat. fat), 128 mg chol., 168 mg sodium,
25 g carbo., 0 g fiber, 8 g pro. **Daily Values:**
23% vit. A, 9% calcium, 8% iron

GRUYÈRE PUFFS

Prep: 25 minutes   Bake: 30 minutes
Stand: 10 minutes   Makes: 18   Oven: 400°F

Serve these cheese puffs filled with chicken salad for a tasty luncheon dish or serve them warm with the salad course when entertaining.

  1 cup water
  ½ cup butter
  ¾ teaspoon dried basil, crushed
  ¼ teaspoon garlic salt
  ⅛ teaspoon ground red pepper
  1 cup all-purpose flour
  4 eggs
  ½ cup shredded Gruyère or Swiss
      cheese (2 ounces)
  2 tablespoons grated Parmesan
      cheese

1 **Grease a baking sheet;** set aside. In a medium saucepan combine water and butter. Add basil, garlic salt, and red pepper. Bring to boiling. Add flour all at once, stirring vigorously. Cook and stir until mixture forms a ball that doesn't separate. Remove from heat. Cool for 5 minutes.

2 **Add eggs,** one at a time, beating well with a wooden spoon after each addition until smooth. Stir in Gruyère.

3 **Drop dough** by rounded tablespoons into 18 mounds 2 inches apart onto the prepared baking sheet. Sprinkle with Parmesan cheese.

4 **Bake in a 400°F oven** for 30 to 35 minutes or until golden. Turn off oven; let puffs stand in oven 10 minutes. Serve hot. (To make ahead, bake and cool puffs completely. Place in airtight container and refrigerate for up to 2 days or freeze up to 1 month. To reheat for serving, place the chilled or frozen puffs on an ungreased baking sheet. Heat in a 350°F oven for 5 to 10 minutes or until warm.)

Nutrition Facts per puff: 101 cal., 7 g total fat
(4 g sat. fat), 65 mg chol., 118 mg sodium, 5 g carbo.,
0 g fiber, 3 g pro. **Daily Values:** 8% vit. A, 4% calcium,
3% iron

STRUDEL DOUGH

Prep: 1 hour   Rest: 1½ hours

1½ to 1¾ cups all-purpose flour
¼ teaspoon salt
¼ cup butter
1 beaten egg yolk
⅓ cup warm water (110°F to 115°F)
½ cup butter, melted

1 **In a large bowl stir** together 1½ cups of the flour and the salt. Cut in ¼ cup butter until pieces are the size of small peas. In a small bowl stir together egg yolk and the water. Add egg yolk mixture to flour mixture. Stir until combined.

2 **Turn dough out** onto a lightly floured surface. Knead dough for 5 minutes. If necessary, knead in some or all of the remaining flour if dough is sticky. Cover with plastic wrap; let dough stand at room temperature for 1 hour.

3 **Cover a large surface** (at least 4×3 feet) with a cloth or sheet. Lightly flour cloth. On the cloth roll the dough into a 15-inch square. Brush with 2 tablespoons of the melted butter. Cover dough with plastic wrap. Let dough rest for 30 minutes.

4 **To stretch dough,** use palms of your hands and work underneath dough (see top photo, right). Starting from the middle and working toward edges, gently lift and pull your hands apart. At the same time, pull dough away from middle toward yourself. Continue stretching until dough is paper thin, forming a 40×20-inch rectangle. Use scissors to trim uneven edges. Brush with remaining melted butter. Fill; shape as directed in recipes on page 93.

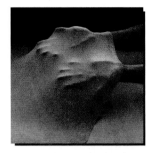

Gently lift and stretch the strudel dough with the palms of your hands, pulling your hands apart and away from middle of dough.

Use the cloth under the strudel dough to lift and roll the pastry over the filling and then to roll up the dough.

Shortcut Phyllo Strudel: To substitute frozen phyllo dough for Strudel Dough, thaw 12 sheets of frozen phyllo dough. Cover a large surface with a cloth. Lightly flour the cloth. Unfold sheets of phyllo dough. Remove 6 sheets, keeping rest covered with plastic wrap. Arrange the 6 sheets of phyllo on floured cloth, overlapping the stacks as necessary to form a rectangle about 40×20 inches. Brush each sheet of phyllo with some of the melted butter; press to seal the seams. Top with 6 more sheets of phyllo dough, brushing each sheet with remaining butter and overlapping as necessary (but do not overlap in the same places where the bottom layer overlaps). Fill and shape as for homemade dough.

STRUDEL 101

Ultra-flaky strudel starts with a large, paper-thin sheet of pulled dough that is filled and rolled into multiple layers. It can be a bit challenging, but it's worth the effort. Follow these tips for success:

■ Prepare filling while the dough is resting.
■ A fabric sheet makes a good pastry cloth.
■ Keep strudel dough covered with a lightly damp cloth when you're not working on it.

■ Remove any jewelry before stretching your dough—the thin dough tears easily.
■ If you're stretching strudel dough with a friend, work on opposite sides of the dough so you are stretching across from each other. The stretching should take about 5 minutes. If you are working alone, place a heavy rolling pin on one edge of the dough and pull from the opposite side; it will take about 15 minutes.

APPLE STRUDEL

Prep: 20 minutes plus dough   **Bake:** 30 minutes
Makes: 12 to16 servings   **Oven:** 350°F

*Apple is one of the most traditional fillings for
this German-Austrian favorite.*

>   1 **recipe Strudel Dough or phyllo
>   dough (see recipe, page 92)**
>   3 **cups thinly sliced, peeled tart
>   apples**
> ⅓ **cup packed brown sugar**
> ⅓ **cup raisins**
> ¼ **cup chopped walnuts or pecans**
> ¾ **teaspoon ground cinnamon**
>   1 **slightly beaten egg white**
>   1 **tablespoon water**
>   **Powdered sugar**

1 Prepare Strudel Dough as directed. For filling,
in a large mixing bowl toss together apples,
brown sugar, raisins, nuts, and cinnamon; set aside.
Lightly grease a large baking sheet; set aside.

2 To assemble strudel, stretch dough as directed
in recipe. Beginning 4 inches from one of the
20-inch sides of dough, spoon filling across the
dough in a 4-inch-wide band.

3 Using the cloth beneath dough as a guide, gently
lift 4-inch section of dough and lay it over filling
(see bottom photo, page 92). Slowly and evenly lift
cloth and tightly roll up dough and filling, in a spiral. If needed, cut excess dough from ends to within
1 inch of the filling. Fold ends under to seal.

4 Carefully transfer the strudel roll to the prepared baking sheet. Curve the ends to form a
crescent shape. Combine egg white and water; brush
over top of strudel. (If using phyllo dough, roll up
and seal but do not curve into a crescent shape on
baking sheet. Brush with 2 tablespoons melted butter instead of egg mixture.)

5 Bake in a 350°F oven for 30 to 35 minutes or
until golden. Carefully remove strudel from pan
and cool on a wire rack. Just before serving, sift
powdered sugar over strudel.

Nutrition Facts per serving: 235 cal., 14 g total fat
(7 g sat. fat), 48 mg chol., 170 mg sodium,
27 g carbo., 1 g fiber, 3 g pro. **Daily Values:**
13% vit. A, 1% calcium, 7% iron

SAVORY TOMATO-OLIVE STRUDEL

Prep: 25 minutes plus dough   **Bake:** 30 minutes
Makes: 40 appetizers   **Oven:** 350°F

>   1 **recipe Strudel Dough or phyllo
>   dough (see recipe, page 92)**
> ½ **cup oil-packed dried tomatoes**
>   1 **8-ounce package cream cheese,
>   softened**
> ½ **cup finely chopped pitted ripe
>   olives**
> ¼ **cup sliced green onions**
>   1 **egg yolk**
> ½ **teaspoon dried basil, crushed**
>   1 **slightly beaten egg white
>   Grated Parmesan cheese**

1 Prepare Strudel Dough as directed. For filling,
drain tomatoes, reserving oil. Chop tomatoes. In
a medium bowl combine tomatoes, cream cheese,
olives, onions, egg yolk, basil, and ½ teaspoon pepper. If necessary, stir in enough reserved tomato oil
(about 1 tablespoon) to make of spreading consistency. Lightly grease a large baking sheet; set aside.

2 To assemble strudel, stretch dough as directed
in recipe. Beginning 4 inches from one of the
20-inch sides of dough, spread filling across the
dough in a 4-inch-wide band.

3 Using the cloth beneath dough as a guide, gently
lift 4-inch section of dough and lay it over filling
(see bottom photo, page 92). Slowly and evenly lift
cloth and tightly roll up dough and filling, into a spiral shape. If needed, cut excess dough from ends to
within 1 inch of the filling. Fold ends under to seal.

4 Transfer to prepared baking sheet. Curve the
ends to form a crescent shape. Combine egg
white and 1 tablespoon water; brush over top. (If
using phyllo dough, roll up and seal but do not
curve. Brush with 2 tablespoons melted butter
instead of egg mixture.) Sprinkle with Parmesan.

5 Bake in a 350°F oven for 30 to 35 minutes or
until golden. Carefully remove strudel from pan
and cool on a wire rack. Serve warm or at room temperature. Cut into 1-inch-wide appetizer slices.

Nutrition Facts per appetizer: 78 cal., 7 g total fat
(4 g sat. fat), 26 mg chol., 92 mg sodium, 4 g carbo.,
0 g fiber, 1 g pro. **Daily Values:** 7% vit. A, 2% vit. C,
1% calcium, 2% iron

BAKLAVA

Prep: 50 minutes   **Bake:** 35 minutes
Makes: 60 servings   **Oven:** 325°F

To cut diamond shapes, make several cuts the length of the baking pan, then make diagonal crosswise cuts. The corners and end pieces will yield odd-shaped pieces.

> 4 **cups walnuts, finely chopped (1 pound)**
> 2 **cups sugar**
> 1 **teaspoon ground cinnamon**
> 1¼ **cups butter, melted**
> 1 **16-ounce package frozen phyllo dough, thawed**
> 1 **cup water**
> ¼ **cup honey**
> ½ **teaspoon finely shredded lemon peel**
> 2 **tablespoons lemon juice**
> 2 **inches stick cinnamon**
>   **Grape leaves (optional)**

1 **For filling,** in a large bowl stir together chopped walnuts, ½ cup of the sugar, and the ground cinnamon. Set aside.

2 **Brush the bottom** of a 15×10×1-inch baking pan with some of the melted butter. Unfold phyllo dough. Keep phyllo covered with plastic wrap, removing sheets as you need them. Layer one-fourth (about 5) of the phyllo sheets in the pan, generously brushing each sheet with melted butter as you layer, and allowing phyllo to extend up the sides of the pan. Sprinkle about 1½ cups of the filling on top of the phyllo. Repeat layering the phyllo sheets and filling 2 more times.

3 **Layer remaining phyllo sheets** on the third layer of filling, brushing each sheet with butter before adding the next phyllo sheet. Drizzle any remaining butter over the top layers. Trim edges of phyllo to fit the pan. Using a sharp knife, cut through all the layers to make 60 diamond-, triangle-, or square-shaped pieces.

4 **Bake in a 325°F oven** for 35 to 45 minutes or until golden. Slightly cool in pan on a wire rack.

5 **Meanwhile, for syrup,** in a medium saucepan stir together the remaining 1½ cups sugar, the water, honey, lemon peel, lemon juice, and stick cinnamon. Bring to boiling; reduce heat. Simmer, uncovered, for 20 minutes. Remove cinnamon. Pour honey mixture over slightly cooled baklava in the pan. Cool completely. If desired, serve pieces on a grape-leaf-lined platter.

Nutrition Facts per piece: 138 cal., 9 g total fat (3 g sat. fat), 10 mg chol., 76 mg sodium, 13 g carbo., 0 g fiber, 2 g pro. **Daily Values:** 4% vit. A, 1% vit. C, 1% calcium, 3% iron

---

PHYLLO-DOUGH KNOW-HOW

Frozen phyllo dough is not as difficult to work with as its delicate nature suggests. Follow these techniques for success:

- Allow frozen phyllo dough to thaw while it is still wrapped and sealed.
- Once unwrapped, sheets of phyllo dough can dry out quickly and crumble. To preserve, keep the opened stack of dough covered with a moist cloth or plastic wrap until needed.
- Brush each sheet you lay down with melted butter, margarine, or—in the case of a savory dish—olive oil.
- Rewrap tightly any remaining sheets of the dough and return them to the freezer.

Baklava: Layers of paper-thin phyllo dough, walnut filling, and a glistening honey-lemon syrup make up this traditional Greek sweet.

Strawberry Turnovers: Stuffed inside these golden pastries discover a simple filling of fresh strawberries mixed with strawberry preserves. Fork marks make the decorative trim on the edges.

STRAWBERRY TURNOVERS

Prep: 25 minutes plus dough **Rise:** 45 minutes
Bake: 15 minutes **Makes:** 18 **Oven:** 375°F

  1 recipe Quick-Method Croissant Dough (see recipe, page 79)
  ½ cup strawberry preserves or peach preserves
  ½ cup chopped strawberries
  1 egg
  1 tablespoon water
  Sifted powdered sugar (optional)

1 Prepare and chill Quick-Method Croissant Dough as directed.

2 To shape turnovers, cut the chilled dough crosswise in half. On a lightly floured surface roll each half of dough into a 12-inch square. Cut each square into nine 4-inch squares (18 squares total). Spoon about 2 teaspoons of the preserves onto the center of each square. Top with several pieces of the chopped strawberries.

3 In a small bowl beat egg and water using a fork. Lightly brush edges of dough with some of the egg mixture. Fold squares in half to form triangles; seal edges with tines of a fork. Place the triangles 4 inches apart on ungreased baking sheets. Cover and let rise in a warm place until nearly double (45 to 60 minutes).

4 Brush turnovers with additional egg mixture. Bake in a 375°F oven about 15 minutes or until golden. Remove turnovers from baking sheets. Cool slightly on wire racks. If desired, sprinkle powdered sugar over warm turnovers. Serve warm or cool.

Nutrition Facts per turnover: 298 cal., 16 g total fat (10 g sat. fat), 66 mg chol., 201 mg sodium, 33 g carbo., 1 g fiber, 5 g pro. **Daily Values:** 16% vit. A, 4% vit. C, 2% calcium, 11% iron

cakes

Triple-Layer Lemon
Cake, recipe page 130

CAKES

YELLOW CAKE

Prep: 20 minutes   **Bake:** 30 minutes
Cool: 1 hour   **Makes:** 12 servings   **Oven:** 375°F

Your grandmother may have served this cake—a version of this classic has appeared in every edition of the Better Homes and Gardens® Cook Book since it was published in 1930.

2½ **cups all-purpose flour**
2½ **teaspoons baking powder**
 ½ **teaspoon salt**
⅔ **cup butter**
1¾ **cups sugar**
1½ **teaspoons vanilla**
 2 **eggs**
1¼ **cups milk**

1 **Grease and lightly flour** two 8×1½-inch or 9×1½-inch round baking pans or grease one 13×9×2-inch baking pan; set pan(s) aside. Stir together flour, baking powder, and salt; set aside.

2 **In a mixing bowl beat** butter with an electric mixer on medium to high speed for 30 seconds. Add sugar and vanilla; beat until well combined. Add eggs, 1 at a time, beating 1 minute after each. Add flour mixture and milk alternately to butter mixture, beating on low speed after each addition just until combined. Pour batter into pan(s).

3 **Bake in a 375°F oven** for 30 to 35 minutes or until a wooden toothpick comes out clean. Cool layer cakes in pans on wire racks for 10 minutes. Remove from pans. Cool thoroughly on wire racks. Or, place 13×9-inch cake in pan on a wire rack; cool thoroughly. Frost with desired frosting.

Nutrition Facts per serving (cake only): 316 cal., 12 g total fat (7 g sat. fat), 65 mg chol., 292 mg sodium, 49 g carbo., 1 g fiber, 4 g pro. **Daily Values:** 12% vit. A, 9% calcium, 9% iron

Citrus Yellow Cake: Prepare as above, except stir 2 teaspoons finely shredded orange peel or lemon peel into batter.

WHITE CAKE

Prep: 20 minutes   **Bake:** 30 minutes
Cool: 1 hour   **Makes:** 12 servings   **Oven:** 350°F

Frost it green on St. Patrick's Day or pink for Valentine's Day, or top it with candles for a birthday. With the right decoration and frosting, this traditional cake fits any occasion.

 2 **cups all-purpose flour**
 1 **teaspoon baking powder**
 ½ **teaspoon baking soda**
 ⅛ **teaspoon salt**
 ½ **cup shortening or butter**
1¾ **cups sugar**
 1 **teaspoon vanilla**
 4 **egg whites**
1⅓ **cups buttermilk or sour milk**
    (see tip, page 208)

1 **Grease and lightly flour** two 8×1½-inch or 9×1½-inch round baking pans or grease one 13×9×2-inch baking pan; set aside. Combine flour, baking powder, baking soda, and salt; set aside.

2 **In a large mixing bowl beat** shortening with an electric mixer on medium to high speed for 30 seconds. Add sugar and vanilla; beat until well combined. Add egg whites, 1 at a time, beating well after each. Add flour mixture and buttermilk to shortening mixture, beating on low speed after each addition just until combined. Pour batter into the prepared pan(s).

3 **Bake in a 350°F oven** for 30 to 35 minutes or until a wooden toothpick comes out clean. Cool layer cakes in pans on wire racks for 10 minutes. Remove from pans. Cool thoroughly on racks. Or, place 13×9-inch cake in pan on a wire rack; cool thoroughly. Frost with desired frosting.

Nutrition Facts per serving (cake only): 275 cal., 9 g total fat (2 g sat. fat), 1 mg chol., 149 mg sodium, 45 g carbo., 1 g fiber, 4 g pro. **Daily Values:** 5% calcium, 6% iron

DEVIL'S FOOD CAKE

Prep: 20 minutes **Bake:** 35 minutes
Cool: 1 hour **Makes:** 12 servings **Oven:** 350°F

The first devil's food recipe appeared almost a century ago and was named so because of its chocolaty richness. This cake fits the name, too.

2¼ **cups all-purpose flour**
 ½ **cup unsweetened cocoa powder**
1½ **teaspoons baking soda**
 ¼ **teaspoon salt**
 ½ **cup shortening**
1¾ **cups sugar**
 1 **teaspoon vanilla**
 3 **eggs**
1⅓ **cups cold water**

1 Grease and lightly flour two 9×1½-inch round baking pans or grease one 13×9×2-inch baking pan; set pan(s) aside. Stir together flour, cocoa powder, baking soda, and salt; set aside.

2 In a large mixing bowl beat shortening with an electric mixer on medium to high speed for 30 seconds. Add sugar and vanilla; beat until well combined. Add eggs, 1 at a time, beating well after each. Add flour mixture and water alternately to shortening mixture, beating on low speed after each addition just until combined. Pour batter into the prepared pan(s).

3 Bake in a 350°F oven for 35 to 40 minutes or until a wooden toothpick comes out clean. Cool layer cakes in pans on wire racks for 10 minutes. Remove from pans. Cool thoroughly on wire racks. Or, place 13×9-inch cake in pan on a wire rack; cool thoroughly. Frost with desired frosting.

Nutrition Facts per serving (cake only): 302 cal., 11 g total fat (3 g sat. fat), 53 mg chol., 219 mg sodium, 48 g carbo., 1 g fiber, 5 g pro. **Daily Values:** 2% vit. A, 4% calcium, 11% iron

CLASSIC CHOCOLATE CAKE

Prep: 25 minutes **Bake:** 30 minutes
Cool: 1 hour **Makes:** 12 servings **Oven:** 350°F

2¼ **cups all-purpose flour**
 1 **teaspoon baking powder**
 ¾ **teaspoon baking soda**
 ¼ **teaspoon salt**
 ⅔ **cup butter**
1¾ **cups sugar**
 2 **eggs**
 3 **ounces unsweetened chocolate,**
    melted and cooled
 1 **teaspoon vanilla**
1¼ **cups water**

1 Grease and lightly flour two 9×1½-inch round baking pans or grease one 13×9×2-inch baking pan; set pan(s) aside. Stir together flour, baking powder, baking soda, and salt; set aside.

2 In a large mixing bowl beat the butter with an electric mixer on medium to high speed for 30 seconds. Add sugar; beat until well combined. Add eggs, 1 at a time, beating well after each. Beat in chocolate and vanilla. Add flour mixture and water alternately to butter mixture, beating on low speed after each addition just until combined. Pour batter into the prepared pan(s).

3 Bake in a 350°F oven for 30 to 35 minutes or until a wooden toothpick comes out clean. Cool layer cakes in pans on wire racks for 10 minutes. Remove from pans. Cool thoroughly on wire racks. Or, place 13×9-inch cake in pan on a wire rack; cool thoroughly. Frost with desired frosting.

Nutrition Facts per serving (cake only): 329 cal., 15 g total fat (8 g sat. fat), 63 mg chol., 269 mg sodium, 48 g carbo., 1 g fiber, 4 g pro. **Daily Values:** 11% vit. A, 3% calcium, 11% iron

A CAKE OF YOUR OWN

Almost any creamed cake (one that starts with beating the sugar and butter or shortening until fluffy) can be made into cupcakes. Just grease and flour a muffin pan (or line the cups with paper bake cups) and fill cups half full. Bake at the same temperature called for in the cake recipe, but reduce baking time by one-third to one-half. A two-layer cake recipe usually yields 24 to 30 cupcakes.

German Chocolate Cake:
All the rage in the 1950s, this layered beauty, with its sweet chocolate flavor and a gooey pecan-coconut topping, has been satisfying sweet tooths ever since.

GERMAN CHOCOLATE CAKE

Prep: 50 minutes   Bake: 30 minutes
Cool: 1 hour   Makes: 12 servings   Oven: 350°F

1½ **cups all-purpose flour**
 ¾ **teaspoon baking soda**
 ¼ **teaspoon salt**
 1 **4-ounce package sweet baking chocolate**
 1 **cup sugar**
 ¾ **cup shortening**
 3 **eggs**
 1 **teaspoon vanilla**
 ¾ **cup buttermilk or sour milk (see tip, page 208)**
 1 **recipe Coconut-Pecan Frosting**
 1 **recipe Chocolate Butter Frosting (optional) (see recipe, page 131)**

1 Grease and lightly flour two 8×1½-inch or 9×1½-inch round baking pans; set pans aside. Stir together flour, baking soda, and salt; set aside.

2 In a saucepan combine chocolate and ½ cup water. Cook and stir over low heat until melted; cool.

3 Beat sugar and shortening with an electric mixer on medium speed until fluffy. Add eggs and vanilla; beat on low speed until combined. Beat on medium speed 1 minute. Beat in chocolate mixture. Add the flour mixture and buttermilk alternately to shortening mixture; beat on low speed after each addi-

tion just until combined. Pour batter into prepared pans.

4 Bake in a 350°F oven for 30 minutes for 9-inch layers, 35 to 40 minutes for 8-inch layers or until a wooden toothpick comes out clean. Cool layers on wire racks for 10 minutes. Remove from pans. Cool thoroughly. Spread Coconut-Pecan Frosting over top of layers; stack. If desired, frost the sides with Chocolate Butter Frosting (see photo, below).

Coconut-Pecan Frosting: In a saucepan slightly beat 1 egg. Stir in one 5-ounce can (⅔ cup) evaporated milk, ⅔ cup sugar, and ¼ cup butter. Cook and stir over medium heat about 12 minutes or until thickened and bubbly. Remove from heat; stir in 1⅓ cups flaked coconut and ½ cup chopped pecans. Cover and cool thoroughly.

Nutrition Facts per serving (with Coconut-Pecan Frosting only): 470 cal., 29 g total fat (11 g sat. fat), 85 mg chol., 214 mg sodium, 51 g carbo., 2 g fiber, 6 g pro. Daily Values: 7% vit. A, 3% vit. C, 5% calcium, 9% iron

Dress up the sides of this classic cake by using a narrow spatula to evenly spread the chocolate frosting. Use smooth, up-and-down strokes.

BUTTERMILK-PINEAPPLE CARROT CAKE

Prep: 30 minutes   Bake: 40 minutes
Cool: 1 hour   Makes: 16 servings   Oven: 350°F

   2 **cups all-purpose flour**
   2 **cups sugar**
   2 **teaspoons baking soda**
1½ **teaspoons ground cinnamon**
   1 **teaspoon baking powder**
 ¼ **teaspoon salt**
   2 **cups finely shredded carrots***
 ¼ **cup buttermilk or sour milk**
        (see tip, page 208)
 ¼ **cup cooking oil**
   1 **8¼-ounce can crushed pineapple,**
        drained
   1 **cup chopped walnuts**
   3 **eggs**
 ½ **cup coconut**
   1 **teaspoon vanilla**
   1 **recipe Buttermilk Glaze**
   1 **recipe Cream Cheese Frosting**
        (see recipe, page 133)
 ½ **cup chopped walnuts**

1 **Grease a** 13×9×2-inch baking pan or grease and lightly flour two 9×1½-inch round baking pans; set aside.

2 **In a large bowl combine** flour, sugar, baking soda, cinnamon, baking powder, and salt. Add shredded carrots, buttermilk. cooking oil, drained pineapple, the 1 cup nuts, eggs, coconut, and vanilla. Stir until combined. Spread batter in prepared pan(s).

3 **Bake in a 350°F oven** for 40 to 45 minutes or until cake(s) spring back when touched lightly. Pour Buttermilk Glaze evenly over top(s) of cake(s). Cool layer cakes in pans on wire racks for 15 minutes. Remove from pans. Cool thoroughly on racks. Or, place 13×9-inch pan on wire rack; cool thoroughly. Frost with Cream Cheese Frosting. Sprinkle with the ½ cup nuts.

Buttermilk Glaze: In a medium saucepan combine ½ cup sugar, ¼ cup buttermilk or sour milk, ¼ cup butter, and 2 teaspoons light-colored corn syrup. Bring to boiling; reduce heat. Cook and stir for 4 minutes. Remove saucepan from heat and stir in ½ teaspoon vanilla.

*Note: The carrots need to be finely shredded or they may sink to the bottom of pan during baking.

Nutrition Facts per serving: 544 cal., 25 g total fat (10 g sat. fat), 75 mg chol., 360 mg sodium, 79 g carbo., 2 g fiber, 6 g pro. **Daily Values:** 53% vit. A, 4% vit. C, 5% calcium, 10% iron

Buttermilk-Pineapple Carrot Cake: A decadent version of the classic, this cake adds pineapple, coconut, and a luscious buttermilk glaze layer. Consider the 13×9-inch size cake when toting.

Pistachio Cake with White Chocolate Buttercream: It's a beauty. Tender cake layers slathered with a sumptuous buttercream frosting and studded with rich pistachios— it all stacks up to an unforgettable dessert.

PISTACHIO CAKE WITH WHITE CHOCOLATE BUTTERCREAM

Prep: 40 minutes   Bake: 30 minutes
Cool: 1 hour   Makes: 12 servings   Oven: 350°F

1⅔ cups all-purpose flour
 4 teaspoons baking powder
 ½ teaspoon baking soda
 ¾ cup butter
 2 cups sugar
 1 teaspoon vanilla
 1 teaspoon almond extract
 1 cup buttermilk or sour milk
 6 egg whites (reserve yolks for White
   Chocolate Buttercream)
1½ cups toasted chopped pistachio
   nuts (see tip, page 181)
 2 teaspoons finely shredded orange peel
 1 recipe White Chocolate
   Buttercream (see recipe, page
   134)
 1 cup toasted chopped pistachio nuts
   (see tip, page 181)

1 **Grease and lightly flour** three 8×1½-inch round baking pans (see tip, page 121); set aside. Stir together flour, baking powder, and baking soda; set aside. Beat butter with an electric mixer on medium to high speed 30 seconds. Add sugar, vanilla, and almond extract to butter; beat until fluffy. Alternately add flour mixture and buttermilk, beating on low to medium speed just until combined.

2 **Thoroughly wash beaters.** In a medium mixing bowl beat egg whites until stiff peaks form (tips stand straight). Gently fold beaten egg whites into batter. Fold in the 1½ cups pistachio nuts and the orange peel. Pour batter into prepared pans.

3 **Bake in a 350°F oven** 30 to 35 minutes or until a wooden toothpick inserted near the center of each cake comes out clean. Cool in pans on wire racks for 10 minutes. Remove cakes from pans and cool thoroughly on wire racks. Frost with White Chocolate Buttercream. If desired, using a decorating bag fitted with a star tip, pipe a scalloped edge around the top of the cake. Press the 1 cup pistachio nuts onto sides of cake. Cover and store cake in the refrigerator for up to 3 days. Let stand at room temperature for 30 minutes before serving.

Nutrition Facts per serving: 753 cal., 47 g total fat (22 g sat. fat), 182 mg chol., 466 mg sodium, 74 g carbo., 3 g fiber, 13 g pro. **Daily Values:** 43% vit. A, 4% vit. C, 17% calcium, 20% iron

BANANA LAYER CAKE

Prep: 30 minutes   Bake: 30 minutes
Cool: 1 hour   Makes: 12 servings   Oven: 350°F

  2 **cups all-purpose flour**
1½ **teaspoons baking powder**
 ¾ **teaspoon baking soda**
 ½ **cup shortening**
1½ **cups sugar**
  1 **teaspoon vanilla**
  2 **eggs**
  1 **cup mashed ripe bananas (3 medium)**
 ½ **cup buttermilk or sour milk**
      (see tip, page 208)

1 **Grease and flour** two 9×1½-inch round baking pans; set aside. Stir together flour, baking powder, baking soda, and ½ teaspoon salt; set aside.

2 **In a large mixing bowl beat** shortening with an electric mixer on medium to high speed for 30 seconds. Add sugar and vanilla; beat until well combined. Add eggs, 1 at a time, beating well after each. Combine bananas and buttermilk. Add flour mixture and buttermilk mixture alternately to egg mixture, beating on low speed after each addition just until combined. Pour into prepared pans.

3 **Bake in 350°F oven** 30 minutes or until wooden toothpick inserted near centers comes out clean. Cool on wire racks 10 minutes. Remove from pans; cool thoroughly on racks. Frost with desired frosting.

Nutrition Facts per serving (cake only): 286 cal., 10 g total fat (3 g sat. fat), 36 mg chol., 235 mg sodium, 47 g carbo., 1 g fiber, 4 g pro. **Daily Values:** 1% vit. A, 4% vit. C, 5% calcium, 7% iron

---

COOL IT!

Before removing a creamed layer cake from its baking pan, let it cool about 10 minutes on a wire rack. To remove, loosen the cake edges from the pan and place an inverted wire rack over the top of the pan. Turn cake and rack over and lift off pan. Place a second rack on cake layer and turn it over again so the baked cake is upright; let it cool completely.

BANANA SPLIT CAKE

Prep: 30 minutes (plus cake)
Makes: 12 servings

  1 **recipe Banana Layer Cake**
      (see recipe, left) or one 2-layer-
      size banana cake mix
  1 **recipe Sweetened Whipped Cream**
      (see page 133) or 6 ounces frozen
      whipped dessert topping, thawed
  1 **cup sliced fresh strawberries**
  1 **8¼-ounce can crushed pineapple,**
      well drained
  1 **11- to 12-ounce jar fudge**
      ice-cream topping
 ½ **cup chopped peanuts**
      Banana slices (optional)

1 **Prepare the** Banana Layer Cake or, if using banana cake mix, prepare according to package directions for a two-layer cake.

2 **For fillings,** divide whipped cream in half. Fold berries into half of the whipped cream. Fold drained pineapple into the other half of the whipped cream. In a small saucepan, heat and stir fudge ice-cream topping over low heat just until warm (not hot).

3 **To assemble,** using a serrated knife, split each cake layer in half horizontally. Place bottom of 1 split layer on serving plate. Top with the strawberry-cream mixture, spreading to edge of the cake layer. Place another split cake layer atop. Spread with half of the warm fudge topping, letting it drizzle down the sides. Sprinkle with half of the nuts.

4 **Top with another** split cake layer. Spread with pineapple-cream mixture. Top with remaining split cake layer. Spread remaining warm fudge topping atop cake, letting some drizzle down sides of cake. Sprinkle top of cake with remaining nuts. Serve immediately. (Or, cover loosely with plastic wrap, placing a few toothpicks in top of the cake so the wrap doesn't stick to the topping, and chill up to 2 hours.) If desired, garnish with banana slices.

Nutrition Facts per serving: 494 cal., 24 g total fat (10 g sat. fat), 63 mg chol., 222 mg sodium, 67 g carbo., 2 g fiber, 7 g pro. **Daily Values:** 11% vit. A, 19% vit. C, 9% calcium, 11% iron

Banana Split Cake:
Looking for a star dessert for
your next social gathering?
This one wins rave reviews
for its soda fountain flavors.

ANGEL FOOD CAKE LOW-FAT

Prep: 50 minutes   **Bake:** 40 minutes
Cool: 2 hours   **Makes:** 12 servings   **Oven:** 350°F

Loosen the cooled cake from the pan by sliding a long metal spatula between the pan and cake. Constantly pressing the spatula against the pan, draw it around the pan in a continuous, not sawing, motion so you don't cut into the cake. For help with techniques, see photos, right.

1½ **cups egg whites (10 to 12 large)**
1½ **cups sifted powdered sugar**
 1 **cup sifted cake flour or sifted**
     all-purpose flour
1½ **teaspoons cream of tartar**
 1 **teaspoon vanilla**
 1 **cup granulated sugar**

1 **In an extra-large mixing bowl allow** egg whites to stand at room temperature for 30 minutes. Meanwhile, sift powdered sugar and flour together 3 times; set aside.

2 **Add cream of tartar** and vanilla to egg whites. Beat with an electric mixer on medium speed until soft peaks form (tips curl). Gradually add granulated sugar, about 2 tablespoons at a time, beating until stiff peaks form (tips stand straight).

3 **Sift about one-fourth** of the flour mixture over beaten egg whites; fold in gently. Repeat, folding in remaining flour mixture by fourths. Pour into an ungreased 10-inch tube pan. Gently cut through batter with a narrow metal spatula or knife to remove large air pockets.

4 **Bake on the lowest rack** in a 350°F oven for 40 to 45 minutes or until top springs back when lightly touched. Immediately invert cake (leave in pan); cool thoroughly. Using a narrow metal spatula, loosen sides of cake from pan; remove cake.

Nutrition Facts per serving: 161 cal., 0 g total fat, 0 mg chol., 46 mg sodium, 37 g carbo., 0 g fiber, 4 g pro. **Daily Values:** 4% iron

Honey Angel Food Cake: Prepare as above, except after beating egg whites to soft peaks, gradually pour ¼ cup honey in a thin stream over the egg white mixture. Continue as above, except beat only ½ cup granulated sugar into the egg whites.

Initially, beat the egg whites, cream of tartar, and vanilla until soft peaks form. This means that the tips will curl when beaters are lifted.

As the granulated sugar is gradually added, continue beating until stiff peaks form. This means that the peaks will stand straight when beaters are lifted.

Sift flour mixture over the stiffly beaten egg white mixture. If you don't have a sifter, you can press the flour mixture through a sieve.

To fold in, cut down through the mixture with a rubber spatula; scrape across the bottom of the bowl and bring spatula up and over, close to surface.

Gently cutting through the cake batter with a narrow metal spatula or table knife helps eliminate any air pockets.

CHOCOLATE ANGEL CAKE WITH COFFEE LIQUEUR GLAZE

LOW-FAT

Prep: 1 hour   Bake: 40 minutes
Cool: 2 hours   Makes: 12 servings
Oven: 350°F

Here's luscious proof that chocolate can fit into a low-fat diet.

1½ cups egg whites (10 to 12 large)
1½ cups sifted powdered sugar
  1 cup sifted cake flour or sifted
      all-purpose flour
 ¼ cup unsweetened cocoa powder
1½ teaspoons cream of tartar
  1 teaspoon vanilla
  1 cup granulated sugar
  1 cup sifted powdered sugar
 ¼ teaspoon vanilla
      Coffee liqueur

1 **In an extra-large mixing bowl allow** egg whites to stand at room temperature for 30 minutes. Meanwhile, sift the 1½ cups powdered sugar, flour, and cocoa powder together 3 times; set aside.

2 **Add cream of tartar** and the 1 teaspoon vanilla to egg whites. Beat with an electric mixer on medium to high speed until soft peaks form (tips curl). Gradually add granulated sugar, about 2 tablespoons at a time, beating on medium to high speed until stiff peaks form (tips stand straight).

3 **Sift about one-fourth** of flour mixture over the beaten egg whites; fold in gently. Repeat, folding in remaining flour mixture by fourths. Pour into an ungreased 10-inch tube pan. Gently cut through the cake batter with a narrow metal spatula or knife.

4 **Bake on the lowest rack** in a 350°F oven for 40 to 45 minutes or until top springs back when lightly touched. Immediately invert cake (leave in the pan); cool thoroughly. Using a narrow metal spatula, loosen the sides of the cake from the pan. Remove cake from the pan.

5 **For glaze,** combine the 1 cup powdered sugar, the ¼ teaspoon vanilla, and enough of the coffee liqueur (about 2 tablespoons), 1 teaspoon at a time, to make of drizzling consistency. Drizzle over top of the cake.

Nutrition Facts per serving: 211 cal., 0 g total fat, 0 mg chol., 47 mg sodium, 47 g carbo., 0 g fiber, 4 g pro. **Daily Values:** 1% calcium, 5% iron

---

ANGEL, SPONGE, AND CHIFFON CAKES MASTERED

For an angel, sponge, or chiffon cake that rises above the rest, keep these tips in mind:

■ Be sure when you separate your eggs that not a speck of egg yolk or any other fat gets into the whites—it can ruin their beating quality. To safeguard against that, separate the whites into a small bowl, then transfer them to a clean glass or metal bowl that is wide enough to keep the beaters from being buried in the egg white as they fluff. Plastic bowls are not recommended for beating egg whites, as even after washing, they can hold an oily film on the interior, minimizing egg white volume.

■ Separate eggs as soon as you take them out of the refrigerator. Let them stand at room temperature for 30 minutes along with other ingredients.

■ Don't over- or under-beat egg whites. They should be stiff but not dry, or your cake may fall.

■ Measure the flour accurately using a dry measuring cup. Sift dry ingredients three times to ensure thorough blending of dry ingredients.

■ Fold dry ingredients into egg white mixture gently with a rubber spatula. Keep the spatula under surface of batter while folding. If you add too much flour or overmix the batter, the volume drops and your cake will be tough.

■ When making a chiffon cake, add egg yolks to flour mixture after the cooking oil. Otherwise, they might bind with the flour and form streaks.

■ When making a sponge cake, beat the egg yolks until they're thick and the color of lemons, or an eggy bottom layer may form.

■ Cool angel, sponge, and chiffon cakes upside down to set their structures.

MARBLE ANGEL FOOD CAKE

LOW-FAT

Prep: 50 minutes   Bake: 40 minutes
Cool: 2 hours   Makes: 12 servings   Oven: 350°F

*To keep this classic low in fat, top with fruit
instead of the whipped cream.*

1½ **cups egg whites (10 to 12 large)**
1½ **cups sifted powdered sugar**
  1 **cup sifted cake flour or sifted
     all-purpose flour**
  2 **tablespoons unsweetened cocoa
     powder**
1½ **teaspoons cream of tartar**
  1 **teaspoon vanilla**
  1 **cup granulated sugar**
  1 **recipe Chocolate Powdered Sugar
     Icing (optional) (see recipe, page
     132)**
    **Sweetened whipped cream
     (optional)**
    Fresh fruit (optional)

1 **In an extra-large mixing bowl allow** egg whites
to stand at room temperature for 30 minutes.

To marble batter, using a folding motion, bring a narrow spatula down through batter and up other side. Go completely around pan, turning pan as you fold. Do not overfold.

Meanwhile, sift powdered sugar and flour together
3 times. Measure 1 cup of the flour mixture; sift
together with the cocoa powder. Set mixtures aside.

2 **Add cream of tartar** and vanilla to the egg
whites. Beat with an electric mixer on medium
speed until soft peaks form (tips curl). Gradually
add the granulated sugar, about 2 tablespoons at a
time, beating until stiff peaks form (tips stand
straight). Transfer one-third of the mixture to
another bowl.

3 **Sift about one-fourth** of the plain flour mixture
over the larger portion of beaten egg whites;
gently fold in. Repeat folding in the remaining plain
flour mixture, using one-fourth of the flour mixture
each time. Sift flour-cocoa mixture, one-third at a
time, over smaller portion of beaten egg whites,
folding in as above.

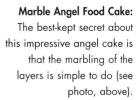

Marble Angel Food Cake:
The best-kept secret about
this impressive angel cake is
that the marbling of the
layers is simple to do (see
photo, above).

4 **Gently spoon one-third** of the white batter evenly into an ungreased 10-inch tube pan. Spoon half of the chocolate batter over white batter in pan. Repeat. Top with remaining white batter. Marble the batter (see top photo, page 108).

5 **Bake on the lowest rack** in a 350°F oven for 40 to 45 minutes or until top springs back when lightly touched. Immediately invert cake (leave in pan). Cool completely. Using a narrow metal spatula, loosen sides of cake from pan. Remove cake from pan. If desired, drizzle with Chocolate Powdered Sugar Icing and serve with sweetened whipped cream or fresh fruit.

Nutrition Facts per serving: 165 cal., 0 g total fat, 0 mg chol., 46 mg sodium, 37 g carbo., 0 g fiber, 4 g pro. Daily Values: 1% calcium, 5% iron

SPONGE CAKE [LOW-FAT]

Prep: 40 minutes **Bake:** 55 minutes
Cool: 2 hours **Makes:** 12 servings **Oven:** 325°F

*A simple drizzle of Powdered Sugar Icing
(page recipe 132) is all it takes to dress up this
golden yellow ring.*

> 6 egg yolks
> 1 tablespoon finely shredded
>   orange peel
> ½ cup orange juice or pineapple juice
> 1 teaspoon vanilla
> 1 cup sugar
> 1¼ cups all-purpose flour
> 6 egg whites
> ½ teaspoon cream of tartar
> ½ cup sugar

1 **In a mixing bowl beat** egg yolks with an electric mixer on high speed about 5 minutes or until thick and lemon colored. Add orange peel, orange juice, and vanilla; beat on low speed until combined. Gradually beat in the 1 cup sugar at low speed. Increase to medium speed; beat until mixture thickens slightly and doubles in volume (about 5 minutes total).

2 **Sprinkle** ¼ cup of the flour over egg yolk mixture; fold in until combined. Repeat with remaining flour, ¼ cup at a time. Set egg yolk mixture aside.

<hr>

ANGEL, SPONGE, AND CHIFFON CAKES— THE EGGS HAVE IT

Q What's the difference in angel, sponge, and chiffon cakes? They seem pretty similar in that they all have beaten eggs.

A Eggs are indeed the common denominator in these airy cakes. They all rely on the power of the beaten egg to make them light as a feather. The main difference in them is that each contains elements of the egg in different measures.

- Angel food cakes—the lightest of the three—contain just beaten egg whites, no yolks. They also do not contain oil.
- Sponge cakes are richer than angel food cakes because they feature egg yolks as well as whites.
- Chiffon cakes are the richest of the three; they contain whole eggs, beaten separately, as well as cooking oil.

<hr>

3 **Thoroughly wash beaters.** In a mixing bowl beat egg whites and cream of tartar on medium speed until soft peaks form (tips curl). Gradually add the ½ cup sugar, beating on high speed until stiff peaks form (tips stand straight). Fold 1 cup of the beaten egg white mixture into the egg yolk mixture; fold yolk mixture into remaining egg white mixture. Pour into an ungreased 10-inch tube pan.

4 **Bake on lowest rack** in a 325°F oven 55 minutes or until cake springs back when lightly touched. Immediately invert cake (leave in pan); cool thoroughly. Loosen sides from pan; remove from pan.

Nutrition Facts per serving: 184 cal., 3 g total fat (1 g sat. fat), 107 mg chol., 32 mg sodium, 36 g carbo., 0 g fiber, 4 g pro. Daily Values: 16% vit. A, 9% vit. C, 1% calcium, 6% iron

Lemon Sponge Cake: Prepare as above, except substitute 2 teaspoons finely shredded lemon peel for the orange peel and ¼ cup lemon juice plus ¼ cup water for the orange juice.

Chocolate Sponge Cake: Prepare as above, except omit orange peel. Reduce flour to 1 cup. Stir ⅓ cup unsweetened cocoa powder into flour.

SHERRY-ALMOND SPONGE CAKE

Prep: 1 hour **Bake:** 25 minutes **Cool:** 1 hour
Chill: 2 hours **Makes:** 12 servings **Oven:** 325°F

4 egg yolks
⅓ cup dry or cream sherry
⅔ cup sugar
⅔ cup all-purpose flour
¼ cup ground toasted almonds
    (see tip, page 181)
4 egg whites
½ teaspoon cream of tartar
⅓ cup sugar
1 cup whipping cream
1 tablespoon sugar
2 to 3 teaspoons dry or cream
    sherry
½ cup strawberry or seedless
    raspberry preserves
2 tablespoons coarsely chopped toasted
    almonds (see tip, page 181)
    Edible flowers (optional)
    (see tip, page 18)

1 **Beat egg yolks** with electric mixer on high speed about 5 minutes or until thick and lemon colored. Add the ⅓ cup sherry. Beat on low speed until combined. Gradually beat in the ⅔ cup sugar. Increase speed to medium; beat until mixture thickens slightly and doubles in volume (about 5 minutes total).

2 **Sprinkle ⅓ cup of flour** over yolk mixture; gently fold in until combined. Repeat with remaining flour. Gently fold in ground almonds. Set aside.

3 **Thoroughly wash beaters.** In a large mixing bowl beat egg whites and cream of tartar on medium speed until soft peaks form (tips curl). Gradually add the ⅓ cup sugar, beating on high speed until stiff peaks form (tips stand straight). Fold about 1 cup beaten egg white mixture into yolk mixture.

4 **Gently fold the yolk mixture** into the remaining white mixture. Pour batter into 2 ungreased 8×1½-inch round cake pans.

5 **Bake in a 325°F oven** about 25 minutes or until top springs back when lightly touched. Invert onto racks (leave in pans); cool. Remove from pans.

6 **In a chilled medium mixing bowl combine** whipping cream, the 1 tablespoon sugar, and the 2 to 3 teaspoons sherry; beat until soft peaks form. Remove cooled cake from pans. Spread preserves between cake layers. Spread whipped cream on top and sides of cake. Pat almonds onto sides. Cover and chill up to 2 hours. If desired, garnish the top with edible flowers.

Nutrition Facts per serving: 256 cal., 11 g total fat (5 g sat. fat), 98 mg chol., 31 mg sodium, 34 g carbo., 1 g fiber, 4 g pro. **Daily Values:** 19% vit. A, 3% calcium, 5% iron

CHIFFON CAKE

Prep: 30 minutes **Bake:** 1 hour 5 minutes
Cool: 2 hours **Makes:** 12 servings **Oven:** 325°F

2¼ cups sifted cake flour or 2 cups
    sifted all-purpose flour
1½ cups sugar
1 tablespoon baking powder
½ cup cooking oil
7 egg yolks
2 teaspoons finely shredded
    orange peel
1 teaspoon finely shredded
    lemon peel
1 teaspoon vanilla
7 egg whites
½ teaspoon cream of tartar

1 **In a large mixing bowl** mix flour, sugar, baking powder, and ¼ teaspoon salt. Make well in center of flour mixture. Add oil, egg yolks, orange and lemon peels, vanilla, and ¾ cup cold water. Beat with electric mixer on low speed until combined. Beat on high speed for 5 minutes more or until satin smooth.

2 **Thoroughly wash beaters.** In an extra-large mixing bowl beat egg whites and cream of tartar on medium speed until stiff peaks form (tips stand straight). Pour batter in a thin stream over beaten egg whites; fold in gently. Pour into an ungreased 10-inch tube pan.

3 **Bake on lowest rack** in a 325°F oven for 65 to 70 minutes or until top springs back when lightly touched. Immediately invert cake (in pan); cool thoroughly. Loosen sides of cake from pan; remove cake.

Nutrition Facts per serving: 298 cal., 12 g total fat (2 g sat. fat), 124 mg chol., 173 mg sodium, 42 g carbo., 0 g fiber, 5 g pro. **Daily Values:** 18% vit. A, 1% vit. C, 8% calcium, 11% iron

Sherry-Almond Sponge Cake: A colorful berry filling nestles between light sponge cake layers. Add to that an infusion of sherry and a sprinkling of almonds, and this cake becomes reminiscent of an elegant Victorian trifle.

GÉNOISE

Prep: 30 minutes   Bake: 25 minutes
Cool: 1 hour   Makes: 12 servings   Oven: 350°F

This fine-crumbed, buttery French sponge cake provides the foundation for many elegant desserts, such as the one at right. It's also lovely served with a fruity sorbet or fresh fruit and whipped cream.

> 1 **cup sugar**
> 6 **slightly beaten eggs**
> 2 **teaspoons vanilla**
> 1 **cup all-purpose flour**
> ½ **cup unsalted butter, melted**
>   **and cooled**

1 Grease two 9×1½-inch or 8×1½-inch round baking pans. Line bottoms with waxed paper or parchment paper; grease paper. Set aside.

2 Place sugar and eggs in a 3- to 4-quart heat-proof mixing bowl.* Place bowl over 1 to 2 inches hot water in a large saucepan (bowl should not touch water). Heat over low heat, stirring occasionally, for 5 to 10 minutes or until egg mixture is lukewarm (105°F to 110°F). Remove bowl from saucepan. Stir in vanilla.

3 Beat egg mixture with an electric mixer on high speed for 10 minutes. Sift about one-third of the flour over egg mixture. Gently fold in flour. Repeat sifting and folding in one-third of the flour at a time. Gently fold in melted butter. Spread batter into prepared pans.

4 Bake in a 350°F oven for 25 to 30 minutes or until a wooden toothpick inserted near the center of each cake comes out clean. Cool cakes in pans on wire racks for 10 minutes. Remove cakes and peel off paper. Cool cakes thoroughly on racks.

*Note: The sugar and egg mixture is heated to help maximize volume while beating.

Nutrition Facts per serving: 207 cal., 10 g total fat (6 g sat. fat), 127 mg chol., 33 mg sodium, 25 g carbo., 0 g fiber, 4 g pro. **Daily Values:** 11% vit. A, 1% calcium, 5% iron

Chocolate Génoise: Prepare Génoise as directed, except melt 3 ounces semisweet chocolate; cool chocolate. Fold the chocolate into the batter with the melted butter.

LEMON TEA CAKES

Prep: 3 hours   Bake: 25 minutes   Cool: 1 hour
Makes: 35 to 40 cakes   Oven: 350°F

> 1 **recipe Génoise (see recipe, left)**
> 1 **tablespoon finely shredded**
>   **lemon peel**
> 1 **tablespoon lemon juice**
> 1 **recipe Lemon Satin Icing**
>   **Melted chocolate, candied violets,**
>   **edible flowers, and/or small**
>   **decorative candies (optional)**

1 Grease a 13×9×2-inch baking pan. Line bottom of pan with waxed paper or parchment paper; grease paper. Set aside.

2 Prepare the Génoise batter as directed, except stir in lemon juice with vanilla and fold in lemon peel with melted butter. Spread batter in prepared pan. Bake in a 350°F oven about 25 minutes or until a wooden toothpick inserted near the center of the cake comes out clean. Cool cake in pan on a wire rack for 10 minutes. Remove cake from pan; peel off paper. Cool thoroughly on the rack.

3 With a serrated knife, trim sides and top of cake to make the edges smooth and straight. Cut cake into 1½-inch squares, diamonds, hearts, and/or circles. Brush off crumbs. Place the cake pieces on wire racks with waxed paper underneath racks.

4 Insert a 2- or 3-pronged, long-handled fork into the side of 1 cake piece. Holding the cake over the saucepan of Lemon Satin Icing, spoon on enough icing to cover sides and top (see bottom photo, page 113). Place frosted cake piece back on the wire rack, making sure it doesn't touch other cake pieces. Repeat with remaining pieces. Let cakes dry 15 minutes. Repeat with a second layer of icing, except set cake pieces on top of the fork prongs (do not spear them). Repeat with a third layer of icing. If necessary, reuse the icing that has dripped onto the waxed paper, straining it to remove crumbs. Tint any remaining icing with food coloring as desired and pipe or drizzle atop cakes. If desired, garnish with piped melted chocolate, candied violets, edible flowers, and/or decorative candies. (Do not eat silver candies, if using.)

Lemon Satin Icing: In a 3-quart saucepan combine 4½ cups granulated sugar, 2¼ cups water, and

Lemon Tea Cakes: Sweet and petite, these teatime gems can be made even more elegant with candied violets and edible flowers. You also can color the Lemon Satin Icing as desired and drizzle or pipe it onto the cakes.

¼ teaspoon cream of tartar. Bring mixture to boiling over medium-high heat, stirring constantly for 5 to 9 minutes or until the sugar dissolves. Reduce heat to medium-low. Clip a candy thermometer to side of the saucepan. Cook until thermometer registers 226°F, stirring only when necessary to prevent sticking. Mixture should boil at a moderate, steady rate over the entire surface (this should take about 15 minutes). Remove saucepan from heat. Cool sugar mixture at room temperature, without stirring, to 110°F (allow about 1 hour).

Stir 1 tablespoon lemon juice or ¼ teaspoon almond extract and 1½ teaspoons clear vanilla into sugar mixture. Stir in 6 to 6¾ cups sifted powdered sugar until icing is easy to drizzle. If necessary, beat the icing with a rotary beater or a wire whisk to remove any lumps. If desired, stir in enough food coloring to make color you want. (If icing gets too thick to drizzle, beat in a few drops hot water.) Makes 5 cups.

Nutrition Facts per cake: 237 cal., 4 g total fat (2 g sat. fat), 44 mg chol., 12 mg sodium, 51 g carbo., 0 g fiber, 1 g pro. **Daily Values:** 4% vit. A, 1% vit. C, 2% iron

To ice cakes, spear 1 cake piece with a fork and hold it over the pan of icing. Spoon icing over cake piece, covering sides and top. Repeat with remaining cakes.

JELLY ROLL *LOW-FAT*

Prep: 30 minutes   Bake: 12 minutes
Cool: 1 hour   Makes: 10 servings   Oven: 375°F

Can a Victorian dessert actually be low in fat? Sure, when it's a light, spongy jelly roll. This basic recipe, filled with jelly, has only 2 grams of fat per serving.

½ **cup all-purpose flour**
1 **teaspoon baking powder**
4 **egg yolks**
½ **teaspoon vanilla**
⅓ **cup granulated sugar**
4 **egg whites**
½ **cup granulated sugar**
    Sifted powdered sugar
½ **cup jelly or jam**

1 Grease and lightly flour a 15×10×1-inch jelly-roll pan; set aside. Combine flour and baking powder; set aside. In a medium mixing bowl beat egg yolks and vanilla with an electric mixer on high speed for 5 minutes or until thick and lemon colored. Gradually add the ⅓ cup granulated sugar, beating on high speed until sugar is almost dissolved.

2 Thoroughly wash the beaters. In a mixing bowl beat egg whites on medium speed until soft peaks form (tips curl). Gradually add the ½ cup granulated sugar, beating until stiff peaks form (tips stand straight). Fold egg yolk mixture into beaten egg whites. Sprinkle flour mixture over egg mixture; fold in gently just until combined. Spread batter evenly in the prepared pan.

3 Bake in a 375°F oven for 12 to 15 minutes or until top springs back when lightly touched. Immediately loosen edges of cake from pan; turn cake out onto a towel sprinkled with powdered sugar. Roll towel and cake, into a spiral, starting from a short side (see photos, above right). Cool on a wire rack. Unroll cake; remove towel. Spread cake with jelly or jam to within 1 inch of edges. Roll up cake.

Nutrition Facts per serving: 162 cal., 2 g total fat (1 g sat. fat), 85 mg chol., 64 mg sodium, 33 g carbo., 0 g fiber, 3 g pro. **Daily Values:** 12% vit. A, 1% vit. C, 3% calcium, 5% iron

Chocolate Cake Roll: Prepare as above, except reduce flour to ⅓ cup and omit baking powder. Add ¼ cup

Starting from a short side of the warm cake, roll it up with the powdered sugar-coated towel. Let the cake cool.

After carefully unrolling the cooled cake and towel, spread the desired filling over the cake. Leave a 1-inch border around the edges.

Roll up the cake and filling (without the towel), again starting from a short side.

unsweetened cocoa powder and ¼ teaspoon baking soda to flour. Substitute 2 cups whipped cream or cooled chocolate pudding for the jelly. Roll up cake; chill up to 2 hours.

Pumpkin Cake Roll: Prepare as at left, except add 2 teaspoons pumpkin pie spice to flour mixture and stir ½ cup canned pumpkin into egg yolk mixture. Substitute 1 recipe Cream Cheese Frosting (see page 133) for the jelly. Sprinkle cake roll with additional sifted powdered sugar; chill.

Lemon Cake Roll: Prepare as at left, except substitute 1 recipe Lemon Curd (see page 132) for the jelly. Sprinkle cake roll with additional sifted powdered sugar; chill up to 2 hours.

Ice-Cream Cake Roll: Prepare as at left, except substitute 2 cups of your choice of ice cream, softened, for the jelly. Store in the freezer.

Pumpkin-Pear Cake:
No frosting needed!
When you invert this
upside-down-style cake,
a smooth, caramel syrup
oozes over the pears and
warm pumpkin cake.

PUMPKIN-PEAR CAKE

Prep: 20 minutes   Bake: 35 minutes
Cool: 5 minutes   Makes: 10 servings
Oven: 350°F

$\frac{1}{3}$ cup packed brown sugar
2 tablespoons butter, melted
1 tablespoon water
2 medium pears, cored, peeled,
   and sliced
1$\frac{1}{4}$ cups all-purpose flour
1$\frac{1}{4}$ teaspoons baking powder
1 teaspoon pumpkin pie spice*
$\frac{1}{4}$ teaspoon baking soda
3 egg whites
$\frac{3}{4}$ cup granulated sugar
$\frac{3}{4}$ cup canned pumpkin
$\frac{1}{3}$ cup cooking oil
2 tablespoons water
1 teaspoon vanilla
   Orange peel curls (optional)

1 In a small bowl combine brown sugar, melted butter, and the 1 tablespoon water. Pour into an ungreased 9×1½-inch round baking pan. Arrange pear slices in pan. Set pan aside.

2 In a small bowl combine flour, baking powder, pumpkin pie spice, and baking soda; set aside.

In another mixing bowl beat egg whites with electric mixer on medium speed until soft peaks form (tips curl). Gradually add granulated sugar, beating until stiff peaks form (tips stand straight). Using low speed, blend in pumpkin, oil, the 2 tablespoons water, and vanilla. Fold flour mixture into pumpkin mixture just until moistened; carefully spoon over pears. Spread mixture evenly with back of spoon.

3 Bake in a 350°F oven about 35 minutes or until a wooden toothpick inserted near center comes out clean. Cool in pan on wire rack for 5 minutes. Loosen from sides of pan; invert onto serving plate. Serve warm. If desired, garnish with orange peel curls.

*Note: Pumpkin pie spice is available at most grocery stores in the spice aisle.

Nutrition Facts per serving: 250 cal., 10 g total fat
(3 g sat. fat), 6 mg chol., 120 mg sodium,
39 g carbo., 2 g fiber, 3 g pro. **Daily Values:**
42% vit. A, 3% vit. C, 5% calcium, 8% iron

AMAZING BANANA NUT ROLL

BEST-LOVED

Prep: 30 minutes   **Bake:** 15 minutes
Cool: 1 hour   **Makes:** 10 servings   **Oven:** 375°F

½ cup all-purpose flour
½ teaspoon baking powder
¼ teaspoon baking soda
1 8-ounce package cream cheese,
    softened
1 3-ounce package cream cheese,
    softened
½ cup granulated sugar
1 egg
3 tablespoons milk
4 egg yolks
½ teaspoon vanilla
⅓ cup granulated sugar
1 large banana, mashed (about ½ cup)
½ cup finely chopped walnuts or
    pecans
4 egg whites
½ cup granulated sugar
    Sifted powdered sugar
1 recipe Vanilla Cream Cheese
    Frosting
    Chocolate-flavored syrup (optional)

1 **Lightly grease a** 15×10×1-inch baking pan. Line bottom with waxed paper; grease paper. Set aside. In a medium bowl stir together flour, baking powder, and baking soda; set aside.

2 **For filling,** in a small mixing bowl combine cream cheese and the ½ cup granulated sugar; beat with an electric mixer on medium speed until smooth. Add whole egg and milk; beat until combined. Spread in the prepared pan; set aside.

3 **In a medium mixing bowl beat** egg yolks and vanilla on medium speed about 5 minutes or until thick and lemon colored. Gradually add the ⅓ cup granulated sugar, beating until sugar is dissolved. Stir in banana and nuts.

4 **Thoroughly wash the beaters.** In a large mixing bowl beat the egg whites on medium speed until soft peaks form (tips curl). Gradually add the ½ cup granulated sugar, beating on high speed until stiff peaks form (tips stand straight). Fold yolk mixture into egg whites. Sprinkle the flour mixture evenly over egg mixture; fold in just until blended.

5 **Carefully spread the batter** evenly over the filling in the pan. Bake in a 375°F oven for 15 to 20 minutes or until the top springs back when lightly touched.

6 **Immediately loosen cake** from sides of pan and turn out onto a towel sprinkled with powdered sugar. Carefully peel off paper. Starting with a short side, roll up cake, using towel as a guide but not rolling towel into cake. Cool completely on rack.

7 **Spread top** with Vanilla Cream Cheese Frosting. If desired, drizzle with chocolate-flavored syrup.

Vanilla Cream Cheese Frosting: In a small mixing bowl combine half of a 3-ounce package cream cheese, softened, and ½ teaspoon vanilla; beat with an electric mixer on medium speed until light and fluffy. Gradually beat in 1 cup unsifted powdered sugar. Beat in enough milk (1 to 2 tablespoons) to make a frosting of spreading consistency. Makes about ½ cup frosting.

Nutrition Facts per serving: 400 cal., 19 g total fat (9 g sat. fat), 146 mg chol., 162 mg sodium, 51 g carbo., 1 g fiber, 8 g pro. **Daily Values:** 29% vit. A, 2% vit. C, 4% calcium, 9% iron

---

THE RISE OF CAKES

The first cakes can be traced back thousands of years to the Middle East, where they were flat baked mixtures of coarsely ground grain and water. Later, honey and sugar became standard ingredients, then sweet spices such as cinnamon, cloves, and nutmeg. When cakes made their way to Europe, they evolved to the status of sweetened breads, leavened with yeast. It wasn't until the 17th century, though, that cakes took on the rich, delicate qualities we've come to know and love.

Amazing Banana Nut Roll:
Some jelly-roll cakes require
rolling twice. Not this one!
The layers bake together
creating a wonderful banana
cake and cream cheese
filling, which are easily rolled
into one memorable dessert.

Granny Cake: Also known as the "hummingbird cake," this old-fashioned, church-social-style goody is one of those recipes that's been traded over backyard fences for years.

GRANNY CAKE

BEST-LOVED

Prep: 20 minutes **Bake:** 70 minutes
Cool: 2 hours **Makes:** 12 servings **Oven:** 325°F

> 3 **cups all-purpose flour**
> 2 **cups granulated sugar**
> 1 **teaspoon baking soda**
> 1 **teaspoon ground nutmeg**
> ½ **teaspoon salt**
> ½ **teaspoon ground cloves**
> ¾ **cup butter**
> 2 **cups mashed ripe bananas**
> 1 **8-ounce can crushed pineapple**
> 3 **eggs**
> 2 **teaspoons vanilla**
> 1 **cup finely chopped pecans**
> **Paper doily (optional)**
> **Powdered sugar (optional)**

1 **Grease and flour** a 10-inch fluted tube pan; set aside. In a medium bowl stir together flour, granulated sugar, baking soda, nutmeg, salt, and cloves; set aside.

2 **In large mixing bowl beat** butter with an electric mixer on medium speed for 30 seconds. Add bananas, undrained pineapple, eggs, and vanilla. Beat until combined. Add flour mixture. Beat on low speed until combined. Beat on medium speed 1 minute. Fold in pecans. Spread in prepared pan.

3 **Bake in a 325°F oven** for 70 to 75 minutes or until a wooden toothpick inserted near the center comes out clean. Cool cake in pan on a wire rack for 10 minutes. Remove cake from pan. Cool thoroughly on wire rack.

4 **If desired, decorate cake** with a powdered-sugar design. Place doily on top of cake. Sift powdered sugar over the doily to fill cutout designs. Carefully remove and discard the doily.

Nutrition Facts per serving: 481 cal., 19 g total fat (8 g sat. fat), 84 mg chol., 328 mg sodium, 74 g carbo., 2 g fiber, 6 g pro. **Daily Values:** 13% vit. A, 12% vit. C, 2% calcium, 13% iron

CHOCOLATE COOKIE CAKE

Prep: 50 minutes **Bake:** 40 minutes
Cool: 1 hour **Makes:** 16 servings **Oven:** 350°F

> 2⅔ **cups all-purpose flour**
> 2¼ **cups sugar**
> 1¼ **teaspoons baking soda**
> ¾ **teaspoon salt**
> ½ **teaspoon baking powder**
> 1⅓ **cups milk**
> 1 **8-ounce carton dairy sour cream**
> 5 **ounces unsweetened chocolate, melted and cooled**

⅓ **cup butter, softened**

3 **eggs**

2 **teaspoons vanilla**

1 **recipe Cookie Filling**

1 **recipe Chocolate-Sour Cream Frosting (see recipe, page 134)**

4 **chocolate sandwich cookies, crushed**

1 Grease and lightly flour two 8×1½-inch or 9×1½-inch round cake pans. Set pans aside.

2 In an extra-large mixing bowl combine flour, sugar, baking soda, salt, and baking powder. Add milk, sour cream, melted chocolate, butter, eggs, and vanilla. Beat with an electric mixer on low speed about 1 minute or until mixture is combined. Beat on high speed 3 minutes, scraping sides of bowl occasionally.

3 Place half of the batter in a medium bowl; cover and chill. Divide remaining half of batter evenly between the prepared pans. Bake in a 350°F oven for 20 to 25 minutes for 9-inch layers and 25 to 30 minutes for 8-inch layers or until a wooden toothpick inserted near centers comes out clean. Cool cakes in pans on wire racks for 10 minutes. Remove cakes from pans. Cool layers thoroughly on wire racks.

4 Wash the 2 cake pans. Grease and lightly flour pans. Divide reserved, chilled batter evenly between pans. Bake and cool as directed above.

5 Prepare Cookie Filling, reserving the ¾ cup filling (without crumbs) for the cake garnish.

6 To assemble the cake, put a cake layer on a serving plate and top with one-third of the remaining cookie filling, spreading filling evenly over layer. Add a second layer of cake and spread with another one-third portion of the cookie filling. Add another cake layer and spread with remaining cookie filling. Top with remaining cake layer.

7 Prepare the Chocolate-Sour Cream Frosting. Spread top and sides of cake with frosting. Stir reserved Cookie Filling and enough milk (about 2 to 3 teaspoons) to make it a drizzling consistency. Spoon onto center top of cake. Carefully spread filling to force some down sides of cake. Garnish top of cake with the 4 crushed chocolate sandwich cookies.

Cookie Filling: In large mixing bowl combine 4 cups sifted powdered sugar; ⅓ cup butter, softened; 2 tablespoons milk; and 1 teaspoon vanilla. Beat with electric mixer on low speed until combined; beat on medium speed until very smooth. Beat in enough additional milk (1 to 2 tablespoons) until frosting is easy to spread. Set aside ¾ cup of mixture. Crush 10 chocolate sandwich cookies; stir into remaining mixture.

Nutrition Facts per serving: 638 cal., 26 g total fat (12 g sat. fat), 79 mg chol., 408 mg sodium, 102 g carbo., 1 g fiber, 7 g pro. **Daily Values:** 18% vit. A, 7% calcium, 14% iron

Chocolate Cookie Cake: Definitely an indulgence, this chocolate-and-cream cake is perfect for a birthday party or any other special occasion.

CARAMEL-ALMOND TORTE

BEST-LOVED

Prep: 25 minutes   Bake: 25 minutes
Cool: 1 hour   Makes: 12 servings   Oven: 325°F

  6 egg yolks
1½ cups sugar
  ½ cup apple cider or apple juice
  1 teaspoon baking powder
  1 teaspoon vanilla
  ½ teaspoon ground cinnamon
  6 egg whites
  2 cups graham cracker crumbs
  1 cup ground almonds
  1 recipe Caramel Sauce
      (see recipe, page 121) (reserve
      ½ cup for Caramel Cream
      Filling)
  1 recipe Caramel Cream Filling
      (see recipe, page 121)
  1 recipe Sweetened Whipped Cream
      (see recipe, page 133)

1 **Generously grease and flour** three 8×1½-inch round baking pans (see tip, page 121); set aside. In a medium mixing bowl combine egg yolks, 1 cup of the sugar, the apple cider, baking powder, vanilla, and cinnamon. Beat with an electric mixer on medium speed about 3 minutes or until thickened and light.

2 **Thoroughly wash the beaters.** In an extra-large mixing bowl beat egg whites on medium speed until soft peaks form (tips curl). Gradually add the remaining sugar, beating on high speed until stiff peaks form (tips stand straight).

3 **Fold the egg yolk mixture** into the egg white mixture. Fold cracker crumbs and almonds into egg mixture, one-fourth at a time. Divide batter evenly among the prepared pans.

4 **Bake in a 325°F oven** for 25 to 30 minutes or until top springs back when lightly touched near the center. Cool on wire racks for 10 minutes. Loosen sides; remove cake layers from pans. Cool thoroughly on wire racks.

Caramel-Almond Torte: Love caramel? This torte gets a triple dose of the smooth, sweet ingredient—in the filling, the frosting, and with its drizzled finish.

<table>
<tr><td>

**TWO PANS—
THREE LAYERS**

The high and mighty Caramel-Almond Torte on page 120 has three layers and calls for three baking pans. However, if you only have two pans, don't let that stop you from making this exquisite dessert. Simply chill one-third of the batter while two of the three layers bake. For the third layer, bake the remaining chilled batter as directed.

</td></tr>
</table>

5 **Place a cake layer** on a cake plate; spread with half of the Caramel Cream Filling. Top with second layer; spread with the remaining filling. Top with third layer. Frost the top and sides with the Sweetened Whipped Cream. Drizzle with the remaining Caramel Sauce.

Caramel Sauce: In a small saucepan combine ⅔ cup packed brown sugar and 1 tablespoon cornstarch. Add ¼ cup apple cider or apple juice and ¼ cup butter. Cook and stir over medium heat until thickened and bubbly. Cook and stir for 2 minutes more. Remove from heat. In a small bowl beat 1 egg yolk; gradually stir in ½ cup of the hot brown sugar mixture. Add the egg mixture to the saucepan. Cook and stir until bubbly; reduce heat. Cook and stir for 2 minutes more. Remove from heat; cover and cool. Use ½ cup of the Caramel Sauce for the Caramel Cream Filling. Use remaining sauce to drizzle over the Sweetened Whipped Cream. If necessary, thin the remaining Caramel Sauce with 1 to 2 teaspoons apple cider or apple juice to make a topping of drizzling consistency. Makes ¾ cup.

Caramel Cream Filling: In a bowl beat one 8-ounce package cream cheese until fluffy. Gradually beat in ½ cup of the Caramel Sauce.

Nutrition Facts per serving: 490 cal., 28 g total fat (13 g sat. fat), 183 mg chol., 247 mg sodium, 54 g carbo., 2 g fiber, 9 g pro. **Daily Values:** 39% vit. A, 9% calcium, 13% iron

HICKORY NUT CAKE

Prep: 25 minutes   **Bake:** 35 minutes
Cool: 1 hour   **Makes:** 12 servings   **Oven:** 375°F

Find hickory nuts at farmers' markets or through mail-order catalogs.

2¾ cups all-purpose flour
  1 cup ground hickory nuts or pecans
2½ teaspoons baking powder
  ¼ teaspoon salt
  ½ cup butter
1¾ cups sugar
1½ teaspoons vanilla
  2 eggs
1¼ cups half-and-half, light cream,
    or milk
  1 recipe Cream Cheese Frosting
    (see recipe, page 133) or
  1 recipe Browned Butter Frosting
    (see recipe, page 133)
  ½ cup finely chopped hickory nuts
    or pecans

1 **Grease and lightly flour** two 8×1½-inch round baking pans; set aside. In a bowl stir together flour, the 1 cup ground nuts, baking powder, and salt; set aside.

2 **In a large mixing bowl beat** butter with an electric mixer on medium to high speed about 30 seconds or until softened. Add sugar and vanilla; beat until combined. Add eggs, 1 at a time, beating on medium speed until combined. Alternately add flour mixture and half-and-half, beating on low to medium speed after each addition just until combined. Spread batter in the prepared pans.

3 **Bake in a 375°F oven** for 35 to 40 minutes or until a wooden toothpick comes out clean. Cool cakes in pans on wire racks for 10 minutes. Remove cakes from pans. Cool thoroughly on the racks.

4 **To assemble,** place a layer on serving plate. Spread with some of the frosting. Sprinkle with half of the finely chopped nuts. Top with second layer. Spread top and sides with remaining frosting; sprinkle top with remaining chopped nuts. Store in the refrigerator.

Nutrition Facts per serving: 680 cal., 33 g total fat (16 g sat. fat), 101 mg chol., 339 mg sodium, 92 g carbo., 2 g fiber, 8 g pro. **Daily Values:** 25% vit. A, 10% calcium, 13% iron

Pecan Cake with Tangerine Cream Filling: It's hard to believe a cake this stunning is mixed together easily in the blender. Finishing touches include a sweet and simple filling and a luscious whipped cream frosting.

PECAN CAKE WITH TANGERINE CREAM FILLING

Prep: 35 minutes   **Bake:** 25 minutes
Cool: 1 hour   **Makes:** 12 servings   **Oven:** 350°F

2½ cups broken pecans, toasted
     (see tip, page 181)
  3 tablespoons all-purpose flour
  4 teaspoons baking powder
  6 eggs
  1 cup granulated sugar
  1 8-ounce package cream cheese,
     softened
¼ cup butter
½ cup packed brown sugar
  1 teaspoon finely shredded tangerine
     peel or orange peel
  1 teaspoon vanilla

  1 recipe Tangerine Whipped Cream
     Frosting (see recipe, page 133)
    Edible roses (optional)
    (see tip, page 18)

1 Grease two 8×1½-inch round baking pans. Line the bottoms with waxed paper or parchment paper. Grease the paper. Lightly flour pans; set aside. Place half the pecans in a food processor/blender container. Cover; process until coarsely ground. Repeat with remaining nuts.

2 In a bowl combine pecans, flour, and baking powder. Place eggs and granulated sugar in food processor/blender container. Cover; process until smooth. Add nut mixture. Cover; blend or process until smooth, stopping and scraping sides as needed to mix evenly (mixture may be foamy). Spread evenly in prepared pans.

3 Bake in a 350°F oven for 25 to 30 minutes or until light brown and tops spring back when lightly touched (centers may dip slightly). Cool in pans on wire racks for 10 minutes. Remove from pans; cool thoroughly on racks.

4 **For tangerine filling,** in a small mixing bowl beat cream cheese and butter with an electric mixer on medium to high speed until fluffy. Gradually add brown sugar, beating for 3 to 4 minutes or until smooth. Stir in citrus peel and vanilla.

5 **To assemble,** with a serrated knife, cut cakes in half horizontally. Place 1 split cake layer, cut side up, on a platter. Spread one-third of the filling on top cake. Place another split cake layer, cut side down, on filling. Spread top with another one-third of the filling. Repeat with remaining cake layers and filling, ending with a cake layer on top.

6 **Frost top and sides** of cake with Tangerine Whipped Cream Frosting, reserving some of the frosting for piping, if desired. To decorate top of cake with piped frosting, place reserved frosting in a decorating bag fitted with a large star tip. Pipe frosting atop cake in a ring. If desired, decorate with edible roses. Refrigerate frosted cake for up to 4 hours.

Nutrition Facts per serving: 533 cal., 43 g total fat (18 g sat. fat), 192 mg chol., 265 mg sodium, 34 g carbo., 2 g fiber, 7 g pro. Daily Values: 34% vit. A, 1% vit. C, 15% calcium, 10% iron

BLACK FOREST CHERRY CAKE

Prep: 1¾ hours   Bake: 22 minutes
Cool: 1 hour   Makes: 16 servings   Oven: 350°F

As if this favorite chocolate-and-cherry treat weren't already exquisite enough, it is made even more so with two luscious frostings.

2¼ cups all-purpose flour
  1 teaspoon baking powder
¾ teaspoon baking soda
¼ teaspoon salt
⅔ cup butter
1¾ cups sugar
  2 eggs
  3 ounces unsweetened chocolate, melted and cooled
  1 teaspoon vanilla
1½ recipes Chocolate Butter Frosting (see recipe, page 131)

  1 recipe Tart Cherry Filling
  1 recipe Sweetened Whipped Cream (see recipe, page 133)

1 **Grease and lightly flour** three 8×1½-inch round baking pans (see tip, page 121); set aside. Stir together flour, baking powder, baking soda, and salt; set aside.

2 **In a large mixing bowl beat** butter on medium to high speed for 30 seconds. Add sugar; beat until well combined. Add eggs, 1 at a time, beating well after each. Beat in chocolate and vanilla. Add flour mixture and 1¼ cups water alternately to egg mixture, beating on low speed after each addition just until combined. Pour into prepared pans.

3 **Bake in a 350°F oven** for 22 minutes or until a wooden toothpick inserted near centers of the cakes comes out clean. Cool the cakes in pans on wire racks for 10 minutes. Remove cakes from pans. Cool thoroughly on wire racks.

4 **To assemble,** place a cake layer on a large serving plate. Using about ⅔ cup of the Chocolate Butter Frosting, spread a ½-inch-wide and ¾-inch-high border around the top edge. Spread half of the Tart Cherry Filling in the center (about ¾ cup). Top with the second cake layer. Using ⅔ cup Chocolate Butter Frosting, repeat spreading a border on top edge of cake and spread remaining filling in center. Top with remaining cake layer. Frost sides with remaining butter frosting; frost top with the Sweetened Whipped Cream. Refrigerate up to 2 hours. Let stand at room temperature 30 minutes before serving.

Tart Cherry Filling: In a medium saucepan stir together ½ cup sugar and 2 tablespoons cornstarch. Stir in ¼ cup water. Add 2 cups fresh or frozen pitted tart red cherries. Cook and stir over medium heat until thickened and bubbly. Cook and stir for 2 minutes more. Remove from heat. Stir in 1 tablespoon cherry liqueur. Cover surface with plastic wrap; cool. Makes about 1¾ cups.

Nutrition Facts per serving: 486 cal., 21 g total fat (12 g sat. fat), 78 mg chol., 249 mg sodium, 74 g carbo., 1 g fiber, 4 g pro. Daily Values: 21% vit. A, 3% vit. C, 6% calcium, 11% iron

DOUBLE CHOCOLATE-ORANGE TORTE

Prep: 40 minutes   Bake: 35 minutes
Cool: 1 hour   Makes: 10 servings   Oven: 350°F

For a nonalcoholic version, replace the liqueur with orange juice.

      3 squares (3 ounces) unsweetened
           chocolate, coarsely chopped
    ¾ cup all-purpose flour
   1½ teaspoons baking powder
    ½ teaspoon baking soda
    ½ teaspoon salt
    ½ cup butter
      1 cup sugar
      4 eggs
      2 tablespoons orange liqueur
    ½ cup water
      1 tablespoon finely shredded
           orange peel
      1 tablespoon orange liqueur
      1 tablespoon orange juice
    ½ cup orange marmalade
      1 recipe Bittersweet Chocolate Icing
           Chocolate curls (optional)
           (see tip, below)

1 **Grease and flour** an 8×8×2-inch baking pan; set aside. In a heavy saucepan place chopped unsweetened chocolate over low heat, stirring constantly, until chocolate just starts to melt. Remove from heat. Stir until smooth; cool. Stir together the flour, baking powder, baking soda, and salt; set aside.

2 **In a large mixing bowl beat** the butter with an electric mixer on medium to high speed for 30 seconds. Add sugar; beat until well combined. Add eggs, 1 at a time, beating well after each. Beat in chocolate and the 2 tablespoons liqueur. Add flour mixture and water alternately to egg mixture, beating on low speed after each addition just until combined. Stir in orange peel. Pour batter into the prepared pan.

3 **Bake in a 350°F oven** about 35 minutes or until a wooden toothpick inserted near the center comes out clean. Cool cake on a wire rack for 10 minutes. Loosen edges of cake with a spatula. Invert onto wire rack. Remove the pan. Cool cake thoroughly on wire rack.

4 **Combine the 1 tablespoon liqueur** and orange juice. Split cake in half horizontally. Sprinkle each cut side with half of the liqueur mixture. Place bottom half of cake, cut side up, on a platter; spread the marmalade evenly on top. Top with remaining cake layer, cut side down.

5 **Frost the cake** with Bittersweet Chocolate Icing. (You can frost the cake several hours before serving.) If desired, decorate the sides of the frosted cake with chocolate curls pressed into icing.

Bittersweet Chocolate Icing: In a heavy small saucepan combine ⅓ cup whipping cream and 1 tablespoon light-colored corn syrup. Bring just to boiling, stirring constantly. Remove from heat. Stir in 6 ounces semisweet chocolate, finely chopped, or 1 cup semisweet chocolate pieces, stirring until chocolate is melted and mixture is smooth. Cool to room temperature. Stir before using.

Nutrition Facts per serving: 429 cal., 24 g total fat (13 g sat. fat), 121 mg chol., 350 mg sodium, 54 g carbo., 3 g fiber, 6 g pro. **Daily Values:** 16% vit. A, 4% vit. C, 7% calcium, 14% iron

Chocolate-Raspberry Torte: Prepare as above, except substitute raspberry liqueur for the orange liqueur and seedless raspberry preserves for the orange marmalade.

CHOCOLATE CURLS

Chocolate curls—whether used as a smattering on top of a cream pie or as a border around a cake—make exquisite dessert decorations. To make curls, carefully draw a vegetable peeler across a bar of chocolate (milk chocolate works best). For narrow curls, use the short side of the bar; for wide curls, use the broad surface. See page 19 for chocolate curl photos and more information.

Double Chocolate-Orange Torte: This incredibly rich, bittersweet torte is equally dazzling with orange or raspberry flavorings.

RASPBERRY TRUFFLE CAKE

BEST-LOVED

Prep: 25 minutes **Bake:** 25 minutes
Cool: 2 hours **Chill:** 4 hours
Makes: 12 servings **Oven:** 350°F

*Don't worry if this nearly flourless cake seems
soft after baking; it firms up when chilled.*

    16 ounces semisweet or bittersweet
        chocolate, cut up
    ½ cup butter
    1 tablespoon sugar
    1½ teaspoons all-purpose flour
    1 teaspoon raspberry liqueur
        (optional)
    4 eggs, separated
    1 12-ounce jar seedless raspberry
        jam (1 cup)
    Sweetened whipped cream
        (optional)
    Fresh raspberries (optional)

1 Grease an 8-inch springform pan; set aside. In a large heavy saucepan, combine chocolate and butter. Cook and stir over low heat until chocolate melts. Remove from heat. Stir in sugar, flour, and, if desired, liqueur. Using a spoon, beat in egg yolks, 1 at a time, until combined. Set aside.

2 In a medium mixing bowl beat egg whites with an electric mixer on high speed until stiff peaks form. Fold into chocolate mixture. Pour batter into prepared pan.

3 Bake in a 350°F oven 25 to 30 minutes or until edges puff. Cool in pan on a wire rack for 30 minutes. Remove sides of pan; cool thoroughly. Chill, covered, for 4 to 24 hours.

4 To serve, allow cake to come to room temperature (about 45 minutes). Heat jam just until melted. Drizzle jam on each dessert plate; top with cake slice. If desired, top with sweetened whipped cream and fresh raspberries.

Nutrition Facts per serving: 358 cal., 22 g total fat (10 g sat. fat), 81 mg chol., 95 mg sodium, 44 g carbo., 3 g fiber, 5 g pro. **Daily Values:** 10% vit. A, 2% calcium, 12% iron

Raspberry Truffle Cake: Ideal for entertaining, this is a very rich, dense dessert—almost like a fudge brownie but much more elegant. It's also surprisingly easy to make.

IS IT DONE YET?

A cake baking in the oven can cause trepidation when it comes time to test its doneness. (Remember those warnings from your mother about not opening the oven door or jumping around the house too much when she had a cake in the oven lest it fall?) But now you can relax. The doneness tests for creamed and foam cakes (angel, sponge, and chiffon), though different, are easy:

- To test whether a foam cake is done, touch the top lightly. The cake is finished baking if the top springs back.
- To test a creamed cake for doneness, insert a wooden toothpick into the cake near the center. If it comes out clean, it's done. If it comes out wet, bake the cake a few minutes longer; test in another spot near the center.

LADY BALTIMORE CAKE

Prep: 45 minutes Bake: 30 minutes
Cool: 1 hour Makes: 12 servings Oven: 350°F

One of the South's most famous desserts, this candied-fruit-studded treat is truly a charmer.

> 1 **cup raisins**
> 8 **dried figs, snipped (½ cup)**
> ¼ **cup brandy**
> 2½ **cups all-purpose flour**
> 2 **cups sugar**
> 1 **teaspoon baking powder**
> 1 **teaspoon finely shredded orange peel**
> ½ **teaspoon baking soda**
> ⅛ **teaspoon salt**
> 1⅓ **cups buttermilk or sour milk (see tip, page 208)**
> ½ **cup shortening or butter, softened**
> 1 **teaspoon vanilla**
> 4 **egg whites**
> 1 **cup toasted chopped pecans (see tip, page 181)**
> ⅓ **cup finely chopped candied red or green cherries**
> ⅓ **cup finely chopped candied pineapple or mixed candied fruits and peels**
> 1 **recipe Seven-Minute Frosting (see recipe, page 132)**

1 **In a medium bowl combine** raisins, figs, and brandy; let stand at room temperature 2 hours or until brandy is absorbed, stirring occasionally.

2 **Meanwhile, grease and flour** three 8×1½-inch round baking pans (see tip, page 121); set aside. Combine flour, sugar, baking powder, orange peel, baking soda, and salt. Add the buttermilk, shortening, and vanilla. Beat with an electric mixer on low speed for 30 seconds, scraping sides of bowl. Beat on medium to high speed for 2 minutes, scraping bowl often. Add egg whites; beat 2 minutes more, scraping bowl. Pour batter into prepared pans.

3 **Bake in a 350°F oven** about 30 minutes or until a wooden toothpick inserted near center comes out clean. Cool in pans on wire racks for 10 minutes. Loosen from sides; remove from pans. Cool thoroughly on wire racks. (At this point, you may cover and freeze the cake layers for up to 6 months.)

4 **For filling,** stir pecans, fruits, and about one-third (1½ cups) of the Seven-Minute Frosting into the raisin mixture.

5 **To assemble,** place a cake layer on a platter; spread half of the filling on top. Add another cake layer and the remaining filling. Top with the remaining cake layer. Frost tops and sides with the remaining Seven-Minute Frosting.

Nutrition Facts per serving: 569 cal., 15 g total fat (3 g sat. fat), 1 mg chol., 165 mg sodium, 103 g carbo., 3 g fiber, 7 g pro. **Daily Values:** 1% vit. C, 7% calcium, 12% iron

ITALIAN CRÈME CAKE

Prep: 40 minutes Bake: 25 minutes
Cool: 1 hour Makes: 14 servings Oven: 350°F

Cakes infused or showered with coconut are a southern Italian favorite.

1¾ cups all-purpose flour
1½ teaspoons baking powder
¼ teaspoon baking soda
½ cup butter
⅓ cup shortening
1¾ cups sugar
4 egg yolks
1 teaspoon vanilla
¾ cup buttermilk or sour milk
1 3½-ounce can flaked coconut
1 cup chopped pecans
4 egg whites
1 recipe Pecan Frosting
Pecan halves (optional)

1 **Grease and flour** three 8×1½-inch round baking pans (see tip, page 121); set aside. Combine flour, baking powder, and baking soda; set aside.

2 **In a large mixing bowl beat** butter and shortening with an electric mixer on medium to high speed for 30 seconds. Add sugar; beat until fluffy. Add egg yolks and vanilla; beat on medium speed until combined. Add flour mixture and buttermilk alternately to egg yolk mixture, beating on low speed after each addition just until combined. Fold in coconut and chopped pecans.

3 **Thoroughly wash the beaters.** In a small mixing bowl beat egg whites until stiff peaks form (tips stand straight). Fold about one-third of the egg whites into cake batter to lighten. Fold in remaining whites. Spread batter evenly into prepared pans.

4 **Bake in a 350°F oven** for 25 to 30 minutes or until a wooden toothpick inserted near centers comes out clean. Cool in pans on wire racks 10 minutes; remove from pans. Cool thoroughly on racks.

5 **When cool,** spread the top of a cake layer with frosting. Top with another layer, frost, and top with the third layer. Frost top and sides of cake with remaining frosting. If desired, decorate cake with pecan halves. Chill cake until serving time. Store any leftover cake, covered, in the refrigerator up to 2 days.

Pecan Frosting: In a bowl beat 12 ounces cream cheese, softened; 6 tablespoons butter, softened; and 1½ teaspoons vanilla until smooth. Gradually add 6 cups sifted powdered sugar, beating until smooth. Stir in ½ cup chopped pecans. Makes 4 cups.

Nutrition Facts per serving: 682 cal., 37 g total fat (17 g sat. fat), 119 mg chol., 284 mg sodium, 86 g carbo., 2 g fiber, 7 g pro. **Daily Values:** 30% vit. A, 7% calcium, 11% iron

MINIATURE AMARETTO CAKES

Prep: 45 minutes Bake: 20 minutes
Cool: 1 hour Makes: 24 servings Oven: 325°F

¾ cup butter
3 eggs
1½ cups all-purpose flour
1 teaspoon baking powder
¼ teaspoon ground nutmeg
¾ cup granulated sugar
¼ cup amaretto
1 teaspoon finely shredded lemon peel
½ teaspoon vanilla
⅓ cup granulated sugar
¼ cup water
2 tablespoons brown sugar
2 tablespoons light-colored corn syrup
½ cup amaretto

1 **Allow butter and eggs to stand** at room temperature 30 minutes. Generously grease and flour six 4-inch fluted tube pans or one 6-cup fluted tube pan. Combine flour, baking powder, and nutmeg; set aside.

2 **In a large mixing bowl beat** butter with electric mixer on medium speed for 30 seconds. Beat on medium-high speed, adding the ¾ cup granulated sugar, 2 tablespoons at a time, about 6 minutes or until mixture is very light and fluffy.

3 **Stir in** the ¼ cup amaretto, lemon peel, and vanilla. Add eggs, 1 at a time, beating for 1 minute after each addition and scraping bowl often. Gradually add flour mixture to egg mixture, beating on medium-low speed just until combined. Pour into prepared pans.

4 **Bake in a 325°F oven** for 20 to 25 minutes for the 4-inch pans (40 to 45 minutes for the 6-cup

Miniature Amaretto Cakes: When holiday gift-giving season rolls around, remember these amaretto-soaked cakes. They make luscious gifts, and the recipients can enjoy them for weeks to come.

fluted pan) or until a wooden toothpick inserted near the center(s) comes out clean. Cool in pans on wire racks for 10 minutes. Remove from pans. Cool thoroughly on rack(s). Prick fluted top and sides of each cake generously with tines of a fork.

5 **For syrup,** in a medium saucepan combine the ⅓ cup granulated sugar, the water, brown sugar, and corn syrup. Cook and stir over medium heat until bubbly and most of the sugar is dissolved; remove from heat. Stir in ½ cup amaretto. Cool for 5 minutes.

6 **Dip fluted top and sides** of each cooled 4-inch cake into syrup. Place cakes on wire racks above a large tray or baking sheet. Spoon or brush any remaining syrup over tops of cakes. (If using 6-cup pan, do not dip cake into syrup. Place cake on wire rack over tray or baking sheet; spoon or brush syrup over top and sides of cake, reusing syrup on tray.) Cool cake(s).

7 **Wrap cakes individually** in plastic wrap or cellophane; chill, fluted side up, for up to 3 weeks. (Or, transfer to a tightly covered container and chill for up to 3 weeks.)

Nutrition Facts per serving: 157 cal., 7 g total fat (2 g sat. fat), 34 mg chol., 78 mg sodium, 20 g carbo., 0 g fiber, 2 g pro. **Daily Values:** 6% vit. A, 1% calcium, 3% iron

---

LET THEM CUT CAKE

Once it is frosted and decorated, your cake becomes a feast for the eyes. But the best is yet to come: sharing your masterpiece with your guests. To do so as neatly as possible, let the frosted cake stand for at least 1 hour before cutting it (unless otherwise specified). When cutting a cake with a fluffy icing, a creamed cake, or a cheesecake, it will be considerably easier if you dip the knife in hot water and shake it to remove excess water (don't dry it completely) between cuts.

TRIPLE-LAYER LEMON CAKE
BEST-LOVED

Prep: 35 minutes **Bake:** 25 minutes
Cool: 1 hour **Makes:** 12 servings **Oven:** 350°F

Tart lemon curd fills this showy cake. Make your own or look for it with jams at the supermarket (see photo, page 97).

2⅓ cups all-purpose flour
1½ teaspoons baking powder
 ½ teaspoon baking soda
 ¼ teaspoon salt
 1 cup butter
 2 cups sugar
 2 teaspoons finely shredded lemon
    peel
 2 tablespoons lemon juice
 4 eggs
 1 cup buttermilk or sour milk
    (see tip, page 208)
 1 recipe Lemon Curd
    (see recipe, page 132) or
    1 cup purchased lemon curd
 1 recipe Lemon Cream Cheese
    Frosting
    Lemon peel curls (optional)

1 **Grease and lightly flour** three 9×1½-inch round baking pans (see tip, page 121). Combine flour, baking powder, soda, and salt. Set aside.

2 **In a large mixing bowl beat** butter with an electric mixer on medium to high speed for 30 seconds. Add sugar, lemon peel, and lemon juice; beat until well combined. Add eggs, 1 at a time, beating well after each. Add flour mixture and buttermilk or alternately to butter mixture, beating on

low speed after each addition just until combined. Pour into prepared pans.

3 **Bake in a 350°F oven** for 25 to 30 minutes or until a wooden toothpick inserted near the center of each cake layer comes out clean. Cool cakes in pans on wire racks for 10 minutes. Remove cakes from pans. Cool thoroughly on wire racks.

4 **To assemble,** place a cake layer on a cake plate. Spread with half of the Lemon Curd. Top with second layer; spread with the remaining Lemon Curd. Top with third layer. Frost top and sides with Lemon Cream Cheese Frosting. (If desired, pipe frosting on sides of cake as shown in photo on page 97 using a decorating bag fitted with a star tip). Cover and store cake in the refrigerator for up to 3 days. Let stand at room temperature for 30 minutes before serving. If desired, garnish with lemon peel curls.

Lemon Cream Cheese Frosting: Finely shred 1 teaspoon lemon peel; set aside. In a medium mixing bowl combine two 3-ounce packages cream cheese, softened; ½ cup butter, softened; and 1 teaspoon lemon juice; beat with electric mixer on low to medium speed until light and fluffy. Gradually add 2 cups sifted powdered sugar, beating well. Gradually beat in 2½ to 2¾ cups additional powdered sugar to make frosting that is easy to spread. Stir in the lemon peel.

Nutrition Facts per serving: 721 cal., 36 g total fat (11 g sat. fat), 158 mg chol., 484 mg sodium, 96 g carbo., 1 g fiber, 7 g pro. **Daily Values:** 37% vit. A, 8% vit. C, 8% calcium, 11% iron

BUTTER FROSTING

Start to finish: 15 minutes   **Frosts:** tops and sides of two 8- or 9-inch cake layers, top of one 13x9-inch cake, or 24 cupcakes

One creamy, sweet master recipe provides the base for seven festive frosting variations.

> ⅓ **cup butter**
> 4½ **cups sifted powdered sugar**
> ¼ **cup milk**
> 1½ **teaspoons vanilla**
>   **Additional milk**
>   **Food coloring (optional)**

1 In a large mixing bowl beat butter until fluffy. Gradually add 2 cups of the powdered sugar, beating well. Slowly beat in ¼ cup milk and vanilla.

2 Gradually add remaining powdered sugar, beating until combined. If necessary, beat in a little additional milk to make frosting that is easy to spread. Tint with food coloring as desired, or use as a base for any of the variations below. Transfer unused frosting to a storage container and chill for up to 1 week.

Nutrition Facts per serving (¹⁄₁₂ of a recipe): 97 cal., 3 g total fat (2 g sat. fat), 7 mg chol., 27 mg sodium, 19 g carbo., 0 g fiber, 0 g pro. **Daily Values:** 2% vit. A

Peanut Butter Crunch
Substitute creamy peanut butter for the butter. Sprinkle chopped candy-coated peanut butter pieces or chopped peanuts over frosting.

Mocha Cocoa
Reduce powdered sugar to 4 cups and add ½ cup unsweetened cocoa powder along with the first 2 cups powdered sugar. Add 1 tablespoon instant coffee crystals to the ¼ cup milk. Let stand 3 minutes; stir until dissolved.

Maraschino Cherry
Substitute 3 tablespoons maraschino cherry juice for the milk; add ⅓ cup chopped maraschino cherries with the cherry juice.

Vanilla Polka Dot
Stir 2 to 3 tablespoons candy sprinkles in the Butter Frosting before using. (Pictured in center.)

Mini Mint Chip
Add ¼ teaspoon mint extract and a few drops green food coloring with the milk. Stir in ⅓ cup miniature semisweet chocolate pieces before using.

Double Orange
Substitute fresh orange juice for the milk; add 1 teaspoon finely shredded orange peel after all the powdered sugar is added. If desired, top with thin strips of orange peel.

Chocolate Butter Frosting Reduce powdered sugar to 4 cups and add ½ cup unsweetened cocoa powder along with the first 2 cups powdered sugar. If desired, top with chocolate curls.

LEMON CURD

Prep: 5 minutes   **Cook:** 8 minutes
Cool: 45 minutes   **Makes:** about 1 cup

Translucent, tart, and tangy, this makes a great filling for almost any cake.

- ⅓ **cup sugar**
- 2 **teaspoons cornstarch**
- 2 **teaspoons finely shredded lemon peel**
- ¼ **cup lemon juice**
- ¼ **cup butter**
- 2 **beaten eggs**

1 **In saucepan combine** sugar and cornstarch. Stir in peel and juice. Add butter. Cook and stir until thickened and bubbly. Stir half lemon mixture into eggs. Pour egg mixture into the pan. Cook and stir 2 minutes more. Cover with waxed paper; cool.

Nutrition Facts per serving (¹⁄₁₂ of a recipe): 53 cal., 3 g total fat (3 g sat. fat), 42 mg chol., 41 mg sodium, 5 g carbo., 0 g fiber, 1 g pro. **Daily Values:** 4% vit. A, 3% vit. C

RASPBERRY FILLING

Prep: 10 minutes   **Cool:** 30 minutes
Chill: 2 hours   **Makes:** ⅔ cup

Use this to add a lovely red ribbon between white cake layers.

- 1 **10-ounce package frozen raspberries in syrup, thawed**
- 4 **teaspoons cornstarch**

1 **In small saucepan combine** berries and syrup with cornstarch. Cook and stir until thickened and bubbly. Reduce heat; cook and stir 2 minutes more. Remove from heat. Immediately press through sieve; discard seeds. Transfer to bowl. Cover surface of filling with plastic wrap. Cool without stirring. Chill at least 2 hours; for maximum stiffness, chill overnight.

Nutrition Facts per serving (¹⁄₁₂ of a recipe): 33 cal., 0 g total fat, 0 mg chol., 0 mg sodium, 8 g carbo., 1 g fiber, 0 g pro. **Daily Values:** 7% vit. C, 1% iron

POWDERED SUGAR ICING

Start to finish: 5 minutes   **Makes:** ½ cup (enough to drizzle over 10-inch tube cake)

This simple drizzle adds dazzle to angel, sponge, and chiffon cakes.

- 1 **cup sifted powdered sugar**
- ¼ **teaspoon vanilla**
- 1 **tablespoon milk or orange juice**

1 **Combine** powdered sugar, vanilla, and milk. Stir in additional milk or juice, 1 teaspoon at a time, until icing is easy to drizzle.

Nutrition Facts per serving (¹⁄₁₂ of a recipe): 33 cal., 1 mg sodium, 8 g carbo.

Chocolate Powdered Sugar Icing: Prepare as above, except add 2 tablespoons unsweetened cocoa powder to powdered sugar. Do not use orange juice.

SEVEN-MINUTE FROSTING

Start to finish: 25 minutes   **Frosts:** tops and sides of two 8- or 9-inch layers or one 10-inch tube cake

Beat well for a fluffy, marshmallowlike topper.

- 1½ **cups sugar**
- 2 **egg whites**
- ¼ **teaspoon cream of tartar or 2 teaspoons light-colored corn syrup**
- 1 **teaspoon vanilla**

1 **In top of double boiler combine** sugar, ⅓ cup cold water, egg whites, and cream of tartar or syrup. Beat with portable electric mixer on low speed for 30 seconds. Place over boiling water (upper pan should not touch water). Cook, beating constantly with mixer on high speed, about 7 minutes or until stiff peaks form. Remove from heat; add vanilla. Beat 2 to 3 minutes more or until easy to spread.

Nutrition Facts per serving (¹⁄₁₂ of a recipe) 100 cal., 0 g total fat, 0 mg chol., 10 mg sodium, 25 g carbo., 0 g fiber, 1 g pro.

CREAMY WHITE FROSTING

Start to finish: 25 minutes   Frosts: tops and sides of two 8- or 9-inch cake layers

  1 **cup shortening**
1½ **teaspoons vanilla**
 ½ **teaspoon lemon extract, orange**
       extract, or almond extract
4½ **cups sifted powdered sugar**
  3 **to 4 tablespoons milk**

1 **Beat shortening, vanilla, and extract** with an electric mixer on medium speed for 30 seconds. Slowly add half of the sugar, beating well. Add 2 tablespoons of the milk. Gradually beat in remaining sugar and enough milk to make frosting that is easy to spread.

Nutrition Facts per serving (1/12 of a recipe): 300 cal., 17 g total fat (4 g sat. fat), 0 mg chol., 2 mg sodium, 38 g carbo., 0 g fiber, 0 g pro.

CREAM CHEESE FROSTING

Start to finish: 20 minutes   Frosts: tops and sides of two 8- or 9-inch cake layers

  2 **3-ounce packages cream cheese,**
     softened
 ½ **cup butter, softened**
  2 **teaspoons vanilla**
4½ **to 4¾ cups sifted powdered sugar**

1 **Beat cream cheese, butter, and vanilla** with an electric mixer until light and fluffy. Gradually add 2 cups sifted powdered sugar, beating well. Gradually beat in enough of the remaining sifted powdered sugar to make frosting that is easy to spread. (Cover and store cake in refrigerator.)

Nutrition Facts per serving (1/12 of a recipe): 263 cal., 13 g total fat (8 g sat. fat), 36 mg chol., 120 mg sodium, 38 g carbo., 0 g fiber, 1 g pro. **Daily Values:** 13% vit. A, 1% calcium, 1% iron

Orange Cream Cheese Frosting: Prepare as above, except omit vanilla; beat in 1 tablespoon apricot brandy or orange juice with the cream cheese mixture. After frosting is of spreading consistency, stir in ½ teaspoon finely shredded orange peel.

SWEETENED WHIPPED CREAM

Start to finish: 10 minutes   Makes: 2 cups

As a frosting or topping, this provides a smooth, rich contrast to lighter cakes, such as angel, chiffon, and sponge cakes.

1 **cup whipping cream**
1 **to 2 tablespoons sugar**
1 **teaspoon vanilla (optional)**

1 **In a small chilled mixing bowl combine** whipping cream, sugar, and vanilla, if desired. Beat with chilled beaters of an electric mixer on medium speed until soft peaks form. Do not overbeat.

Nutrition Facts per tablespoon: 28 cal., 3 g total fat (2 g sat. fat), 10 mg chol., 3 mg sodium, 1 g carbo., 0 g fiber, 0 g pro. **Daily Values:** 3% vit. A

Tangerine Whipped Cream Frosting: Prepare as above, except increase whipping cream to 2 cups and sugar to 2 tablespoons. Omit vanilla and add ¾ teaspoon finely shredded tangerine or orange peel with sugar. Use frosting immediately.

BROWNED BUTTER FROSTING

Start to finish: 20 minutes   Frosts: tops and sides of two 8- or 9-inch cake layers

½ **cup butter**
4 **cups sifted powdered sugar**
2 **tablespoons milk**
1 **teaspoon vanilla**

1 **In a small saucepan heat** butter over low heat until melted. Continue heating until butter turns a delicate brown. Remove from heat; pour into small mixing bowl. Add powdered sugar, milk, and vanilla. Beat with an electric mixer on low speed until combined. Beat on medium to high speed, adding more milk, if necessary, to make frosting that is easy to spread.

Nutrition Facts per serving (1/12 of a recipe): 197 cal., 8 g total fat (5 g sat. fat), 21 mg chol., 79 mg sodium, 34 g carbo., 0 g fiber, 0 g pro. **Daily Values:** 9% vit. A

CHOCOLATE-SOUR CREAM FROSTING

Start to finish: 25 minutes   **Frosts:** tops and sides of two 8- or 9-inch cake layers

  1 **6-ounce package (1 cup) semisweet chocolate pieces**
  ¼ **cup butter**
  ½ **cup dairy sour cream**
  2½ **cups sifted powdered sugar**

1 In a saucepan melt chocolate and butter over low heat, stirring frequently. Cool about 5 minutes. Stir in sour cream. Gradually add powdered sugar, beating until smooth and easy to spread. (Cover and store in the refrigerator.)

Nutrition Facts per serving (1/12 of a recipe): 211 cal., 8 g total fat (3 g sat. fat), 14 mg chol., 53 mg sodium, 35 g carbo., 0 g fiber, 1 g pro. **Daily Values:** 4% vit. A, 2% calcium, 2% iron

BUTTERCREAM

Prep: 30 minutes   **Cool:** 30 minutes   **Frosts:** tops and sides of two 8- or 9-inch cake layers

Just as you might expect, this pastry-shop favorite is lusciously buttery and creamy—perfect for frosting and decorating cakes.

  ⅔ **cup sugar**
  ¼ **cup water***
  4 **slightly beaten egg yolks**
  1 **teaspoon vanilla**
  1 **cup unsalted butter, softened**

1 In a heavy medium saucepan combine sugar and water. Bring to boiling; remove from heat. Gradually stir about half of the sugar mixture into the egg yolks. Return all of egg yolk mixture to saucepan. Bring to a gentle boil; reduce heat. Cook and stir for 2 minutes. Remove from heat. Stir in vanilla. Cool to room temperature. In a large mixing bowl beat butter with an electric mixer on high speed until fluffy. Add cooled sugar mixture, beating until combined. If necessary, chill until easy to spread.

*Note: If desired, flavor Buttercream with 1 tablespoon liqueur, decreasing water to 3 tablespoons. Stir in liqueur with vanilla.

Nutrition Facts per serving (1/12 of a recipe): 200 cal., 17 g total fat (10 g sat. fat), 113 mg chol., 5 mg sodium, 12 g carbo., 0 g fiber, 1 g pro. **Daily Values:** 25% vit. A, 0% vit. C, 1% calcium, 1% iron

WHITE CHOCOLATE BUTTERCREAM

Prep: 30 minutes   **Cool:** 30 minutes   **Frosts:** tops and sides of two 8- or 9-inch cake layers

  ½ **cup sugar**
  2 **tablespoons all-purpose flour**
  6 **egg yolks**
  1½ **cups milk**
  1 **6-ounce package white baking bar, chopped**
  1½ **teaspoons vanilla**
  ½ **teaspoon almond extract**
  1 **cup butter, softened**

1 In a medium mixing bowl combine sugar and flour; add the egg yolks. Beat mixture with a wire whisk until combined; set aside. In a heavy medium saucepan heat milk over medium heat just to boiling. Remove from heat. Gradually beat hot milk into egg mixture with the wire whisk; return entire mixture to saucepan. Cook over medium heat until bubbly, whisking constantly. Cook for 2 minutes more. Remove from heat. Add white baking bar, vanilla, and almond extract. Let stand 1 minute; stir until smooth.

2 Transfer mixture to a bowl. Cover surface with plastic wrap to prevent skin from forming; cool to room temperature. In a medium mixing bowl beat butter on medium to high speed until fluffy. Add cooled baking bar mixture, one-fourth at a time, beating on low speed after each addition until combined.

Nutrition Facts per serving (1/12 of a recipe): 298 cal., 23 g total fat (14 g sat. fat), 155 mg chol., 189 mg sodium, 19 g carbo., 0 g fiber, 4 g pro. **Daily Values:** 32% vit. A, 5% calcium, 2% iron

cookies

Pistachio Nut Stars of India,
recipe page 152

COOKIES

CHOCOLATE CHIP COOKIES

Prep: 25 minutes   **Bake:** 8 minutes per batch
Makes: 60 cookies   **Oven:** 375°F

The Toll House restaurant added chopped chocolate to a basic dough in the 1930s. The result? The most popular cookie in the country.

½ cup shortening
½ cup butter
1 cup packed brown sugar
½ cup granulated sugar
½ teaspoon baking soda
2 eggs
1 teaspoon vanilla
2½ cups all-purpose flour
1 12-ounce package (2 cups) semisweet chocolate pieces
1½ cups chopped walnuts, pecans, or hazelnuts (optional)

1 In a large mixing bowl beat the shortening and butter with an electric mixer on medium to high speed for 30 seconds. Add the brown sugar, granulated sugar, and baking soda. Beat mixture until combined, scraping sides of bowl occasionally. Beat in the eggs and vanilla until combined. Beat in as much of the flour as you can with the mixer. Using a wooden spoon, stir in any remaining flour. Stir in chocolate pieces and, if desired, nuts. Drop the dough by rounded teaspoons 2 inches apart on an ungreased cookie sheet.

2 Bake in a 375°F oven for 8 to 10 minutes or until edges are lightly browned. Transfer cookies to a wire rack and let cool.

Nutrition Facts per cookie: 93 cal., 5 g total fat (1 g sat. fat), 11 mg chol., 29 mg sodium, 12 g carbo., 0 g fiber, 1 g pro. **Daily Values:** 1% vit. A, 3% iron

Giant Chocolate Chip Cookies: Prepare as at left, except use a ¼-cup dry measure or scoop to drop mounds of dough about 4 inches apart on an ungreased cookie sheet. Bake in a 375°F oven for 11 to 13 minutes or until edges are lightly browned. Makes about 20 cookies.

Macadamia Nut and White Chocolate Cookies: Prepare as at left, except substitute chopped white baking bars or white chocolate baking squares for the semisweet chocolate pieces. Stir in one 3½-ounce jar macadamia nuts, chopped, with the white chocolate.

Chocolate Chip Cookie Bars: Prepare as at left, except press dough into an ungreased 15×10×1-inch baking pan. Bake in a 375°F oven for 15 to 20 minutes or until golden. Cool in pan on a wire rack. Cut into bars. Makes 48 bars.

DROP EVERYTHING!

Drop cookies are so easy to make, the time they take out of your day is a drop in the bucket. These tips will help make homemade cookies a staple at your house:

- If a recipe calls for greased cookie sheets, use only a very light coating or your cookies may spread too far when baking. If a recipe specifies ungreased cookie sheets, use regular or nonstick sheets—but don't grease them.
- If your electric mixer begins to strain while mixing dough, stir the last bit of flour in with a wooden spoon.
- Drop the dough using spoons from your flatware—not measuring spoons—to get the right number of cookies from each batch. Make sure the mounds are rounded and about the same size so they'll bake evenly.
- Let cookie sheets cool between batches so the dough doesn't spread too much.
- Bake on only one oven rack at a time for even browning.
- Drop cookies are done when the dough looks set and the edges and bottoms of the baked cookies are lightly browned.

Browned Butter Cookies (front) and Pecan Drops: Each of these simple cookies is dressed up with a pretty topping that tastes good. Browned Butter Cookies get a nutty nuance from frosting flavored with lightly browned butter. Pecan Drops get a flavor and texture boost from the real thing.

BROWNED BUTTER COOKIES

Prep: 25 minutes   **Bake:** 10 minutes per batch
Makes: 56 cookies   **Oven:** 350°F

The French term for browned butter is "beurre noisette," referring to butter cooked to a light hazelnut color. Browned butter has a nutty flavor too.

  ½ **cup butter**
1½ **cups packed brown sugar**
  1 **teaspoon baking soda**
  ½ **teaspoon baking powder**
  ¼ **teaspoon salt**
  2 **eggs**
  1 **teaspoon vanilla**
2½ **cups all-purpose flour**
  1 **8-ounce carton dairy sour cream**
  1 **cup coarsely chopped walnuts**
  1 **recipe Browned Butter Icing**

1 Grease a cookie sheet; set aside. In a large mixing bowl beat butter with an electric mixer on medium speed for 30 seconds. Beat in brown sugar, baking soda, baking powder, and salt until combined. Beat in eggs and vanilla until fluffy. Add flour to beaten mixture along with the sour cream, mixing well. Stir in walnuts. Drop dough by rounded teaspoons 2 inches apart on prepared cookie sheet.

2 Bake in a 350°F oven about 10 minutes or until set. Transfer cookies to a wire rack and let cool. Frost with Browned Butter Icing.

Browned Butter Icing: In a small saucepan heat ¼ cup butter over medium heat until butter turns the color of light brown sugar. Remove saucepan from heat. Stir in 2 cups sifted powdered sugar and enough boiling water (1 to 2 tablespoons) to make icing smooth and easy to spread. Frost the cooled cookies immediately after preparing frosting. If the frosting becomes grainy, soften with a few more drops of hot water.

Nutrition Facts per cookie: 97 cal., 5 g total fat (2 g sat. fat), 16 mg chol., 66 mg sodium, 13 g carbo., 0 g fiber, 1 g pro. **Daily Values:** 3% vit. A, 1% calcium, 2% iron

PECAN DROPS

Prep: 30 minutes   **Bake:** 8 minutes per batch
Makes: 36 cookies   **Oven:** 375°F

Pick out the nicest pecan halves to use for the cookie tops and chop the rest to stir into the dough (see photo, page 138).

  ½ **cup butter**
  2 **cups sifted powdered sugar**
1¾ **cups all-purpose flour**
  ⅓ **cup milk**
  1 **egg**
  1 **teaspoon baking powder**
  1 **teaspoon vanilla**
  1 **cup coarsely chopped pecans**
     Granulated sugar
     Pecan halves (optional)

1 **Lightly grease a cookie sheet;** set aside. In a large mixing bowl beat butter with an electric mixer on medium to high speed for 30 seconds. Add powdered sugar, about half of the flour, half of the milk, the egg, baking powder, and vanilla. Beat until thoroughly combined, scraping sides of bowl occasionally. Beat or stir in remaining flour and milk. Stir in chopped pecans.

2 **Drop dough** by rounded teaspoons 2 inches apart on the prepared cookie sheet. Sprinkle with granulated sugar. If desired, lightly press a pecan half in the center of each cookie.

3 **Bake in a 375°F oven** for 8 to 10 minutes or until edges are slightly golden. Transfer cookies to a wire rack and let cool.

Nutrition Facts per cookie: 90 cal., 5 g total fat (1 g sat. fat), 9 mg chol., 36 mg sodium, 11 g carbo., 0 g fiber, 1 g pro. **Daily Values:** 2% vit. A, 1% calcium, 2% iron

TRIPLE-CHOCOLATE CHUNK COOKIES

BEST-LOVED

Prep: 25 minutes   **Bake:** 12 minutes per batch
Makes: 22 cookies   **Oven:** 350°F

For the true chocophile, there is no such thing as too much chocolate. These chunky, oversize treats contain a trio of chocolates.

  1 **cup butter**
  ¾ **cup granulated sugar**
  ¾ **cup packed brown sugar**
  1 **teaspoon baking soda**
  2 **eggs**
  1 **teaspoon vanilla**
  3 **ounces unsweetened chocolate, melted and cooled**
  2 **cups all-purpose flour**
  8 **ounces semisweet chocolate, cut into ½-inch pieces, or 1⅓ cups large semisweet chocolate pieces**
  6 **ounces white baking bar, cut into ½-inch pieces, or 1 cup white baking pieces**
  1 **cup chopped black walnuts or pecans (optional)**

1 **Lightly grease a cookie sheet;** set aside. In a large mixing bowl beat butter with an electric mixer on medium to high speed for 30 seconds. Beat in granulated sugar, brown sugar, and baking soda until combined. Beat in eggs and vanilla until combined. Stir in melted chocolate. Beat in as much of the flour as you can with the mixer. Stir in any remaining flour. Stir in chocolate and white baking pieces and, if desired, nuts.

2 **Using a ¼-cup dry measure** or scoop, drop mounds of dough about 4 inches apart on the prepared cookie sheet.

3 **Bake in a 350°F oven** for 12 to 14 minutes or until edges are firm. Cool on cookie sheet for 1 minute. Transfer cookies to a wire rack; let cool.

Nutrition Facts per cookie: 280 cal., 17 g total fat (10 g sat. fat), 44 mg chol., 158 mg sodium, 33 g carbo., 1 g fiber, 3 g pro. **Daily Values:** 8% vit. A, 2% calcium, 8% iron

APRICOT-OATMEAL
COOKIES

Prep: 30 minutes   **Bake:** 10 minutes per batch
Makes: 48 cookies   **Oven:** 375°F

*Homey oatmeal cookies take on an elegant air
with the addition of sweet and chewy dried
apricots and hazelnuts.*

¾ **cup snipped dried apricots**
¾ **cup butter**
1 **cup packed brown sugar**
½ **cup granulated sugar**
1 **teaspoon baking powder**
½ **teaspoon ground cinnamon**
¼ **teaspoon baking soda**
1 **egg**
1 **teaspoon vanilla**
1¾ **cups all-purpose flour**
2 **cups rolled oats**
½ **cup chopped hazelnuts or walnuts**
1 **recipe Powdered Sugar Icing**
    (optional) (see recipe, page 151)

1 In a small mixing bowl combine apricots and
enough boiling water to cover. Let stand for
5 minutes. Drain.

2 In a large mixing bowl beat the butter with an
electric mixer on medium to high speed for
30 seconds. Add brown sugar, granulated sugar,
baking powder, cinnamon, and baking soda; beat
until combined. Beat in egg and vanilla until combined. Beat in as much flour as you can with the
mixer. Using a wooden spoon, stir in drained apricots, rolled oats, nuts, and any remaining flour.

3 Drop dough by rounded teaspoons 2 inches
apart on an ungreased cookie sheet.

4 Bake in a 375°F oven about 10 minutes or
until edges are golden. Transfer cookies to a wire
rack and let cool. If desired, drizzle cooled cookies
with Powdered Sugar Icing.

Nutrition Facts per cookie: 90 cal., 4 g total fat
(2 g sat. fat), 12 mg chol., 46 mg sodium, 13 g carbo.,
1 g fiber, 1 g pro. **Daily Values:** 4% vit. A, 1% calcium,
3% iron

SHEET SMARTS

All cookie sheets are not created equal.
Here's what to look for when you go
shopping for your next cookie sheet:
- Heavy-gauge aluminum with low sides or no
  sides at all.
- Lighter-colored cookie sheets. If they are too
  dark, cookies can overbrown.
- A dull finish so cookie bottoms brown evenly.
  (For cookies that should not brown on the
  bottoms—such as shortbread—choose a shiny
  cookie sheet.)

- If you don't want to grease your sheets, use a
  nonstick cookie sheet. The dough won't spread
  as much, though, so you'll get thicker cookies.
- Insulated cookie sheets are fine if you want
  pale drop cookies with soft centers. You might
  have trouble using them for cookies high in
  butter, shaped cookies, and some drop cookies
  because the butter may start to melt and leak
  out before the dough is set. Because dough
  spreads before it sets, you're also likely to have
  cookies with thin edges.

Apricot-Hazelnut Biscotti: After the first baking of the biscotti logs, use a serrated knife to cut the logs into slices. Reduce the oven temperature and continue baking the cookie slices until they are dry and crisp. For a shiny surface, mix an egg yolk with a little water and brush over the top of the biscotti logs before the first baking.

APRICOT-HAZELNUT BISCOTTI

Prep: 35 minutes   **Chill:** 1 hour (if necessary)
Bake: 41 minutes per batch   **Cool:** 1 hour
Makes: 32 cookies   **Oven:** 375°F/325°F

  ⅓ **cup butter**
  ⅔ **cup sugar**
  2 **teaspoon baking powder**
  ½ **teaspoon ground cardamom or**
      cinnamon
  2 **eggs**
  1 **teaspoon vanilla**
  2 **cups all-purpose flour**
  ¾ **cup toasted chopped hazelnuts**
      or almonds
  ¾ **cup finely snipped dried apricots**

1 **In a large bowl beat** butter with an electric mixer on medium speed for 30 seconds. Add sugar, baking powder, and cardamom; beat until combined. Beat in eggs and vanilla. Beat in as much flour as you can with mixer. Stir in any remaining flour, the nuts, and apricots. Divide dough in half. If necessary, cover and chill until easy to handle.

2 **Lightly grease a cookie sheet;** set aside. Shape each portion of dough into a 9-inch log. Place 4 inches apart on the prepared cookie sheet. Flatten logs slightly until about 2 inches wide.

3 **Bake in a 375°F oven** for 25 to 30 minutes or until a wooden toothpick inserted near the centers comes out clean. Cool logs on the cookie sheet on a wire rack for 1 hour. With a serrated knife, cut each log diagonally into ½-inch slices (see photo, above). Lay slices, cut side down, on an ungreased cookie sheet.

4 **Bake in a 325°F oven** for 8 minutes. Turn slices over; bake for 8 to 10 minutes more or until dry and crisp (do not underbake). Transfer cookies to a wire rack and let cool.

Nutrition Facts per cookie: 96 cal., 5 g total fat (1 g sat. fat), 18 mg chol., 51 mg sodium, 13 g carbo., 1 g fiber, 2 g pro. **Daily Values:** 5% vit. A, 1% calcium, 4% iron

ONE BISCOTTO, PLEASE

In Italy, "biscotti" refers to all kinds of cookies—not just the crunchy, twice-baked variety it implies on this side of the Atlantic. Biscotti is the plural of "biscotto," or biscuit. Try serving biscotti the Tuscan way: Dip them into coffee, tea, or a dessert wine, such as Vin Santo.

Giant Cherry-Oatmeal Cookies: Tart dried cherries stand in for more traditional raisins in these super-size, spicy drop cookies. They're perfect with a cup of rich, full-flavored coffee.

GIANT CHERRY-OATMEAL COOKIES

Prep: 30 minutes Bake: 8 minutes per batch
Makes: 14 large cookies Oven: 375°F

½ **cup shortening**
½ **cup butter**
¾ **cup packed brown sugar**
½ **cup granulated sugar**
2 **teaspoons apple pie spice or pumpkin pie spice**
½ **teaspoon baking powder**
¼ **teaspoon baking soda**
¼ **teaspoon salt**
2 **eggs**
1 **teaspoon vanilla**
1⅓ **cups all-purpose flour**
2½ **cups regular rolled oats**
1½ **cups snipped dried tart cherries or raisins**
1 **teaspoon finely shredded orange peel**

1 **Grease a cookie sheet;** set aside. In a large mixing bowl beat shortening and butter for 30 seconds. Add brown sugar, granulated sugar, pie spice, baking powder, baking soda, and salt. Beat until fluffy. Add eggs and vanilla; beat thoroughly. Beat in flour. Using a wooden spoon, stir in oats, dried cherries, and orange peel.

2 **Generously fill** a ⅓-cup dry measure with dough and drop onto a greased cookie sheet. Press into a 4-inch circle. Repeat with the remaining dough, placing cookies 3 inches apart.

3 **Bake in a 375°F oven** for 8 to 10 minutes or until edges are golden. Let stand 1 minute. Transfer cookies to a wire rack and let cool.

Nutrition Facts per cookie: 345 cal., 16 g total fat (6 g sat. fat), 48 mg chol., 141 mg sodium, 47 g carbo., 2 g fiber, 5 g pro. **Daily Values:** 15% vit. A, 2% calcium, 0% iron

HICKORY NUT MACAROONS

BEST-LOVED

Prep: 20 minutes   **Bake:** 15 minutes per batch
Makes: 36 cookies   **Oven:** 325°F

This recipe was first published in Better Homes and Gardens® *magazine in 1925, and it has been an all-time favorite ever since.*

  4 **egg whites**
  4 **cups sifted powdered sugar**
  2 **cups chopped hickory nuts, black walnuts, or toasted pecans**

1 **Grease a cookie sheet;** set aside. In a large mixing bowl beat egg whites with an electric mixer on high speed until stiff, but not dry, peaks form. Gradually add powdered sugar, about ¼ cup at a time, beating at medium speed just until combined. Beat for 1 to 2 minutes more or until combined. Using a wooden spoon, fold in nuts. Drop mixture by rounded teaspoons 2 inches apart on the prepared cookie sheet.

2 **Bake in a 325°F oven** about 15 minutes or until edges are very lightly browned. Transfer cookies to a wire rack and let cool.

Note: It is normal for these cookies to split around the edges as they bake.

Nutrition Facts per cookie: 86 cal., 4 g total fat (0 g sat. fat), 0 mg chol., 6 mg sodium, 12 g carbo., 1 g fiber, 1 g pro.

SANDIES

Prep: 25 minutes   **Bake:** 20 minutes per batch
Makes: 36 cookies   **Oven:** 325°F

Sometimes called wedding cakes or snowballs, these powdered sugar cookies are always a hit.

  1 **cup butter**
  ⅓ **cup granulated sugar**
  1 **tablespoon water**
  1 **teaspoon vanilla**
  2¼ **cups all-purpose flour**
  1 **cup chopped pecans**
  1 **cup sifted powdered sugar**

1 **In a large mixing bowl beat** butter with an electric mixer on medium to high speed for 30 seconds. Add granulated sugar. Beat until combined, scraping sides of bowl occasionally. Beat in the water and vanilla until combined. Beat in as much flour as you can with mixer. Using a wooden spoon, stir in any remaining flour and the pecans.

2 **Shape dough** into 1-inch balls or 2×½-inch logs. Place the balls or logs about 1 inch apart on an ungreased cookie sheet.

3 **Bake in a 325°F oven** for 20 minutes or until bottoms are lightly browned. Transfer cookies to a wire rack and let cool. Gently shake cooled cookies in a plastic bag with the powdered sugar.

Nutrition Facts per cookie: 109 cal., 7 g total fat (3 g sat. fat), 14 mg chol., 52 mg sodium, 11 g carbo., 0 g fiber, 1 g pro. **Daily Values:** 4% vit. A, 2% iron

MARVELOUS MACAROONS

The classic macaroon is the essence of simplicity—ground nuts (usually almonds) mixed with sugar and egg whites. Though our Depression-era macaroons often called for cornflakes instead of nuts, we've returned to the real McCoy. Perhaps macaroons have remained so popular because there's something in them for everyone: They're crisp around the edges and chewy in the center. Some are made with coconut, or flavored with chocolate, maraschino cherries, orange peel, or pistachios. The French like their macaroons on the double—two cookies held together with a rich chocolate filling.

SNICKERDOODLES

Prep: 30 minutes   Chill: 1 hour
Bake: 10 minutes per batch
Makes: 36 cookies   Oven: 375°F

The whimsical name of these cookies that originated in 19th-century New England seems to have no purpose other than fun.

½ **cup butter**
1 **cup sugar**
¼ **teaspoon baking soda**
¼ **teaspoon cream of tartar**
1 **egg**
½ **teaspoon vanilla**
1½ **cups all-purpose flour**
2 **tablespoons sugar**
1 **teaspoon ground cinnamon**

1 In a medium mixing bowl beat the butter with an electric mixer on medium to high speed for 30 seconds. Add the 1 cup sugar, baking soda, and cream of tartar. Beat until combined, scraping sides of bowl occasionally. Beat in the egg and vanilla until combined. Beat in as much of the flour as you can with the mixer. Using a wooden spoon, stir in any remaining flour. Cover and chill for 1 hour.

2 Combine the 2 tablespoons sugar and the cinnamon. Shape dough into 1-inch balls. Roll balls in sugar-cinnamon mixture to coat. Place balls 2 inches apart on an ungreased cookie sheet.

3 Bake in a 375°F oven for 10 to 11 minutes or until edges are golden. Transfer cookies to a wire rack and let cool.

Nutrition Facts per cookie: 66 cal., 3 g total fat (2 g sat. fat), 13 mg chol., 36 mg sodium, 10 g carbo., 0 g fiber, 1 g pro. **Daily Values:** 2% vit. A, 1% iron

PEANUT BUTTER COOKIES

Prep: 30 minutes   Bake: 7 minutes per batch
Makes: 36 cookies   Oven: 375°F

½ **cup butter**
½ **cup peanut butter**
½ **cup granulated sugar**
½ **cup packed brown sugar or**
    ¼ **cup honey**
½ **teaspoon baking soda**
½ **teaspoon baking powder**
1 **egg**
½ **teaspoon vanilla**
1¼ **cups all-purpose flour**
    Granulated sugar

1 In a large mixing bowl beat the butter and peanut butter with an electric mixer on medium to high speed for 30 seconds. Add the granulated sugar, brown sugar, baking soda, and baking powder. Beat until combined, scraping sides of bowl occasionally. Beat in the egg and vanilla until com-

IT'S A MATTER OF DEGREES

For all kinds of baking—cookies included—it's important that your oven temperature is accurate. If you've noticed that your cookies brown too fast or that they seem to take forever to bake and are pale, coarsely textured, and dry when they finally do come out of the oven, your oven might be a little bit off.

To be certain, set your oven at 350°F and let it heat for at least 10 minutes. Place an oven thermometer (available at hardware stores) in the oven and close the door for at least 5 minutes.

If the thermometer reads higher than 350°F, reduce the oven setting specified in the recipe by the number of degrees between 350°F and the thermometer reading. If it's lower, increase the temperature.

If it's off more than 50 degrees in either direction, have your thermostat adjusted.

MIX NOW, BAKE LATER

Forget those tubes of cookie dough in the grocery store—you can do the same thing, only better! Most cookie doughs (except bar cookie batters and meringues) can be mixed then refrigerated or frozen for baking later.

Just pack your favorite dough into freezer containers or shape slice-and-bake dough into rolls and wrap. Store in a tightly covered container in the refrigerator for up to one week or freeze for up to six months.

Before baking, thaw the frozen dough in the container in the refrigerator. If it's too stiff to work with, let the dough stand at room temperature to soften.

---

bined. Beat in as much of the flour as you can with the mixer. Using a wooden spoon, stir in any remaining flour. If necessary, cover and chill dough until easy to handle.

2 Shape dough into 1-inch balls. Roll in additional granulated sugar to coat. Place balls 2 inches apart on an ungreased cookie sheet. Flatten by making crisscross marks with the tines of a fork.

3 Bake in a 375°F oven for 7 to 9 minutes or until bottoms are lightly browned. Transfer cookies to a wire rack and let cool.

Nutrition Facts per cookie: 83 cal., 4 g total fat (2 g sat. fat), 13 mg chol., 68 mg sodium, 10 g carbo., 0 g fiber, 1 g pro. **Daily Values:** 2% vit. A, 2% iron

PEANUT BUTTER BLOSSOMS

Prep: 30 minutes   Bake: 10 minutes per batch
Makes: 54 cookies   Oven: 350°F

Do kid-pleasing peanut butter cookies one better with the addition of a milk chocolate star or kiss in the center of each rich, nutty round.

½ **cup shortening**
½ **cup peanut butter**
½ **cup granulated sugar**
½ **cup packed brown sugar**
1 **teaspoon baking powder**
⅛ **teaspoon baking soda**
1 **egg**
2 **tablespoons milk**

1 **teaspoon vanilla**
1¾ **cups all-purpose flour**
¼ **cup granulated sugar**
   Milk chocolate stars or kisses

1 In a large mixing bowl beat the shortening and peanut butter with an electric mixer on medium speed for 30 seconds. Add the ½ cup granulated sugar, the brown sugar, baking powder, and baking soda. Beat until combined, scraping sides of bowl. Beat in egg, milk, and vanilla until combined. Beat in as much of the flour as you can with the mixer. Using a wooden spoon, stir in any remaining flour.

2 Shape dough into 1-inch balls. Roll balls in the ¼ cup granulated sugar. Place balls 2 inches apart on an ungreased cookie sheet.

3 Bake in a 350°F oven for 10 to 12 minutes or until edges are firm and bottoms are lightly browned. Immediately press a chocolate star or kiss into the center of each cookie. Transfer cookies to a wire rack and let cool.

Nutrition Facts per cookie: 83 cal., 4 g total fat (2 g sat. fat), 4 mg chol., 27 mg sodium, 10 g carbo., 0 g fiber, 1 g pro. **Daily Values:** 1% calcium, 2% iron

Jam Thumbprints: A variety of jewel-toned jams and preserves—in apricot, strawberry, or cherry—lend their beautiful hues to these nut-encrusted treats.

JAM THUMBPRINTS

Prep: 30 minutes   **Chill:** 1 hour
Bake: 10 minutes per batch
Makes: 42 cookies   **Oven:** 375°F

Have these thumbprint cookies baked, cooled, and on hand for drop-in company during the holidays. Fill them right before serving.

  ⅔ **cup butter**
  ½ **cup sugar**
  2 **egg yolks**
  1 **teaspoon vanilla**
1½ **cups all-purpose flour**
  2 **slightly beaten egg whites**
  1 **cup finely chopped walnuts**
  ⅓ **to** ½ **cup strawberry, cherry, or**
      apricot jam or preserves

1 Grease a cookie sheet; set aside. In a large mixing bowl beat butter with an electric mixer on medium to high speed for 30 seconds. Add the sugar and beat until combined, scraping sides of bowl occasionally. Beat in egg yolks and vanilla until combined. Beat in as much of the flour as you can with mixer. Stir in any remaining flour. Cover and chill dough about 1 hour or until easy to handle.

2 Shape dough into 1-inch balls. Roll balls in egg whites; roll in walnuts. Place balls 1 inch apart on the prepared cookie sheet. Press your thumb into the center of each ball.

3 Bake in a 375°F oven for 10 to 12 minutes or until edges are lightly browned. Transfer to a wire rack; cool. Before serving, fill centers with jam.

Nutrition Facts per cookie: 79 cal., 5 g total fat (2 g sat. fat), 18 mg chol., 33 mg sodium, 8 g carbo., 0 g fiber, 1 g pro. **Daily Values:** 4% vit. A, 2% iron

SPRITZ

Prep: 25 minutes   **Bake:** 8 minutes per batch
Makes: about 84 cookies   **Oven:** 375°F

*Use a cookie press to shape these classic
Christmas cookies.*

1½ **cups butter**
 1 **cup sugar**
 1 **teaspoon baking powder**
 1 **egg**
 1 **teaspoon vanilla**
 ¼ **teaspoon almond extract (optional)**
3½ **cups all-purpose flour**
 1 **recipe Powdered Sugar Icing**
    (optional) (see recipe, page 151)

1 **In a large mixing bowl beat** butter with an
electric mixer on medium to high speed for
30 seconds. Add sugar and baking powder. Beat
until combined, scraping sides of bowl occasionally.
Beat in egg, vanilla, and, if desired, almond extract
until combined. Beat in as much flour as you can
with the mixer. Using a wooden spoon, stir in any
remaining flour.

2 **Force unchilled dough** through a cookie press
onto an ungreased cookie sheet.

3 **Bake in a 375°F oven** for 8 to 10 minutes or
until edges are firm but not browned. Transfer
cookies to a wire rack and let cool. If desired, dip
tops into icing.

Nutrition Facts per cookie: 56 cal., 3 g total fat
(2 g sat. fat), 11 mg chol., 38 mg sodium, 6 g carbo.,
0 g fiber, 1 g pro. **Daily Values:** 3% vit. A, 1% iron

Chocolate Spritz: Prepare as above, except reduce
all-purpose flour to 3¼ cups and add ¼ cup
unsweetened cocoa powder with the sugar.

Nutty Spritz: Prepare as above, except reduce sugar
to ⅔ cup and flour to 3¼ cups. After adding flour,
stir in 1 cup finely ground toasted almonds or hazelnuts (see tip, page 181).

OLD-FASHIONED SUGAR COOKIES

Prep: 30 minutes   **Chill:** 2 hours
Bake: 7 minutes per batch
Makes: 60 cookies   **Oven:** 375°F

*For round sugar cookies without making
cutouts, this recipe calls for shaping the cookie
dough into balls. They flatten into rounds as
they bake.*

 1 **cup butter, softened**
1½ **cups sugar**
 2 **eggs**
 2 **teaspoons cream of tartar**
 1 **teaspoon baking soda**
 1 **teaspoon vanilla**
 ¼ **teaspoon salt**
2¾ **cups all-purpose flour**
 ¼ **to ⅓ cup sugar**

1 **In a large mixing bowl beat** the butter with an
electric mixer on medium to high speed for
30 seconds. Add the 1½ cups sugar; beat until combined. Beat in eggs, cream of tartar, baking soda,
vanilla, and salt until combined. Beat in as much of
the flour as you can with the mixer. Using a wood-
en spoon, stir in any remaining flour. Cover and
chill for 2 to 3 hours.

2 **Shape dough** into 1-inch balls. Roll balls in the
¼ cup sugar. Place balls 2 inches apart on an
ungreased cookie sheet.

3 **Bake in a 375°F oven** for 7 to 8 minutes or
until lightly browned. Transfer cookies to a wire
rack and let cool.

Nutrition Facts per cookie: 71 cal., 3 g total fat
(2 g sat. fat), 15 mg chol., 63 mg sodium, 10 g carbo.,
0 g fiber, 1 g pro. **Daily Values:** 3% vit. A, 1% iron

WHERE DID COOKIES COME FROM?

One of the world's best-loved treats was a bit of serendipity that took on a life of its own. The word "cookie" comes from the Dutch word for cake, "koekje." The first cookies were actually tiny cakes baked as a test to make sure the oven temperature was right for baking a large cake. Someone obviously liked the results of the test.

CHOCOLATE CRINKLES

Prep: 30 minutes   Chill: 1 hour
Bake: 8 minutes per batch
Makes: 48 cookies   Oven: 375°F

Snow white powdered sugar on these chocolate cookies gives them a crackly appearance.

    3 eggs
1½ cups granulated sugar
    4 ounces unsweetened chocolate, melted
½ cup cooking oil
    2 teaspoons baking powder
    2 teaspoons vanilla
    2 cups all-purpose flour
        Sifted powdered sugar

1 **In a mixing bowl beat** eggs, granulated sugar, melted chocolate, cooking oil, baking powder, and vanilla with an electric mixer until combined. Beat in as much flour as you can with the mixer. Using a wooden spoon, stir in any remaining flour. Cover and chill 1 to 2 hours or until easy to handle.

2 **Shape dough** into 1-inch balls. Roll balls in powdered sugar to coat generously. Place balls 1 inch apart on an ungreased cookie sheet.

3 **Bake in a 375°F oven** for 8 to 10 minutes or until edges are set and tops are crackled. Transfer cookies to a wire rack and let cool. If desired, sprinkle with additional powdered sugar.

Nutrition Facts per cookie: 80 cal., 4 g total fat (1 g sat. fat), 13 mg chol., 19 mg sodium, 11 g carbo., 0 g fiber, 1 g pro. **Daily Values:** 1% calcium, 3% iron

---

FAIRY DROPS

Prep: 30 minutes   Chill: 30 minutes
Bake: 10 minutes per batch
Makes: 84 cookies   Oven: 350°F

    1 cup butter
    1 cup sifted powdered sugar
    1 cup granulated sugar
    1 teaspoon baking soda
    1 teaspoon cream of tartar
    1 teaspoon salt
    1 cup cooking oil
    2 eggs
    2 teaspoons almond extract
4½ cups all-purpose flour
        Plain or colored granulated sugar
        or one recipe Almond Frosting
        (see recipe, page 149)
        Crushed hard candies (optional)

1 **In a large mixing bowl beat** the butter with an electric mixer on medium to high speed for 30 seconds. Add powdered sugar, granulated sugar, baking soda, cream of tartar, and salt; beat on medium-high speed until fluffy. Add cooking oil, eggs, and almond extract; beat just until combined. Gradually beat in as much of the flour as you can with the mixer. Stir in any remaining flour. Cover and chill dough about 30 minutes or until needed.

2 **Working with one-fourth** of the dough at a time, shape dough into 1¼-inch balls. (The dough will be soft; keep it chilled as you work with a portion.) Arrange balls 2 inches apart on an ungreased cookie sheet. With the palm of your hand or, if desired, the bottom of a glass or a patterned cookie stamp dipped in granulated sugar, gently flatten balls to about ¼ inch thick (see photo below).

One way to flatten balls of dough when making Fairy Drops is to use a cookie stamp that has been dipped into granulated sugar between each stamping.

Fairy Drops: These cookies sparkle like magic when spread with Almond Frosting and sprinkled with crushed candy or trimmed with a simple sprinkling of plain or colored sugar.

Sprinkle with sugar (unless flattened with sugared glass or stamp) or leave plain for frosting.

3 Bake in a 350°F oven for 10 to 12 minutes or until edges just begin to brown. Transfer cookies to a wire rack and let cool. If desired, frost with Almond Frosting and sprinkle with crushed candy.

Almond Frosting: In a small mixing bowl beat ½ cup butter with an electric mixer on medium speed until fluffy. Beat in ½ teaspoon almond extract and ½ teaspoon vanilla. Alternately add 2½ to 3½ cups sifted powdered sugar and 3 tablespoon light cream or milk, beating until smooth and easy to spread. To tint, if desired, stir in a few drops food coloring. Makes about 2 cups.

Nutrition Facts per cookie: 77 cal., 5 g total fat (2 g sat. fat), 10 mg chol., 61 mg sodium, 8 g carbo., 0 g fiber, 1 g pro. **Daily Values:** 2% vit. A, 0% vit. C, 0% calcium, 1% iron

---

BEYOND THE COOKIE JAR

An heirloom cookie jar or pretty tin may be the most aesthetic way to store homemade cookies, but there are better ways to ensure they retain their just-baked freshness.

- **To store cookies short-term,** cool them completely. In an airtight container, arrange unfrosted cookies in single layers separated by sheets of waxed paper. If frosted, store cookies in a single layer or place waxed paper between layers. (Don't mix soft and crisp cookies in the same container or the crisp cookies will soften.) Store them at room temperature for up to three days. If they are frosted with a cream cheese or yogurt icing, you'll need to refrigerate them.

- **To store cookies long-term,** let them cool completely, then package them in freezer bags or containers and freeze for up to three months. Before serving, thaw them in the container for about 15 minutes. If the cookies are to be frosted, glazed, or sprinkled with sugar, wait until they have thawed to decorate them.

GINGERSNAPS

Prep: 30 minutes   **Bake:** 8 minutes per batch
Makes: 48 cookies   **Oven:** 375°F

  ¾ **cup shortening**
  1 **cup packed brown sugar**
  1 **teaspoon baking soda**
  1 **teaspoon ground ginger**
  1 **teaspoon ground cinnamon**
  ½ **teaspoon ground cloves**
  ¼ **cup molasses**
  1 **egg**
2¼ **cups all-purpose flour**
  ¼ **cup granulated sugar**

1 In a large mixing bowl beat shortening with an electric mixer on medium to high speed for 30 seconds. Add brown sugar, baking soda, ginger, cinnamon, and cloves. Beat until combined. Beat in molasses and egg. Beat in as much of the flour as you can with the mixer. Stir in any remaining flour.

2 Shape dough into 1-inch balls. Roll balls in the granulated sugar to coat. Place balls 2 inches apart on an ungreased cookie sheet.

3 Bake in a 375°F oven for 8 to 10 minutes or until edges are set and tops are crackled. Cool cookies on cookie sheet for 1 minute. Transfer cookies to a wire rack and let cool.

Nutrition Facts per cookie: 72 cal., 3 g total fat (1 g sat. fat), 4 mg chol., 29 mg sodium, 10 g carbo., 0 g fiber, 1 g pro. Daily Values: 0% vit. A, 0% vit. C, 0% calcium, 2% iron

BIG SOFT GINGER COOKIES

Prep: 25 minutes   **Bake:** 10 minutes per batch
Makes: 24 large cookies   **Oven:** 350°F

This recipe shared by a Better Homes and Gardens® *reader first appeared in a holiday sweets story called "With Love From Grandma's Kitchen" in the magazine's December 1989 issue.*

2¼ **cups all-purpose flour**
  2 **teaspoons ground ginger**
  1 **teaspoon baking soda**
  ¾ **teaspoon ground cinnamon**
  ½ **teaspoon ground cloves**
  ¾ **cup butter**
  1 **cup sugar**
  1 **egg**
  ¼ **cup molasses**
  2 **tablespoons sugar**

1 In a medium bowl combine the flour, ginger, baking soda, cinnamon, and cloves; set aside.

2 In a large mixing bowl beat butter with an electric mixer on medium speed for 30 seconds. Beat in the 1 cup sugar. Add egg and molasses; beat well. Stir flour mixture into egg mixture.

3 Shape dough into 1½-inch balls, using about 1 heaping tablespoon dough for each. Roll balls in the 2 tablespoons sugar to coat. Place balls about 2½ inches apart on an ungreased cookie sheet.

4 **Bake in a 350°F oven** about 10 minutes or until light brown and still puffed. (Do not over-bake.) Cool cookies on cookie sheet for 2 minutes. Transfer cookies to a wire rack and let cool.

Nutrition Facts per cookie: 138 cal., 6 g total fat (4 g sat. fat), 24 mg chol., 114 mg sodium, 20 g carbo., 0 g fiber, 1 g pro. Daily Values: 5% vit. A, 4% iron

SUGAR COOKIE CUTOUTS

Prep: 45 minutes   Chill: 3 hours (if necessary)
Bake: 7 minutes per batch
Makes: 36 to 48 cookies   Oven: 375°F

⅓ **cup butter**
⅓ **cup shortening**
¾ **cup sugar**
 1 **teaspoon baking powder**
    Dash salt
 1 **egg**
 1 **teaspoon vanilla**
 2 **cups all-purpose flour**
 1 **recipe Powdered Sugar Icing**
    (optional)

1 **In a medium mixer bowl beat** butter and shortening with an electric mixer on medium to high speed for 30 seconds. Add sugar, baking powder, and salt. Beat until combined, scraping sides of bowl occasionally. Beat in egg and vanilla. Beat in as much of the flour as you can with the mixer. Using a wooden spoon, stir in any remaining flour. Divide dough in half. If necessary, cover and chill the dough for 3 hours or until it is easy to handle.

2 **On a lightly floured surface roll** half of the dough at a time to ⅛-inch thickness. Using a 2½-inch cookie or biscuit cutter, cut into desired shapes. Place on ungreased cookie sheet.

3 **Bake in a 375°F oven** for 7 to 8 minutes or until edges are firm and bottoms are very lightly browned. Transfer cookies to a wire rack and let cool. If desired, frost with Powdered Sugar Icing.

Powdered Sugar Icing: In a mixing bowl combine 1 cup sifted powdered sugar, ¼ teaspoon vanilla, and 1 tablespoon milk. Stir in additional milk, 1 teaspoon at a time, until icing is easy to drizzle. Makes ½ cup.

Nutrition Facts per cookie: 74 cal., 4 g total fat (2 g sat. fat), 10 mg chol., 33 mg sodium, 9 g carbo., 0 g fiber, 1 g pro. Daily Values: 1% vit. A, 1% calcium, 2% iron

CUTOUT COOKIE KNOW-HOW

There's no end to the versatility and fun of cutout cookies. Here are a few ways to ensure their success:
■ When rolling and cutting, work with half of the cookie dough at a time. Keep the other half of the dough refrigerated until you're ready to roll it out.
■ Keep the cookie dough from sticking to the countertop by lightly sprinkling the surface with all-purpose flour. A pastry stocking and pastry cloth also can help prevent the dough from sticking.

■ Dip the cutter in flour between uses to keep dough from sticking to it.
■ Leave little space between cutouts to get the greatest number of cookies from the dough.
■ After you've cut out your cookies, combine any scraps and reroll on a very lightly floured surface. Handle and roll the dough as little as possible to keep the cookies tender.
■ Cutout cookies are done when the bottoms are very lightly browned and edges are firm.
■ Cool cookies completely before storing them so they don't lose their shape.

PISTACHIO NUT
STARS OF INDIA

Prep: 40 minutes **Chill:** 2 hours
Bake: 6 minutes per batch
Makes: 36 cookies **Oven:** 375°F

Indian cooks spice rice with cinnamon and cardamom. Here, the flavors infuse after-dinner treats with warmth (see photo, page 135).

  1 **cup butter, softened**
  ½ **cup granulated sugar**
  ¼ **cup packed brown sugar**
  2 **tablespoons vanilla yogurt**
  1 **egg**
2½ **cups all-purpose flour**
  1 **teaspoon ground cinnamon**
  ¼ **to ½ teaspoon ground cardamom**
  ¼ **teaspoon salt**
  2 **cups finely chopped pistachio nuts**
      or almonds
  1 **slightly beaten egg white**
  ½ **cup orange marmalade**
  2 **tablespoons powdered sugar**

1 **In a large mixing bowl beat** butter, granulated sugar, brown sugar, and yogurt with an electric mixer on medium to high speed until creamy. Add egg; beat well. Beat in flour, cinnamon, cardamom, and salt. Using a wooden spoon, stir in nuts. Divide dough in half. Cover and chill for 2 hours.

2 **Lightly grease a cookie sheet**; set aside. On a floured surface, roll half of dough at a time to ⅛-inch thickness. Using a 3-inch star cookie cutter, cut out 36 stars from each half of dough, rerolling trimmings as needed. Place on prepared cookie sheet. With a small star-shaped cutter, cut stars from centers of half of stars. Brush all cookies with egg white.

3 **Bake in a 375°F oven** for 6 to 8 minutes or until lightly browned. Transfer cookies to a wire rack and let cool.

4 **To assemble cookies,** spread dull side of each whole star with ½ teaspoon marmalade. Top each with a cutout cookie, shiny side up. Press cookies together gently. Sift powdered sugar lightly over tops of filled cookies.

Nutrition Facts per cookie: 146 cal., 9 g total fat (4 g sat. fat), 20 mg chol., 72 mg sodium, 16 g carbo., 1 g fiber, 3 g pro. **Daily Values:** 5% vit. A, 1% vit. C, 1% calcium, 6% iron

CASHEW-SUGAR
COOKIES

Prep: 35 minutes **Bake:** 8 minutes per batch
Makes: 42 cookies **Oven:** 375°F

These shortbread-style sweets are perfect with a cup of afternoon tea.

1¼ **cups all-purpose flour**
  ½ **cup ground lightly salted cashews**
      or ground almonds
  ¼ **cup granulated sugar**
  ¼ **cup packed brown sugar**
  ½ **cup butter**
     Granulated sugar
     Whole cashews or toasted blanched
     whole almonds
     (see tip, page 181)

1 **In a medium bowl combine** flour, ground nuts, granulated sugar, and brown sugar. Using a pastry blender, cut in butter until mixture resembles fine crumbs. Form mixture into a ball and knead gently until smooth.

2 **On a lightly floured surface roll** dough to ¼-inch thickness. Cut into 1½-inch circles. Place 1 inch apart on an ungreased cookie sheet. Lightly sprinkle with the granulated sugar. Lightly press a whole nut in the center of each cookie.

3 **Bake in a 375°F oven** for 8 to 10 minutes or until. Transfer cookies to a wire rack and let cool.

Nutrition Facts per cookie: 62 cal., 4 g total fat (1 g sat. fat), 3 mg chol., 41 mg sodium, 6 g carbo., 0 g fiber, 1 g pro. **Daily Values:** 2% vit. A, 2% iron

DECORATING 101

Cookies are wonderful because they satisfy that craving for just a bite of something sweet; you can have one (or more) all to yourself; and with *a few simple tools and techniques, they become miniature works of art. Apply one of these fun effects to the next batch of cookies you bake.*

Stenciling
A condiment bottle filled with colored sugar is handy for applying stencils. It's easy to control the flow of sugar and have precise aim.

Stenciling
Sift powdered sugar over a waxed-paper snowflake pattern. Or, use a tiny cookie cutter and spoon colored sugar inside the cutter.

Chocolate Trims To make chocolate-mint curls, draw a vegetable peeler at an angle across room-temperature, layered mint candies. To make marble cutouts, swirl melted chocolate and white candy coating together, let chill 10 minutes, and cut into diamonds.

Painting Paint with cocoa paint (equal parts unsweetened cocoa powder and water) on glazed baked cookies. Or, brush egg paint (1 egg yolk, 1 teaspoon water, and food coloring) on unbaked cookies and bake.

Candy Trims
Nothing's easier—and sweeter—than a quick candy trim. Try sliced gumdrops and red cinnamon candy to make bells or holly and berries, or crushed peppermint for a cool and colorful finish.

Two-Color Glaze
Spoon one color of icing evenly over the cookie. While the first color is still wet, apply a small amount of a second color, then use a toothpick to pull the icing and make a design.

Candlewicking
To get this embroidered French-knot effect, fit a decorating tube with a small writing tip. Pipe dots in a pattern, using a swirl action so each dot looks like a thread knot.

Dips and Drizzles
Start by melting 6 ounces chocolate with 2 teaspoons shortening. Dip half or all of each cooled cookie in the melted mixture or drizzle it over the tops of the cookies.

LEMON-ALMOND TEA COOKIES

LOW-FAT

Prep: 20 minutes   **Chill:** 4 hours
Bake: 8 minutes per batch
Makes: 64 cookies   **Oven:** 375°F

½ cup butter
½ cup granulated sugar
⅛ teaspoon baking soda
1 egg yolk
1 tablespoon milk
2 teaspoons finely shredded lemon peel
1 teaspoon almond extract
½ teaspoon vanilla
1½ cups all-purpose flour
2 tablespoons butter
1 cup sifted powdered sugar
1 tablespoon milk
½ teaspoon lemon juice
½ cup toasted, sliced almonds
    (see tip, page 181)

1 In a medium mixing bowl beat the ½ cup butter with an electric mixer on medium to high speed for 30 seconds. Add the granulated sugar and baking soda. Beat until combined. Beat in the egg yolk, 1 tablespoon milk, lemon peel, almond extract, and vanilla. Beat in as much of the flour as you can with the mixer. Stir in any remaining flour.

2 Shape dough into an 8-inch-long roll. Wrap in waxed paper or plastic wrap. Chill the dough at least 4 hours.

3 Cut dough into ⅛-inch slices. Place slices 2 inches apart on an ungreased cookie sheet.

4 Bake in a 375°F oven 8 to 10 minutes or until edges are firm and bottoms are lightly browned. Transfer cookies to a wire rack and let cool.

5 For frosting, in a small bowl beat 2 tablespoons butter with an electric mixer on medium to high speed for 30 seconds. Beat in half the powdered sugar. Beat in the 1 tablespoon milk and the lemon juice. Mix thoroughly. Gradually beat in the remaining powdered sugar. Spread about 1 teaspoon of frosting atop each cookie. Sprinkle with almonds.

Nutrition Facts per cookie: 45 cal., 2 g total fat
(1 g sat. fat), 8 mg chol., 21 mg sodium, 5 g carbo.,
0 g fiber, 1 g pro. **Daily Values:** 2% vit. A, 1% iron

RED RASPBERRY TWIRLS

LOW-FAT

Prep: 30 minutes   **Chill:** 5 hours
Bake: 9 minutes per batch
Makes: 60 cookies   **Oven:** 375°F

½ cup butter
1 cup sugar
½ teaspoon baking powder
1 egg
3 tablespoons milk
¼ teaspoon almond extract (optional)
2¾ cups all-purpose flour
½ cup seedless red raspberry jam
1½ teaspoons cornstarch
½ cup toasted almonds, ground
    (see tip, page 181)

1 In a large mixing bowl beat the butter with an electric mixer on medium to high speed for 30 seconds. Add sugar and baking powder. Beat until combined, scraping sides of bowl occasionally. Beat in egg, milk, and, if desired, almond extract. Beat in as much flour as you can with the mixer. Using a wooden spoon, stir in any remaining flour. Cover; chill 1 hour or until dough is easy to handle.

2 Meanwhile, for filling, in a saucepan combine jam and cornstarch. Cook and stir until thickened and bubbly. Cook and stir for 1 minute more. Stir in almonds. Cover and set aside to cool.

3 Divide dough in half. On waxed paper use a floured rolling pin to roll each portion into a 12×8-inch rectangle. Spread with filling. From short side, roll up each, into a spiral, removing waxed paper as you roll. Moisten edges and pinch to seal. Wrap in waxed paper or clear plastic wrap. Chill for 4 to 24 hours.

4 Line a cookie sheet with foil. Grease foil; set aside. Using a thin-bladed knife, cut dough into ¼ slices. Place 2 inches apart on the prepared cookie sheet.

5 Bake in a 375°F oven for 9 to 11 minutes or until edges are firm and bottoms are lightly browned. Transfer cookies to a wire rack; let cool.

Nutrition Facts per cookie: 62 cal., 2 g total fat
(0 g sat. fat), 6 mg chol., 19 mg sodium, 10 g carbo.,
0 g fiber, 1 g pro. **Daily Values:** 1% vit. A, 2% iron

Red Raspberry Twirls: These pretty, swirled cookies have the flavors of the classic Austrian dessert, linzertorte (raspberry and almonds) all wrapped up in a sweet you can eat with your fingers.

SHORTBREAD

Prep: 15 minutes
Bake: 25 minutes per batch
Makes: 16 cookie wedges   **Oven:** 325°F

1¼ cups all-purpose flour
  3 tablespoons granulated sugar
½ cup butter

1 **In a medium mixing bowl combine** flour and sugar. Using a pastry blender, cut in butter until mixture resembles fine crumbs and starts to cling. Form mixture into a ball and knead until smooth.

To make shortbread wedges: On an ungreased cookie sheet pat or roll the dough into an 8-inch circle. Make a scalloped edge (see photo, top right). Cut circle into 16 wedges (see middle photo, right). Leave wedges in the circle. Bake in a 325°F oven for 25 to 30 minutes or until bottom just starts to brown and center is set. Cut circle into wedges again while warm. Cool on the cookie sheet for 5 minutes. Transfer to a wire rack and let cool.

To make shortbread rounds: On a lightly floured surface roll the dough to ½-inch thickness. Use a 1½-inch cookie cutter to cut 24 rounds. Place them 1 inch apart on an ungreased cookie sheet and bake in the 325°F oven for 20 to 25 minutes.

To make shortbread strips: On a lightly floured surface roll dough into an 8×6-inch rectangle about ½ inch thick. Using a knife, cut into twenty-four 2×1-inch strips (see bottom photo, right). Place 1 inch apart on an ungreased cookie sheet. Bake in the 325°F oven for 20 to 25 minutes.

Nutrition Facts per cookie wedge: 92 cal., 6 g total fat (4 g sat. fat), 15 mg chol., 58 mg sodium, 9 g carbo., 0 g fiber, 1 g pro. **Daily Values:** 5% vit. A, 2% iron

Butter-Pecan Shortbread: Prepare Shortbread as above, except substitute brown sugar for the granulated sugar. After cutting in butter, stir in 2 tablespoons finely chopped pecans. Sprinkle mixture with ½ teaspoon vanilla before kneading.

For a scalloped edge, use your thumb on the inside hand and thumb and index finger on the other and carefully crimp a scalloped edge around dough.

To cut shortbread into wedges, use a long, sharp knife to carefully cut dough circle into pie-shaped wedges of equal size.

For shortbread strips, mark the long sides of the rectangle at 1-inch intervals and mark the short sides at 2-inch intervals. Cut with a sharp knife or pizza cutter.

Lemon-Poppy Seed Shortbread: Prepare Shortbread as at left, except stir 1 tablespoon poppy seed into flour mixture and add 1 teaspoon finely shredded lemon peel with the butter.

Oatmeal Shortbread: Prepare Shortbread as at left, except reduce flour to 1 cup. After cutting in butter, stir in ⅓ cup quick-cooking rolled oats.

Spiced Shortbread: Prepare Shortbread as at left, except substitute brown sugar for the granulated sugar and stir ½ teaspoon ground cinnamon, ¼ teaspoon ground ginger, and ⅛ teaspoon ground cloves into the flour mixture.

brownies
and bars

Ultimate Bar Cookies, recipe page 162
Creamy, Fudgy, Nutty Brownies, recipe page 163

BROWNIES AND BARS

Brickle Bars: Give the traditional fudgy brownie treat a crunchy topping by sprinkling almond brickle and chocolate pieces over the batter before baking.

EASY FUDGE **BROWNIES**

Prep: 30 minutes   Bake: 30 minutes
Makes: 24 brownies   Oven: 350°F

These no-mixing-bowl brownies are a breeze to make. Mix them in a saucepan, pour them in a baking pan, and enjoy them in no time.

  ½ **cup butter**
  2 **ounces unsweetened chocolate,**
        chopped
  1 **cup sugar**
  2 **eggs**
  1 **teaspoon vanilla**
  ¾ **cup all-purpose flour**
  ½ **cup chopped nuts**

1 Grease an 8×8×2-inch baking pan; set aside. In a medium saucepan melt butter and chocolate over low heat. Remove from heat. Stir in sugar, eggs, and vanilla. Using a wooden spoon, lightly beat the mixture just until combined (don't overbeat or brownies will rise too high then fall). Stir in flour and chopped nuts. Spread batter in prepared pan.

2 Bake in a 350°F oven for 30 minutes. Cool in pan on a wire rack. Cut into bars.

Nutrition Facts per brownie: 113 cal., 7 g total fat (3 g sat. fat), 28 mg chol., 44 mg sodium, 12 g carbo., 0 g fiber, 2 g pro. **Daily Values:** 4% vit. A, 3% iron

Brickle Bars: Prepare as above, except omit the nuts. Spread the batter in the prepared pan and sprinkle ¾ cup almond brickle pieces and ½ cup miniature semisweet chocolate pieces evenly over top of batter. Bake. Cool in pan on a wire rack. Cut into bars.

WHEN IN SYDNEY ...

Is there anything better than a soft, chewy brownie and a glass of milk? Those nutty, much-beloved cookies that are claimed to be as American as apple pie actually evolved from cocoa scones, a variation of Scottish tea cakes. In Australia if you ask for a brownie, you'll be served raisin bread traditionally eaten on cattle ranches at a "smoke oh," or morning break.

IRISH CREAM BROWNIES

Prep: 25 minutes   Bake: 15 minutes
Cool: 2 hours   Makes: 36 brownies
Oven: 350°F

Your family and friends will feel they have the luck of the Irish when you make these extra-special, Irish cream-infused brownies.

1¼ cups sugar
¾ cup butter
½ cup unsweetened cocoa powder
2 eggs
1 teaspoon vanilla
1½ cups all-purpose flour
1 teaspoon baking powder
¼ teaspoon baking soda
1 cup milk
1 cup chopped walnuts or pecans
¼ cup Irish cream liqueur or crème de cacao
1 recipe Liqueur Glaze
1 recipe Powdered Sugar Frosting (optional)

1 Grease a 15×10×1-inch baking pan; set aside. In a large saucepan heat sugar, butter, and cocoa powder over medium heat until butter melts, stirring constantly. Remove from heat; cool slightly. Add eggs, one at a time, and vanilla. Using a wooden spoon, lightly beat mixture just until combined. In a bowl combine flour, baking powder, and baking soda. Add flour mixture and milk alternately to chocolate mixture, beating by hand after each addition. Stir in nuts. Pour into the prepared pan.

2 Bake in a 350°F oven for 15 to 20 minutes or until a wooden toothpick inserted near center comes out clean. Place pan on a wire rack. While brownies are still hot, use a pastry brush to brush liqueur or crème de cacao evenly over top. Cool. Spread with Liqueur Glaze. If desired, pipe with Powdered Sugar Frosting. Cut into bars.

Liqueur Glaze: In a medium bowl combine 2½ cups sifted powdered sugar, 2 tablespoons unsweetened cocoa powder, and ¼ teaspoon vanilla. Stir in 1 tablespoon Irish cream liqueur or crème de cacao. Stir in 3 to 4 teaspoons milk, 1 teaspoon at a time, until of drizzling consistency.

Powdered Sugar Frosting: Stir together ½ cup sifted powdered sugar and enough milk (about 1½ teaspoons) to make of piping consistency.

Nutrition Facts per brownie: 149 cal., 7 g total fat (1 g sat. fat), 17 mg chol., 62 mg sodium, 20 g carbo., 0 g fiber, 2 g pro. **Daily Values:** 4% vit. A, 3% calcium, 3% iron

FUDGE BROWNIE TARTS

Prep: 25 minutes   Bake: 10 minutes
Makes: 30 tarts   Oven: 350°F

5 ounces unsweetened chocolate, chopped
⅓ cup butter
1 cup sugar
2 beaten eggs
1 teaspoon vanilla
½ cup all-purpose flour
Pecan halves (optional)

1 Line 1¾-inch muffin cups with 1¾-inch paper bake cups or grease the muffin cups; set aside. In a heavy medium saucepan melt unsweetened chocolate and butter over low heat until smooth, stirring constantly. Remove from heat.

2 Stir in sugar, eggs, and vanilla. Using a wooden spoon, lightly beat the mixture just until combined. Stir in flour. Spoon about 1 tablespoon batter into each prepared muffin cup. If desired, top with a pecan half.

3 Bake in a 350°F oven for 10 to 12 minutes or until edges appear set (centers should be soft). Cool in pan on a wire rack for 5 minutes. Transfer tarts, in the paper bake cups, to a wire rack to cool.

Nutrition Facts per tart: 80 cal., 5 g total fat (2 g sat. fat), 17 mg chol., 23 mg sodium, 10 g carbo., 0 g fiber, 1 g pro. **Daily Values:** 2% vit. A, 3% iron

THINK OUTSIDE THE SQUARE

Bar cookies—including brownies—are called that because they're generally served in the shape of a bar of gold, a square, or a rectangle. You'll get the most equally sized pieces if you use a ruler to measure and toothpicks to mark the lines. Also, it's easier to get the cookies out of the pan if you remove a corner piece first.

But there's certainly more than one way to cut bars and brownies into the proper pieces:

- To make triangles, cut bars into 2- or 2½-inch squares. Cut each square in half diagonally. Or, cut bars into rectangles; cut each diagonally for triangles.
- To make diamonds, first cut parallel lines 1 or 1½ inches apart down the length of the pan. Then cut diagonal lines 1 or 1½ inches apart across the pan, forming a diamond pattern.

TRILEVEL BROWNIES

Prep: 40 minutes **Bake:** 35 minutes
Makes: 32 brownies **Oven:** 350°F

A favorite that first appeared in Better Homes and Gardens® *cookbooks during the days of bell-bottoms and the Beach Boys, these triple-layered treats are always a hit.*

1 **cup quick-cooking rolled oats**
½ **cup all-purpose flour**
½ **cup packed brown sugar**
¼ **teaspoon baking soda**
½ **cup butter, melted**
1 **egg**
¾ **cup granulated sugar**
⅔ **cup all-purpose flour**
¼ **cup milk**
¼ **cup butter, melted**
1 **ounce unsweetened chocolate, melted and cooled**
1 **teaspoon vanilla**
¼ **teaspoon baking powder**
½ **cup chopped walnuts**
1 **ounce unsweetened chocolate**
2 **tablespoons butter**
1½ **cups sifted powdered sugar**
½ **teaspoon vanilla**
Walnut halves (optional)

1 **For bottom layer,** stir together oats, the ½ cup flour, the brown sugar, and baking soda. Stir in the ½ cup melted butter. Press mixture into bottom of an ungreased 11×7×1½-inch baking pan. Bake in a 350°F oven for 10 minutes.

2 **Meanwhile, for middle layer,** stir together egg, granulated sugar, the ⅔ cup flour, milk, the ¼ cup melted butter, 1 ounce melted chocolate, the 1 teaspoon vanilla, and baking powder until smooth. Fold in chopped walnuts. Spread batter over baked layer in pan. Bake in the 350°F oven about 25 minutes more or until a wooden toothpick inserted near the center comes out clean. Place the pan on a wire rack while preparing top layer.

3 **For top layer,** in a medium saucepan heat and stir the 1 ounce chocolate and the 2 tablespoons butter until melted. Stir in the powdered sugar and the ½ teaspoon vanilla. Stir in enough hot water (1 to 2 tablespoons) to make a mixture that is almost pourable. Spread over brownies. If desired, garnish with walnut halves. Cool in pan on a wire rack. Cut into bars.

Nutrition Facts per brownie: 140 cal., 7 g total fat (4 g sat. fat), 20 mg chol., 68 mg sodium, 18 g carbo., 1 g fiber, 2 g pro. **Daily Values:** 5% vit. A, 1% calcium, 3% iron

---

BARS IN THE BAG

Bake a batch of bars and stash them in the freezer for the future; you'll be glad you had such discipline when the craving for something sweet hits. Here's how to bake and store bars:

Before spreading the batter in the pan, line it with foil (see tip, page 169). Follow the recipe for baking and cooling. Lift the bars out of the pan on the foil. Place the uncut and unfrosted bars in freezer bags or airtight containers. Seal, label, date, and freeze. Thaw the bars at room temperature for about 15 minutes. Once thawed, the bars can be frosted and cut.

ULTIMATE BAR COOKIES

Prep: 30 minutes **Bake:** 30 minutes
Makes: 36 bars **Oven:** 350°F

Crush any leftover bars and sprinkle over ice cream as a topping (see photo, page 157).

  2 **cups all-purpose flour**
  ½ **cup packed brown sugar**
  ½ **cup butter, softened**
  1 **cup coarsely chopped walnuts**
  1 **3½-ounce jar macadamia nuts,**
      coarsely chopped (1 cup)
  1 **6-ounce package white baking**
      bars, coarsely chopped (1 cup)
  1 **cup milk chocolate pieces**
  ¾ **cup butter**
  ½ **cup packed brown sugar**

1 **In a medium mixing bowl beat** flour, ½ cup brown sugar, and ½ cup butter with an electric mixer on medium speed until mixture forms fine crumbs. Press mixture firmly into the bottom of an ungreased 13×9×2-inch baking pan.

2 **Bake in a 350°F oven** 15 minutes or until lightly browned. Transfer pan to a rack. Sprinkle nuts, baking bars, and milk chocolate pieces over hot crust.

3 **Heat and stir** the ¾ cup butter and ½ cup brown sugar over medium heat until bubbly. Cook and stir for 1 minute more. Pour evenly over layers in pan. Bake in the 350°F oven for 15 minutes more or until just bubbly around edges. Cool in pan on a wire rack. Cut into desired shapes.

Nutrition Facts per bar: 188 cal., 13 g total fat (6 g sat. fat), 18 mg chol., 12 mg sodium, 16 g carbo., 1 g fiber, 2 g pro. **Daily Values:** 6% vit. A, 2% calcium, 4% iron

HAZELNUT BARS

Prep: 20 minutes **Bake:** 50 minutes
Makes: 48 bars **Oven:** 350°F

  2 **cups all-purpose flour**
  2 **3-ounce packages cream cheese,**
      softened
  ½ **cup butter, softened**
  ½ **cup packed brown sugar**
  4 **eggs**
  2 **cups granulated sugar**
  1½ **cups buttermilk or sour milk**
      (see tip, page 208)
  ½ **cup butter, melted**
  ⅓ **cup all-purpose flour**
  2 **teaspoons vanilla**
  ¼ **teaspoon salt**
  2 **cups chopped hazelnuts, toasted**
      (see tip, page 181)

1 **For crust,** beat the 2 cups flour, cream cheese, the ½ cup softened butter, and brown sugar with an electric mixer until well combined. With lightly floured hands, press mixture into bottom and up sides of an ungreased 15×10×1-inch baking pan. Bake in a 350°F oven for 15 minutes.

2 **Meanwhile, for filling,** in a large mixing bowl beat the eggs, granulated sugar, buttermilk, the ½ cup melted butter, the ⅓ cup flour, vanilla, and salt with an electric mixer until combined. Stir in nuts. Pour mixture into prebaked crust. Bake about 35 minutes more or until golden. Cool on a wire rack. Cut into bars. Cover and store in refrigerator.

Nutrition Facts per bar: 146 cal., 9 g total fat (4 g sat. fat), 32 mg chol., 75 mg sodium, 16 g carbo., 1 g fiber, 2 g pro. **Daily Values:** 5% vit. A, 2% calcium, 3% iron

CREAMY, FUDGY, NUTTY BROWNIES

Prep: 25 minutes **Bake:** 50 minutes
Chill: 2 hours **Makes:** 12 brownies
Oven: 350°F

The creamy crown on these brownies is essentially a chocolate cheesecake mixture, so store them in the refrigerator (see photo on page 157).

Use a flexible rubber spatula to easily spread the chocolate-cheese topping on the hot brownies. Continue baking until topping is set.

 4 ounces unsweetened chocolate, chopped
½ cup butter
 1 cup all-purpose flour
½ cup chopped walnuts or pecans, toasted (see tip, page 181)
¼ teaspoon baking powder
1½ cups sugar
 3 eggs
 1 teaspoon vanilla
 3 ounces semisweet chocolate, chopped
 2 3-ounce packages cream cheese, softened
 1 egg
¼ cup sugar
 1 tablespoon milk
½ teaspoon vanilla

1 **Grease and lightly flour** an 8×8×2-inch baking pan; set aside. In a small saucepan melt unsweetened chocolate and butter. Remove from heat; set aside to cool slightly. In a medium bowl stir together flour, nuts, and baking powder; set aside.

2 **In a large bowl stir** together the melted chocolate mixture and the 1½ cups sugar. Add the 3 eggs and 1 teaspoon vanilla. Using a wooden spoon, lightly beat mixture just until combined (don't overbeat or brownies will rise too high then fall). Stir in flour mixture. Spread batter in the prepared pan. Bake in a 350°F oven for 40 minutes.

3 **Meanwhile, for topping,** in a heavy small saucepan melt semisweet chocolate over low heat; cool slightly. In a medium bowl beat the softened cream cheese with melted semisweet chocolate, 1 egg, ¼ cup sugar, 1 tablespoon milk, and ½ teaspoon vanilla until combined.

4 **Carefully spread topping** evenly over hot brownies (see photo, above). Bake in the 350°F oven about 10 minutes more or until topping appears set. Cool thoroughly in pan on a wire rack. Cover and chill in the refrigerator at least 2 hours before serving. Cut into bars. Cover and refrigerate to store.

Nutrition Facts per brownie: 409 cal., 27 g total fat (9 g sat. fat), 97 mg chol., 143 mg sodium, 43 g carbo., 2 g fiber, 7 g pro. **Daily Values:** 17% vit. A, 4% calcium, 14% iron

---

MAKE 'EM MELT

Melting chocolate for drizzling over cookies can be done in one of two ways:
- To melt chocolate on top of the stove, place chocolate pieces or cut-up chocolate in a heavy saucepan. Add 1 teaspoon shortening for each ½ cup (3 ounces) chocolate. (The shortening helps the chocolate set up.) Melt chocolate over low heat; stir often to avoid scorching.

- To melt chocolate in a microwave oven, place ½ cup pieces (3 ounces cut-up chocolate) in a microwave-safe measuring cup or custard cup. Microwave, uncovered, on 100% power (high) 60 to 90 seconds or until soft enough to stir smoothly; stir after 60 seconds (makes about ¼ cup melted chocolate). Pieces or squares of chocolate won't seem melted until stirred.

Raspberry-Citrus Bars: Raspberry and lemon are classically compatible flavors. The tang of the lemon heightens the sweetness of the fresh raspberries that are baked right into the bars.

LEMON BARS DELUXE

Prep: 25 minutes **Bake:** 45 minutes
Cool: 2 hours **Makes:** 30 bars
Oven: 350°F

BEST-LOVED

Who says you can't freshen up a classic? One version of this longtime favorite lemon bar recipe gets a sprinkling of fresh raspberries and orange peel (see right).

　1　cup butter
　½　cup sifted powdered sugar
　2　cups all-purpose flour
　4　beaten eggs
1½　cups granulated sugar
　2　teaspoons finely shredded lemon
　　　peel (set aside)
　⅓　cup lemon juice
　¼　cup all-purpose flour
　½　teaspoon baking powder
　　　Sifted powdered sugar
　　　Citrus peel strips (optional)

1 **In a large mixing bowl beat** the butter with an electric mixer on medium to high speed for 30 seconds. Add the ½ cup powdered sugar and beat until combined. Beat in the 2 cups flour until crumbly. Press mixture into the bottom of an ungreased 13×9×2-inch baking pan. Bake in a 350°F oven for 20 to 25 minutes or until lightly browned.

2 **Meanwhile, beat together** eggs, granulated sugar, and lemon juice. Combine the ¼ cup flour and the baking powder; stir into egg mixture along with the lemon peel. Pour over baked crust.

3 **Bake in the 350°F oven** for 25 minutes more or until lightly browned around edges and center appears set. Cool in pan on a wire rack. Sprinkle with additional powdered sugar. Cut into squares or diamonds. If desired, garnish with strips of citrus peel. Store, covered, in the refrigerator.

Nutrition Facts per bar: 142 cal., 7 g total fat (4 g sat. fat), 45 mg chol., 77 mg sodium, 19 g carbo., 0 g fiber, 2 g pro. **Daily Values:** 6% vit. A, 2% vit. C, 1% calcium, 3% iron

Raspberry-Citrus Bars: Prepare as above, except substitute 2 tablespoons finely shredded orange peel for the lemon peel in the filling. After crust is baked, sprinkle 1½ cups fresh raspberries over crust. Pour filling over berries, arranging berries evenly with a spoon. Bake for 25 to 30 minutes or until set.

Cranberry-Macadamia Bars:
Bake up a batch of these bars for the holidays when fresh cranberries are in season. Like tiny slices of a special tart, they add a different shape and beautiful color to any holiday cookie tray.

CRANBERRY-MACADAMIA BARS

Prep: 40 minutes   Bake: 40 minutes
Makes: 48 bars   Oven: 350°F

1 ¼ cups all-purpose flour
 ¾ cup sugar
 ½ cup butter
 ½ cup finely chopped macadamia
    nuts, hazelnuts (filberts),
    or pecans
1 ¼ cups sugar
 2 beaten eggs
 2 tablespoons milk
 1 teaspoon finely shredded
    orange peel
 1 teaspoon vanilla
 ½ cup finely chopped macadamia
    nuts, hazelnuts (filberts),
    or pecans
 1 cup finely chopped cranberries
 ½ cup coconut

1 **In a bowl stir** together the flour and the ¾ cup sugar. Using a pastry blender, cut in butter until mixture resembles coarse crumbs. Stir in the ½ cup nuts. Press flour mixture into the bottom of an ungreased 13×9×2-inch baking pan. Bake in a 350°F oven for 10 to 15 minutes or until the crust is light brown around the edges.

2 **Meanwhile, in a bowl** combine the 1 ¼ cups sugar, eggs, milk, orange peel, and vanilla. Beat until combined. Pour over the hot crust. Sprinkle with the ½ cup nuts, the cranberries, and coconut.

3 **Bake in the 350°F oven** for 30 minutes more or until golden. Cool slightly in pan on a wire rack. Cut into 24 bars and cut bars in half diagonally while warm. Cool completely in pan.

Nutrition Facts per bar: 88 cal., 4 g total fat
(2 g sat. fat), 14 mg chol., 23 mg sodium, 12 g carbo.,
0 g fiber, 1 g pro. **Daily Values:** 2% vit. A, 1% iron

PAN SIZE COUNTS

As easy as bar cookies are to make, you can't be too casual about the pan in which they bake if you want them to turn out just right. Here are a couple of alternatives:

■ If you don't have a 15×10×1-inch pan, use two 9×9×2-inch baking pans.

■ If you don't have a 13×9×2-inch pan, use two 8×8×2-inch baking pans.

In both substitutions, use the same oven temperature but check the bars for doneness 5 minutes before the minimum baking time given in the recipe is reached.

LAYERED CHOCOLATE-PEANUT BARS

Prep: 30 minutes   **Bake:** 32 minutes
Makes: 42 bars   **Oven:** 350°F

A peanut-buttery crust, a cheesecake-like center, and a chocolate topping add up to the promise of a kid-pleasing favorite.

   ⅓ **cup butter**
   ¼ **cup peanut butter**
   ¾ **cup packed brown sugar**
   1¼ **cups all-purpose flour**
   1 **8-ounce package cream cheese, softened**
   ¼ **cup honey**
   2 **tablespoons all-purpose flour**
   2 **tablespoons brown sugar**
   2 **eggs**
   1½ **cups finely chopped peanuts**
   1 **6-ounce package (1 cup) semisweet chocolate pieces**

1 **In a medium mixing bowl beat** the butter and peanut butter with an electric mixer on medium to high speed for 30 seconds. Add the ¾ cup brown sugar and beat until combined. Add the 1¼ cups flour and beat until combined. Press mixture into the bottom of an ungreased 13×9×2-inch baking pan. Bake in a 350°F oven about 15 minutes or until lightly browned.

2 **Meanwhile, in a medium mixing bowl** combine cream cheese, honey, the 2 tablespoons flour, and the 2 tablespoons brown sugar. Beat on medium speed until smooth. Add eggs and beat on low speed just until combined. Stir in 1 cup of the peanuts. Pour over partially baked crust. Bake in the 350°F oven about 15 minutes more or until set.

3 **Sprinkle the baked layers** evenly with chocolate pieces. Bake in the 350°F oven about 2 minutes more or until chocolate is softened. Remove from oven; transfer to wire rack. Spread softened chocolate evenly over the baked layers. Sprinkle with remaining peanuts. Cool completely. Cut into bars or squares. Store, covered, in the refrigerator.

Nutrition Facts per bar: 132 cal., 8 g total fat
(3 g sat. fat), 18 mg chol., 42 mg sodium, 12 g carbo.,
1 g fiber, 3 g pro. **Daily Values:** 4% vit. A, 1% calcium,
3% iron

BLONDIES *EASY*

Prep: 25 minutes   Bake: 25 minutes
Makes: 36 bars   Oven: 350°F

A saucepan and a spoon are all you need to mix up these butterscotch bars.

    2 cups packed brown sugar
    ⅔ cup butter
    2 eggs
    2 teaspoons vanilla
    2 cups all-purpose flour
    1 teaspoon baking powder
    ¼ teaspoon baking soda
    1 6-ounce package (1 cup) semisweet
        chocolate pieces
    1 cup chopped nuts

1 **Grease a** 13×9×2-inch baking pan; set aside. In a medium saucepan heat brown sugar and butter over medium heat until sugar dissolves, stirring constantly. Cool slightly. Using a wooden spoon, stir in eggs, one at a time, and vanilla. Stir in flour, baking powder, and baking soda. Spread batter in the prepared pan. Sprinkle with chocolate and nuts.

2 **Bake in a 350°F oven** for 25 to 30 minutes or until done. Cool slightly in pan on a wire rack. Cut into bars while warm; cool completely in pan.

Nutrition Facts per bar: 138 cal., 7 g total fat (2 g sat. fat), 21 mg chol., 61 mg sodium, 18 g carbo., 0 g fiber, 2 g pro. **Daily Values:** 3% vit. A, 2% calcium, 5% iron

---

THE SOFT TOUCH

Most recipes that call for cream cheese call for it to be softened. There are two ways to do this.

If you have the time, simply let it stand at room temperature for about 30 minutes. If not, place 3 ounces of cream cheese in a microwave-safe container. Microwave, uncovered, on 100% power (high) for 15 to 30 seconds (30 to 60 seconds for 8 ounces) or until the cheese is softened.

OATMEAL-CARAMEL BARS

Prep: 25 minutes   Bake: 22 minutes
Makes: 60 bars   Oven: 350°F

Enlist help from the kids to unwrap the caramels needed to make the topping (just be sure enough candies go in the bowl).

    1 cup butter
    2 cups packed brown sugar
    2 eggs
    2 teaspoons vanilla
    1 teaspoon baking soda
    2½ cups all-purpose flour
    3 cups quick-cooking rolled oats
    1 cup semisweet chocolate pieces
    ½ cup chopped walnuts or pecans
    30 vanilla caramels (8 ounces)
    3 tablespoons milk

1 **In a large mixing bowl beat** butter with an electric mixer on medium to high speed for 30 seconds. Add the brown sugar. Beat until well combined. Add eggs, vanilla, and baking soda. Beat mixture until combined. Beat or stir in the flour. Stir in the oats.

2 **Press two-thirds** (about 3⅓ cups) of the rolled oats mixture into the bottom of an ungreased 15×10×1-inch baking pan. Sprinkle with chocolate pieces and nuts.

3 **In a medium saucepan combine** caramels and milk. Cook over low heat until caramels are melted. Drizzle caramel mixture over chocolate and nuts. Drop remaining one-third of the rolled-oat mixture by teaspoons over the top.

4 **Bake in a 350°F oven** for 22 to 25 minutes or until top is light brown. Cool in pan on a wire rack. Cut into bars.

Nutrition Facts per bar: 120 cal., 5 g total fat (2 g sat. fat), 15 mg chol., 66 mg sodium, 17 g carbo., 1 g fiber, 2 g pro. **Daily Values:** 3% vit. A, 1% calcium, 4% iron

MOCHA CHEESECAKE DREAMS

Prep: 30 minutes   **Bake:** 35 minutes
Makes: 32 bars   **Oven:** 350°F

1¼ **cups all-purpose flour**
 1 **cup sifted powdered sugar**
 ½ **cup unsweetened cocoa powder**
 ¼ **teaspoon baking soda**
 ¾ **cup butter**
 1 **tablespoon instant coffee crystals**
 1 **tablespoon hot water**
 1 **8-ounce package cream cheese, softened**
 1 **14-ounce can (1¼ cups) sweetened condensed milk**
 2 **eggs**
   Chocolate-flavored syrup (optional)

1 **For crust,** in a large bowl stir together flour, powdered sugar, cocoa powder, and baking soda. Using a pastry blender or fork, cut in butter until crumbly; press flour mixture into the bottom of an ungreased 13×9×2-inch baking pan. Bake in a 350°F oven for 15 minutes.

2 **Meanwhile, dissolve** instant coffee crystals in hot water. Set aside. In a large mixing bowl beat cream cheese with an electric mixer until fluffy. Gradually beat in the sweetened condensed milk. Add the coffee mixture and eggs; beat until combined. Pour over the hot baked crust.

3 **Bake in the 350°F oven** for 20 minutes or until set. Cool in pan on a wire rack. Cut into bars. Store, covered, in the refrigerator. If desired, drizzle bars with chocolate-flavored syrup.

Nutrition Facts per bar: 143 cal., 8 g total fat (7 g sat. fat), 49 mg chol., 94 mg sodium, 14 g carbo., 0 g fiber, 3 g pro. **Daily Values:** 8% vit. A, 4% calcium, 3% iron

Mocha Cheesecake Dreams: These mocha-flavored treats are easy-to-make bar cookies masquerading as cheesecake. Drizzle extra chocolate on your serving plates for a sophisticated presentation.

Apricot-Cardamom Bars: Applesauce fills in for some of the fat in these bars to make them moist and flavorful.

APRICOT-CARDAMOM BARS

LOW-FAT

Prep: 25 minutes **Bake:** 25 minutes
Cool: 2 hours **Makes:** 24 bars
Oven: 350°F

　1　**cup all-purpose flour**
　½　**teaspoon baking powder**
　¼　**teaspoon baking soda**
　¼　**teaspoon ground cardamom or**
　　　　⅛ teaspoon ground cloves
　1　**slightly beaten egg**
　½　**cup packed brown sugar**
　½　**cup apricot nectar or orange juice**
　¼　**cup unsweetened applesauce**
　2　**tablespoons cooking oil**
　½　**cup finely snipped dried apricots**
　1　**recipe Apricot Icing**

1 **In a medium bowl stir** together flour, baking powder, soda, and cardamom; set aside. In another bowl stir together egg, brown sugar, apricot nectar, applesauce, and oil until combined. Add to flour mixture; stir until combined. Stir in apricots.

2 **Spread batter** in an ungreased 11×7×1½-inch baking pan. Bake in a 350°F oven about 25 minutes or until a wooden toothpick inserted near the center comes out clean. Cool in pan on a wire rack. Drizzle with Apricot Icing. Cut into bars.

Apricot Icing: Stir together ½ cup sifted powdered sugar and enough apricot nectar (2 to 3 teaspoons) to make icing that is easy to drizzle.

Nutrition Facts per bar: 63 cal., 1 g total fat
(0 g sat. fat), 9 mg chol., 25 mg sodium, 12 g carbo.,
0 g fiber, 1 g pro. **Daily Values:** 3% vit. A, 3% vit. C,
1% calcium, 3% iron

QUICK CLEANUP

Lining your baking pan with foil not only makes it easier to get the bars or brownies out of the pan when they have finished baking, it makes it easier to clean up, too.

　Simply line the pan with foil, slightly extending the foil over the edges of the pan. If the recipe calls for a greased pan, grease the foil instead. Spread the cookie dough evenly in the pan. Bake and cool the bars in the pan; then pull the foil edges down to the counter and lift the bars out. Cut into whatever shapes you wish (see tip, page 161).

MIXED NUT BARS

Prep: 20 minutes   **Bake:** 25 minutes
Makes: 20 bars   **Oven:** 350°F

Though there's not a trace of chocolate in these nutty bars, they have a rich, fudgy texture.

  1 **cup packed brown sugar**
⅓ **cup butter**
  1 **beaten egg**
½ **teaspoon vanilla**
  1 **cup all-purpose flour**
½ **teaspoon baking powder**
  1 **cup mixed nuts, Brazil nuts, or**
     cashews, coarsely chopped

1 Grease an 8×8×2-inch baking pan; set aside. In a medium saucepan heat brown sugar and butter over medium heat until sugar dissolves, stirring constantly. Remove from heat. Cool slightly.

2 Stir in egg and vanilla. Stir in flour and baking powder just until combined. Stir in nuts. Spread batter in the prepared pan.

3 Bake in a 350°F oven about 25 minutes or until a wooden toothpick inserted near center comes out clean. Cool slightly in pan on a wire rack. Cut into bars while warm; cool completely in pan.

Nutrition Facts per bar: 138 cal., 7 g total fat (1 g sat. fat), 15 mg chol., 45 mg sodium, 17 g carbo., 1 g fiber, 2 g pro. **Daily Values:** 3% vit. A, 2% calcium, 5% iron

---

BEAUTIFUL BARS

Besides their great taste, much of the beauty of bar cookies is their ease: just stir, bake, and eat. If you'd like to dress them up a bit, try one of these simple garnishes:

- For unfrosted bars, lay waxed-paper strips across top in a pattern. Sprinkle with a mixture of powdered sugar and a spice that's called for in the recipe.
- For frosted bars, sprinkle with grated chocolate or chocolate curls, miniature chocolate chips, chopped nuts, or dried or candied fruit.

CARROT-PUMPKIN BARS WITH ORANGE ICING

Prep: 40 minutes   **Bake:** 20 minutes
Cool: 2 hours   **Makes:** 36 bars   **Oven:** 350°F

  2 **cups all-purpose flour**
  2 **teaspoons baking powder**
  1 **teaspoon finely shredded orange**
     peel
½ **teaspoon baking soda**
¼ **teaspoon salt**
  3 **beaten eggs**
1½ **cups packed brown sugar**
  1 **cup canned pumpkin**
⅔ **cup cooking oil**
¼ **cup milk**
  1 **teaspoon vanilla**
  1 **cup finely shredded carrots**
  1 **cup chopped walnuts**
  1 **recipe Orange Icing**
     Walnut halves (optional)

1 Grease a 15×10×1-inch baking pan; set aside. In a large bowl stir together flour, baking powder, orange peel, baking soda, and salt. Set mixture aside.

2 In a medium bowl combine eggs and brown sugar. Stir in pumpkin, cooking oil, milk, and vanilla. Stir in carrots and walnuts. Add egg mixture to flour mixture, stirring with a wooden spoon until combined. Spread batter in the prepared pan.

3 Bake in a 350°F oven for 20 to 25 minutes or until a wooden toothpick inserted near the center comes out clean. Cool in pan on a wire rack. Spread with Orange Icing and cut into triangles or squares. If desired, garnish each with a walnut half. Store, covered, in the refrigerator.

Orange Icing: In a mixing bowl combine 1½ cups sifted powdered sugar and enough orange liqueur or orange juice (1 to 2 tablespoons) to make an icing that is easy to drizzle.

Nutrition Facts per bar: 137 cal., 7 g total fat (1 g sat. fat), 18 mg chol., 63 mg sodium, 18 g carbo., 1 g fiber, 2 g pro. **Daily Values:** 24% vit. A, 1% vit. C, 3% calcium, 4% iron

Carrot-Pumpkin Bars with Orange Icing: Chunky walnut halves make an attractive addition atop these autumnal treats.

BRANDIED CRANBERRY-APRICOT BARS

BEST-LOVED

Prep: 35 minutes **Bake:** 1 hour
Cool: 2 hours **Makes:** 16 bars **Oven:** 350°F

Relatively new to our archives, these rich, cakelike bars were the first Better Homes and Gardens® *Prize-Tested Recipe Grand Prize Winner.*

⅓ **cup golden raisins**
⅓ **cup dark raisins**
⅓ **cup dried cranberries**
⅓ **cup snipped dried apricots**
½ **cup brandy or water**
1 **cup all-purpose flour**
⅓ **cup packed brown sugar**
½ **cup butter**
2 **eggs**
1 **cup packed brown sugar**
½ **cup all-purpose flour**
1 **teaspoon vanilla**
⅓ **cup chopped pecans**
  Powdered sugar

1 **In a saucepan** combine the golden raisins, dark raisins, dried cranberries, apricots, and brandy. Bring to boiling. Remove from heat. Let stand for 20 minutes; drain.

2 **In a medium bowl** stir together the 1 cup flour and ⅓ cup brown sugar. Using a pastry blender, cut in butter until mixture resembles coarse crumbs. Press mixture into the bottom of an ungreased 8×8×2-inch baking pan. Bake in a 350°F oven about 20 minutes or until golden.

3 **Meanwhile, in a medium mixing bowl** beat the eggs with an electric mixer on low speed for 4 minutes. Stir in 1 cup brown sugar, the ½ cup flour, and the vanilla. Stir in the drained fruit and pecans. Pour fruit mixture over crust; spread evenly.

4 **Bake in the 350°F oven** about 40 minutes more or until a toothpick inserted near center comes out clean, covering with foil the last 10 minutes to prevent overbrowning. Cool in pan on a wire rack. Sprinkle powdered sugar over top. Cut into bars.

Nutrition Facts per bar: 221 cal., 8 g total fat (6 g sat. fat), 57 mg chol., 72 mg sodium, 32 g carbo., 1 g fiber, 2 g pro. **Daily Values:** 8% vit. A, 2% calcium, 8% iron

Brandied Cranberry-Apricot Bars: These perfect-for-the-holidays bars prove easy and elegant are possible together.

PIÑA COLADA SQUARES

Prep: 20 minutes **Bake:** 30 minutes
Makes: 48 bars **Oven:** 350°F

Pineapple ice-cream topping makes these island-inspired bar cookies a breeze to bake.

2 **cups all-purpose flour**
2 **cups quick-cooking rolled oats**
1⅓ **cups packed brown sugar**
¼ **teaspoon baking soda**
1 **cup butter**
1 **cup pineapple ice-cream topping**
1 **teaspoon rum extract**
1 **cup coconut**

1 **In a large bowl** combine the flour, oats, brown sugar, and baking soda. Using a pastry blender, cut in butter until mixture resembles coarse crumbs. Reserve 1 cup of the crumb mixture for topping. Press the remaining mixture into the bottom of an ungreased 13×9×2-inch baking pan.

2 **For filling,** in a small bowl combine pineapple topping and rum extract. Spread pineapple mixture evenly over the crust.

3 **For topping,** stir coconut into reserved crumb mixture. Sprinkle topping evenly over the pineapple-rum filling. Bake in a 350°F oven about 30 minutes or until golden. Cool. Cut into bars.

Nutrition Facts per bar: 108 cal., 5 g total fat (3 g sat. fat), 10 mg chol., 52 mg sodium, 16 g carbo., 1 g fiber, 1 g pro. **Daily Values:** 3% vit. A, 6% vit. C, 0% calcium. 3% iron

spectacular
desserts

Mini Molten Chocolate Cakes, recipe page 177

SPECTACULAR DESSERTS

BRANDIED PEACH-PRALINE BASKETS

EASY

Prep: 40 minutes   **Bake:** 8 minutes per batch
Makes: 12 servings   **Oven:** 350°F

½ **cup butter**
1 **cup sugar**
¼ **cup dark-colored corn syrup**
1⅓ **cups toasted, finely chopped**
     pecans (see tip, page 181)
¼ **cup all-purpose flour**
     Melted chocolate (optional)
1½ **quarts butter pecan or other**
     desired ice cream or sorbet
1 **recipe Brandied Peach Sauce**
     Chocolate Leaves and/or gold
     paper leaves (optional)

1 **Line a large** cookie sheet with heavy foil; grease foil. Grease outside bottoms and sides of 4 inverted 6-ounce custard cups. Set sheet and cups aside.

2 **Melt butter** in a medium saucepan; remove from heat. Stir in sugar and corn syrup. Stir in nuts and flour. For each basket, drop 2 tablespoons of the batter 7 inches apart on the prepared cookie sheet; spread batter to 3-inch circles. (Bake only 2 cookies at a time.)

3 **Bake in a 350°F oven** 8 to 10 minutes or until a deep golden brown. Cool on cookie sheet 2 minutes or just until cookies are firm enough to hold their shape. Quickly remove cookies from sheet and place each cookie over a prepared custard cup. Using a wooden spoon, gently fold edges down to form ruffles or pleats. (If cookies harden before shaping, reheat them in oven for 1 minute.) Cool completely. Remove baskets from custard cups. Repeat with remaining batter, wiping excess fat from cookie sheet between batches. Tightly cover and store in a cool, dry place up to 1 week or in freezer up to 6 months.

4 **To serve,** if desired, brush basket edges with melted chocolate. Scoop ice cream into baskets. Top with warm Brandied Peach Sauce. If desired, garnish with Chocolate Leaves and/or gold paper leaves.

Brandied Peach Sauce: In small saucepan combine ½ cup packed brown sugar and 1 tablespoon cornstarch. Add ½ cup whipping cream and 2 teaspoons butter. Cook and stir over medium heat until bubbly. Add 1 cup thinly sliced peaches, ¼ cup toasted chopped pecans, and 1 tablespoon brandy. Cook and stir until bubbly. Cool slightly. Makes 1¾ cups.

Nutrition Facts per serving: 467 cal., 29 g total fat (13 g sat. fat), 65 mg chol., 148 mg sodium, 52 g carbo., 1 g fiber, 4 g pro. **Daily Values:** 20% vit. A, 3% vit. C, 9% calcium, 6% iron

Chocolate Leaves: With a clean, small paintbrush, brush 1 or 2 coats of melted chocolate on the underside of nontoxic leaves such as mint, rose, or lemon. Wipe away any chocolate from top side of leaf. Place the leaves, chocolate side up, on waxed-paper-lined baking sheet until dry. Before using, peel the leaf away from the chocolate.

Brandied Peach-Praline Baskets: Present your guests with an edible basket of goodies as a final course. You can make the nutty, caramelized cups up to six months in advance, freezing until needed. To serve, thaw and fill.

Olive Oil Génoise in Strawberry Champagne Sauce: This airy sponge cake surrounded by a champagne-laced fruit sauce is the definition of simple elegance. The cake is made especially delicate thanks to olive oil.

OLIVE OIL GÉNOISE IN STRAWBERRY CHAMPAGNE SAUCE

Prep: 40 minutes Bake: 30 minutes
Makes: 10 to 12 servings Oven: 350°F

> 6 **eggs**
>   **Granulated sugar**
>   **Cake flour or all-purpose flour**
> ³⁄₄ **cup granulated sugar**
> ¹⁄₃ **cup extra-light or pure olive oil**
>   **(not extra-virgin olive oil)**
> 1¹⁄₃ **cups sifted cake flour or 1¹⁄₄ cups**
>   **sifted all-purpose flour**
>   **Powdered sugar**
> 1 **recipe Strawberry Champagne**
>   **Sauce**
>   **Fresh strawberries (optional)**
>   **Fresh mint (optional)**

1 **Let eggs stand** at room temperature for 30 minutes. Grease bottom and sides of a 9-inch springform pan. Line bottom with parchment paper; grease paper. Sprinkle bottom and sides with granulated sugar; dust with flour. Set pan aside.

2 **In a large mixing bowl combine** eggs and the ³⁄₄ cup granulated sugar. Beat with an electric mixer on high speed for 15 minutes. With mixer running, gradually add oil in a thin, steady stream (this will take 1¹⁄₂ to 2 minutes). Turn off mixer immediately after all of the oil has been added.

3 **Sift flour** over egg mixture; fold until no lumps remain. Pour into the prepared pan; place on a baking sheet.

4 **Bake in a 350°F oven** 30 to 35 minutes or until top springs back when touched. Cool cake completely in the pan on a wire rack.

5 **To assemble,** remove cake from pan; remove and discard parchment paper. Sift powdered sugar atop cake. Cut cake into wedges. Place wedges on plates or in shallow bowls. If desired, sprinkle rims with powdered sugar. Pour Strawberry Champagne Sauce around cake wedges. If desired, garnish with strawberries and mint.

Strawberry Champagne Sauce: In a blender container combine 4 cups strawberries, ²⁄₃ cup champagne or sparkling white wine, and 3 tablespoons sugar. Cover and blend until smooth. (Or, for food processor, combine half of the ingredients at a time; cover and process until smooth.) Cover and chill until needed, up to 24 hours. Makes about 3¹⁄₂ cups.

Nutrition Facts per serving: 273 cal., 11 g total fat (2 g sat. fat), 128 mg chol., 39 mg sodium, 38 g carbo., 1 g fiber, 5 g pro. **Daily Values:** 5% vit. A, 56% vit. C, 2% calcium, 11% iron

MINI MOLTEN CHOCOLATE CAKES

EASY

Prep: 20 minutes Bake: 12 minutes
Makes: 6 servings Oven: 400°F

American restaurants made these rich cakes that ooze with chocolate popular; you'll see how easy they are (pictured on page 173).

  ¾ **cup butter**
  6 **ounces semisweet chocolate,**
      chopped
    Granulated sugar
  3 **eggs**
  3 **egg yolks**
  ⅓ **cup sifted powdered sugar**
  1½ **teaspoons vanilla**
  ¼ **cup all-purpose flour**
  2 **tablespoons unsweetened cocoa**
      powder
  1 **recipe Mocha Cream**
    Chocolate spiral garnishes
      (optional) (see tip, page 185)
    Fresh raspberries (optional)

1 In heavy saucepan combine butter and chopped chocolate; melt over low heat, stirring constantly. Remove from heat; cool. Grease six 1-cup soufflé dishes or 6-ounce custard cups. Coat with granulated sugar. Place in shallow baking pan; set aside.

2 Beat eggs, egg yolks, powdered sugar, and vanilla with an electric mixer on high speed about 5 minutes or until thick and pale yellow. Beat in chocolate mixture on medium speed. Sift flour and cocoa over chocolate mixture; beat on low speed just until blended. Spoon into prepared dishes.

3 Bake in a 400°F oven 12 to 14 minutes or until cakes rise slightly and feel firm at edges and softer in the center when pressed gently. Cool in dishes 5 minutes. Invert with pot holders onto plates. Cool 15 minutes before serving with Mocha Cream. If desired, sprinkle with additional sifted powdered sugar and top with spiral garnishes and raspberries.

Mocha Cream: In a cup stir 1 teaspoon instant espresso powder or 2 teaspoons instant coffee crystals and 1 teaspoon hot water until dissolved. In chilled mixing bowl combine ½ cup cold whipping cream, 2 tablespoons powdered sugar, 1 teaspoon unsweetened cocoa powder, ½ teaspoon vanilla, and espresso mixture. Beat with chilled beaters of electric mixer on medium-high speed until soft peaks form.

Nutrition Facts per serving: 532 cal., 45 g total fat (26 g sat. fat), 302 mg chol., 276 mg sodium, 31 g carbo., 2 g fiber, 8 g pro. **Daily Values:** 50% vit. A, 6% calcium, 14% iron

CHOCOLATE CHOICES

Chocolate lovers take note of these common chocolates types:

■ Unsweetened chocolate is pure chocolate and cocoa butter (no sugar added). Often called baking or bitter chocolate, it is almost used exclusively for baking and cooking.

■ Unsweetened cocoa powder is pure chocolate with most of the cocoa butter removed. It is most often used in baking. Those labeled Dutch-process or European-style have been treated to neutralize natural acids, giving the cocoa powder a mellow flavor and darker, redder color.

■ Semisweet chocolate is pure chocolate with added cocoa butter and sugar. Although it is sometimes referred to as bittersweet chocolate, the latter is usually darker and less sweet than that labeled semisweet. Some European bittersweet chocolates are labeled dark chocolate. Use dark, semisweet, and bittersweet chocolate interchangeably in recipes.

■ Milk chocolate is pure chocolate with added cocoa butter, sugar, and milk or cream. Milk chocolate has a creamier texture, lighter color, and milder flavor than semisweet chocolate.

■ White baking bars or pieces and vanilla-flavored candy coatings often are referred to as white chocolate. This is a misnomer. Because none of these products contains pure chocolate (although some contain cocoa butter), legally they can't be labeled as chocolate in the United States.

SACHER TORTE

Prep: 50 minutes   Stand: 30 minutes
Bake: 35 minutes   Makes: 12 servings
Oven: 350°F

    6 egg whites
    **5 ounces semisweet or bittersweet
        chocolate, chopped**
    ½ cup butter
    6 egg yolks
  1½ teaspoons vanilla
    ½ cup sugar
    ¾ cup all-purpose flour
    ⅔ cup apricot preserves
    1 recipe Chocolate Glaze
        Sweetened whipped cream (optional)
        Apricot Roses (optional)

1 **In a very large mixing bowl allow** egg whites to stand at room temperature 30 minutes. Grease and lightly flour a 9-inch springform pan. Set aside.

2 **In a heavy medium saucepan** melt chocolate and butter; cool. Stir egg yolks and vanilla into the cooled chocolate mixture. Set mixture aside.

3 **Beat egg whites** with an electric mixer on medium to high speed until soft peaks form (tips curl). Gradually add the sugar, about 1 tablespoon at a time, beating about 4 minutes or until stiff peaks form (tips stand straight).

To split cake, mark the halfway point around the cake's side with toothpicks. Use a long, sharp or serrated knife to slice cake with sawing motion. Lift off top with wide spatula.

Place cake on rack over waxed paper to catch glaze drips. Carefully pour cooled glaze over cake and immediately spread to completely cover top and sides.

4 **Fold about 1 cup** of the egg white mixture into chocolate mixture. Fold mixture into remaining egg white mixture. Sift about one-third of the flour over the chocolate-egg mixture; gently fold in. Repeat sifting and folding in one-third of the flour mixture at a time. Spread batter into prepared pan.

5 **Bake in a 350°F oven** 35 to 40 minutes or until a wooden toothpick inserted near the center of the cake comes out clean. Completely cool cake in pan on a wire rack. Remove sides of springform pan. Brush crumbs from edges of cake. (Top crust will be slightly flaky.) Remove bottom of springform pan from cake.

6 **In a small saucepan heat** preserves until melted. Press preserves through a sieve; cool slightly. To assemble, cut cake horizontally into 2 even layers (see top photo, lower left). Set top layer aside. Spread preserves over bottom layer. Top with second cake layer. Spoon Chocolate Glaze over torte, spreading to glaze top and sides completely (see bottom photo, lower left). Let torte stand at room temperature at least 1 hour before serving.* If desired, serve with whipped cream and garnish with Apricot Roses.

*Note: If desired, after Chocolate Glaze is dry, decorate with piped Powdered Sugar Icing (see recipe, page 132) made to piping consistency. For light brown icing, stir in chocolate syrup until desired shade is achieved. Allow piping to dry before serving.

Chocolate Glaze: In a saucepan heat 4 ounces semisweet chocolate, cut up, and 2 tablespoons butter over low heat just until melted, stirring occasionally; set aside. In a heavy small saucepan bring ½ cup whipping cream and 2 teaspoons light-colored corn syrup to a gentle boil. Reduce heat and simmer for 2 minutes. Remove from heat. Stir in chocolate mixture. Cool to room temperature before using.

Nutrition Facts per serving: 356 cal., 23 g total fat
(13 g sat. fat), 146 mg chol., 135 mg sodium,
37 g carbo., 2 g fiber, 6 g pro. **Daily Values:**
29% vit. A, 34% calcium, 10% iron

Apricot Roses: Roll dried apricot halves between waxed paper to ⅛-inch-thick circles. Cut in half. For center of each rose, roll 1 half-circle into a cone shape. For petals, press on as many half-circles around center as desired, curving rounded edges outward and overlapping petals. Trim bottom. Hold together with half a wooden toothpick.

Sacher Torte: Do as some Viennese pastry chefs do: Pipe the word "Sacher" on the torte to show this is the real thing—a celebrated torte of chocolate layers filled with apricot jam and generously covered with a chocolate glaze.

CHOCOLATE-HAZELNUT COOKIE TORTE

BEST-LOVED

Prep: 40 minutes   Bake: 20 minutes
Chill: 2 hours   Makes: 12 servings
Oven: 375°F

You can bake the large cookies and wedges up to a month ahead of time and freeze. Layer the cooled cookies, with waxed paper between each, in a freezer container. Thaw before using. Or, store at room temperature for up to two days.

> 2 cups shelled whole hazelnuts or almonds, toasted (see tip, page 181)
> ⅔ cup sugar
> 1 cup all-purpose flour
> ¾ cup butter, cut in pieces
> ½ teaspoon salt
> 1 egg yolk
>   Sugar
> 1 recipe Chocolate Mousse (see recipe, page 181)
> 1 cup whipping cream
> 1 tablespoon sugar
> 1 teaspoon vanilla
> 2 cups sliced strawberries
> 2 to 3 ounces semisweet chocolate, chopped
> 1 teaspoon shortening
>   Whole strawberries (optional)

1 **Chill two medium mixing bowls** and the beaters of an electric mixer. Place toasted nuts and the ⅔ cup sugar in a food processor bowl (to use a blender, see note on page 181). Cover and process until nuts are finely ground but not oily. Add flour, butter, and salt. Process until combined. Add egg yolk. Process until combined. Divide dough into 4 equal balls. Cover and chill 2 balls until needed.

Brush off any loose cookie crumbs before dipping the edges of the cookie wedge into the warm chocolate.

2 **Grease and lightly flour** 2 baking sheets; place each sheet on a towel to prevent slipping while rolling out dough. On each baking sheet, draw an 8-inch circle with your finger using an 8-inch cake pan as a guide. On 1 of the prepared baking sheets, roll out 1 ball of dough to fit the circle, trimming edges of dough with a knife to make an even circle. Repeat with another ball of dough on the second baking sheet. Score 1 round into wedges, keeping circle intact. Sprinkle both rounds with sugar.

3 **Bake the dough rounds** in a 375°F oven for 10 to 12 minutes or until browned around the edges. Cool the cookies on baking sheets for 5 minutes. Cut the warm, scored cookie into wedges. Carefully transfer cookie and wedges to a wire rack; cool completely. Allow baking sheets to cool completely. Grease and flour baking sheets again. Repeat shaping and baking the remaining 2 balls of dough, except do not score either round.

4 **Use 1 of the chilled mixing bowls** to prepare Chocolate Mousse; chill (for no more than 2 hours). In another chilled mixing bowl, beat whipping cream, the 1 tablespoon sugar, and vanilla on medium speed just until stiff peaks form. Spoon whipped cream into a pastry bag fitted with a large star tip.

5 **To assemble torte,** place a whole cookie on a serving platter. Spread with half of the Chocolate Mousse and top with half of the sliced strawberries. Place another whole cookie atop. Repeat with remaining Chocolate Mousse and sliced strawberries. Top with remaining whole cookie.

6 **Pipe large dollops** of the sweetened whipped cream on top torte, covering the whole top. Cover and chill about 2 hours to soften the cookies.

7 **Place the chocolate** (use the 3 ounces if also dipping berries) and shortening in a heavy small saucepan over low heat, stirring constantly until partially melted. Immediately remove from the heat and stir until smooth. Dip a long side of each cookie wedge into melted chocolate mixture (see photo, left). Set aside on waxed paper until chocolate is set. If desired, dip whole strawberries in remaining melted chocolate. (If your saucepan is not small, you may need additional chocolate to dip.)

8 **Just before serving,** arrange chocolate-dipped cookie wedges atop the sweetened whipped cream on the torte, placing chocolate-dipped edges

Chocolate-Hazelnut Cookie Torte: With a silky chocolate mousse and piped whipped cream, giant shortbread-style cookies go uptown in this showy layered torte. Chocolate-dipped berries come along for the ride.

up and tilting slightly in a pinwheel pattern. Pipe a large star of whipped cream in the center where the cookie wedges meet. If using chocolate-dipped strawberries, place between wedges and on top of the whipped cream star in the center. Serve immediately, cutting into wedges with a serrated knife.

Note: To use a blender instead of a food processor, place half of the nuts in a blender container. Cover and blend until finely ground but not oily. Transfer nuts to a mixing bowl; repeat with remaining nuts. In a mixing bowl beat butter and the ⅔ cup sugar until combined. Beat in egg yolk. Beat in ground nuts and half of the flour. Beat or stir in remaining flour. Continue as directed.

Chocolate Mousse: In a chilled mixing bowl combine ¼ cup sugar and 3 tablespoons unsweetened cocoa powder. Add 1½ cups whipping cream. Beat

with the chilled beaters of an electric mixer on medium speed just until stiff peaks form. Chill until needed. Makes 3 cups.

Nutrition Facts per serving: 536 cal., 45 g total fat (21 g sat. fat), 117 mg chol., 226 mg sodium, 34 g carbo., 3 g fiber, 6 g pro. **Daily Values:** 35% vit. A, 24% vit. C, 7% calcium, 10% iron

TOASTING NUTS, SEEDS, AND COCONUT

Toasting heightens the flavor of nuts, seeds, and coconut. To toast, spread the nuts, seeds, or coconut in a single layer in a shallow baking pan. Bake in a 350°F oven for 5 to 10 minutes or until light golden brown, watching carefully and stirring once or twice to brown evenly.

Battenberg Cake: This was a favorite of Queen Victoria's daughter, Beatrice, whose married name was Battenberg (Anglicized to Mountbatten). Fortunately, you don't need a royal baking staff to enjoy this showpiece—it starts with pound cake mix and finishes with purchased marzipan (see tip, page 183).

BATTENBERG CAKE

Prep: 1 ¼ hours   Bake: according to package
Makes: 8 servings   Oven: according to package

  2 **16-ounce packages pound
      cake mix
     Red paste food coloring**
  2 **tablespoons orange juice**
 ½ **cup seedless red raspberry jam**
  2 **tablespoons light-colored corn
     syrup**
  2 **7-ounce packages marzipan
     Sifted powdered sugar
     Sugared Raspberries and Mint
      Leaves (optional)
      (see page 183)**

1 Grease and flour two 9×5×3-inch loaf pans; set aside. Prepare pound cake mixes according to package directions (make each package separately). Spread batter from 1 mix into 1 of the prepared pans. Tint second batter pink with food coloring; spread into the second pan. Bake cakes according to package directions or until tops spring back when lightly touched. Cool in pans on a rack 10 minutes; remove from pans; cool completely.

2 To assemble, trim crusts from sides, ends, and tops of cakes to make evenly shaped loaves. Trim loaves so each measures 7½×4×1½ inches. Cut the plain loaf into 4 logs measuring 7½×1×¾ inches. Cut pink loaf into 5 logs measuring 7½×1×¾ inches (see top photo, page 183). You will have some cake leftover from each loaf; use for another dessert.

3 Drizzle the 9 logs with orange juice; set aside. In a small saucepan combine the raspberry jam and corn syrup; heat and stir over low heat until jam is melted and mixture is smooth; set aside.

4 **In a bowl knead marzipan** with your hands to soften. Sprinkle both sides of marzipan with powdered sugar; roll between 2 sheets of waxed paper to a 12×8-inch rectangle. (If desired, roll marzipan to a 15×8-inch rectangle; trim 3 inches from a short side and use to cut decorative shapes for garnishes.) Brush off excess sugar.

5 **Remove top sheet** of waxed paper. Brush jam mixture on 1 long side of a plain cake log. Place log crosswise in the center of marzipan sheet, jam side down. Brush jam mixture on the other 3 long sides of log. Brush a long side of 2 pink logs with jam mixture. Place, jam side down, on each side of the plain log. Brush exposed long sides with jam mixture. For second layer, place another pink log on top of first plain log. Brush exposed sides with jam. Place 2 plain logs on either side of the second pink log, brushing exposed sides with jam. Repeat layering with remaining cake logs, alternating colors to make checkerboard pattern. Press logs together.

6 **Bring marzipan** up over sides of cake (see bottom photo, right) so edges meet at top of cake, covering long sides but not ends. Crimp marzipan to seal; decorate top with marzipan trimmings as desired. Transfer to a serving plate. Using a serrated knife, trim cake and marzipan to make ends even.

7 **Let cake stand,** covered, for several hours or overnight before serving. If desired, garnish with Sugared Raspberries and Mint Leaves.

A perfectly shaped dessert starts with evenly sized cake logs. Slice the cake with long, even cuts and measure frequently to assure that your cuts are 1 inch apart.

Press the marzipan to the cake logs as you wrap it around the assembled logs.

Nutrition Facts per serving: 450 cal., 17 g total fat (7 g sat. fat), 66 mg chol.,136 mg sodium, 69 g carbo., 2 g fiber, 6 g pro. **Daily Values:** 10% vit. A, 3% vit. C, 11% calcium, 9% iron

Sugared Raspberries and Mint Leaves: Place 2 teaspoons dried egg whites (available in cake-decorating stores) and ¼ cup water in a 6-ounce custard cup; stir together with a wire whisk or fork. Place superfine or granulated sugar in a shallow dish. Using a pastry brush, brush egg white mixture onto berries and mint leaves; roll in sugar. Allow to dry on a wire rack. Arrange on top marzipan.

SPECTACULAR INGREDIENTS

The desserts in this chapter are made even more spectacular with these inventive basics from several origins:

- **Crème Anglaise:** A rich custard sauce served hot or cold over cake, fresh fruit, and other desserts.
- **Ganache:** Created in Paris around 1850, this exquisitely smooth chocolate icing is made of semisweet or bittersweet chocolate and whipping cream.
- **Marzipan:** A sweet, shapable mixture of almond paste, sugar, and sometimes beaten egg whites, marzipan often is rolled into sheets to cover whole cakes. It also can be tinted and formed into shapes, including miniature fruits or flowers. Marzipan is available in larger supermarkets.
- **Génoise:** Rising out of Genoa, Italy, and adapted by the French, this rich, light, and versatile cake is used in many famous desserts, including petit fours, cake rolls, and baked Alaska.
- **Phyllo:** In Greek, phyllo means "leaf," which is an apt description for these tissue-thin layers of pastry dough. Its most famous use is in baklava.
- **Ladyfingers:** These small, light sponge cakes are used in such desserts as charlottes and tiramisu.

Marjolaine: Bring a French pastry-shop favorite home. Extra-rich mocha ganache nestles between nutty cake layers. The frosting? A smooth, elegant buttercream.

MARJOLAINE

BEST-LOVED

Prep: 50 minutes
Bake: 40 minutes   Chill: 4 hours
Makes: 16 to 20 servings   Oven: 300°F

 6 egg whites
1¾ cups hazelnuts
 2 tablespoons all-purpose flour
 1 cup sugar
 1 recipe Mocha Ganache
 1 recipe Buttercream
  (see recipe, page 134)
  Chocolate lace wedges (optional)
  (see tip, page 185)
  Chocolate-dipped hazelnuts
  (optional)

1 **In a large mixing bowl let** egg whites stand at room temperature for 30 minutes. Meanwhile, grease three 8×1½-inch round baking pans. Line the bottoms with waxed paper; grease paper. Set pans aside.

2 **Place half** of the hazelnuts in a food processor/blender container. Cover; process until finely ground but not oily. Repeat with remaining nuts. In a bowl stir together 2 cups of the ground hazelnuts and the flour. Set nut mixture aside. Reserve remaining ground nuts for garnish.

3 **Beat egg whites** with electric mixer on medium to high speed until soft peaks form (tips curl). Gradually add sugar, 1 tablespoon at a time, beating on high speed about 8 minutes or until stiff peaks form (tips stand straight) and sugar is almost dissolved. By hand, fold hazelnut mixture into egg white mixture. Spread into prepared pans.

4 **Bake in a 300°F oven** for 40 to 45 minutes or until very lightly browned and just set when lightly touched. Cool in pans on racks 10 minutes. Carefully loosen sides from pans. Remove from pans. Peel off waxed paper; cool completely on racks.

5 **To assemble,** place a cake layer on a large serving plate. Spread half of the Mocha Ganache on top of cake layer to within ¼ inch of the edge. Chill in the freezer for 5 minutes. Spread ½ cup of the Buttercream on top of the Mocha Ganache. Top with second cake layer. Spread with remaining Mocha Ganache. Top with remaining cake layer. Spread remaining Buttercream on sides and top of cake.

6 **To garnish,** gently press remaining ground nuts into Buttercream two-thirds up sides of torte. Lightly cover; refrigerate 4 to 24 hours. To serve, let stand at room temperature for 10 minutes. If desired, garnish with chocolate lace wedges and whole nuts.

Mocha Ganache: In a heavy medium saucepan combine 8 ounces coarsely chopped semisweet chocolate, 1 cup whipping cream, 3 tablespoons unsalted butter, and 2 teaspoons instant espresso coffee powder or coffee crystals. Heat and stir over low heat until chocolate is melted. Remove from heat. Place the saucepan in a bowl of ice water. Using a rubber spatula, stir almost constantly for 6 to 8 minutes or until mixture thickens and is easy to spread. Remove the saucepan from the bowl of ice water. Makes about 2 cups.

Nutrition Facts per serving: 450 cal., 35 g total fat (16 g sat. fat), 111 mg chol., 154 mg sodium, 34 g carbo., 3 g fiber, 5 g pro. **Daily Values:** 27% vit. A, 4% calcium, 8% iron

LIME PHYLLO
NAPOLEONS *EASY*

Prep: 30 minutes   **Bake:** 8 minutes   **Chill:** 2 hours
Makes: 8 servings   **Oven:** 350°F

Lime curd makes it opulent; phyllo makes it easy.

  4 sheets frozen phyllo dough, thawed
  ¼ cup butter, melted
  ¼ cup sugar
  3 tablespoons toasted coconut
      (see tip, page 181)
  3 tablespoons toasted, finely chopped
      almonds (see tip, page 181)
  1 recipe Lime Curd
  1 recipe Tropical Fruit Salsa

1 Lightly grease 2 large baking sheets. Unfold phyllo dough. Remove a sheet, keeping remaining phyllo dough covered with plastic wrap or waxed paper and a damp towel. Place sheet on a large cutting board. Brush with some of the melted butter. Sprinkle with 1 tablespoon each sugar, coconut, and almonds. Repeat layers twice. Top with remaining phyllo sheet; brush with butter. Sprinkle with remaining sugar.

2 Cut sheets lengthwise into 4 equal strips and again crosswise into 4 pieces, making 16 rectangles. Transfer to prepared baking sheets.

3 Bake in a 350°F oven 8 to 10 minutes or until golden. Transfer rectangles to wire rack to cool.

4 Spread 1 to 2 tablespoons Lime Curd on 12 of the rectangles. Stack 3 of the 12 filled rectangles; top with 1 of the remaining unfilled rectangles. Repeat stacking to make 4 layered Napoleons; care-

fully cut each stack in half crosswise. Serve immediately with Tropical Fruit Salsa.

Lime Curd: Finely shred 1 teaspoon lime peel; set aside. In a medium saucepan stir together ¾ cup sugar and 1 tablespoon cornstarch. Add ¼ cup fresh lime juice and ¼ cup water. Cook and stir over medium heat until thickened and bubbly. Slowly stir about half of the lime mixture into 3 beaten egg yolks. Return all of the egg yolk mixture to saucepan. Bring to a gentle boil. Cook and stir 1 minute. Remove from heat and stir in 3 tablespoons butter until melted. Cover surface with plastic wrap. Chill until set and cold, about 2 hours. In a chilled mixing bowl beat ⅓ cup whipping cream with an electric mixer on medium speed until stiff peaks form. Gently fold whipped cream and the finely shredded lime peel into lime filling.

Tropical Fruit Salsa: Combine 2 cups tropical fruits such as kiwifruit, mango, pineapple, strawberries, and/or oranges cut into ¼-inch pieces; 2 tablespoons light-colored corn syrup; 1 tablespoon rum (if desired); and 1 tablespoon orange or lime juice.

Nutrition Facts per serving: 361 cal., 18 g total fat (6 g sat. fat), 106 mg chol., 154 mg sodium, 49 g carbo., 1 g fiber, 4 g pro. **Daily Values:** 38% vit. A, 37% vit. C, 3% calcium, 7% iron

---

CHOCOLATE TOUCHES

Here's how to make the chocolate garnishes in this chapter: Melt 6 ounces chocolate and 1 tablespoon shortening; cool the mixture slightly. Place the mixture in a plastic bag with a small hole snipped in a corner.

■ For the Marjolaine, page 184, pipe about 10 pie-wedge shapes on a waxed-paper-lined baking sheet; drizzle chocolate randomly within outlines.

■ For the Mini Molten Chocolate Cakes, page 177, pipe spiral shapes.

For both garnishes, let designs stand until dry; peel garnishes from waxed paper. For best results, do not chill the garnishes.

PASSION FRUIT TARTS

Prep: 1¼ hours   **Bake:** 30 minutes
Cool and Chill: 3½ to 6½ hours
Makes: 4 small tarts or 1 large tart   **Oven:** 350°F

Make the fruit puree by blending or processing the fruit pulp in a blender or food processor until smooth. Or, check food specialty shops for frozen puree.

  2 egg whites
  1 recipe Sweet Tart Pastry
     (see tip, page 187)
¾ cup sugar
½ cup fresh or frozen passion fruit
     puree or mango puree
⅓ cup unsalted butter
  3 eggs
½ teaspoon vanilla
⅛ teaspoon cream of tartar

1 Let egg whites stand at room temperature for 30 minutes. Divide the chilled tart pastry into 4 portions. On a lightly floured surface, roll each portion to ⅛-inch thickness. Cut into a 5½-inch round. Fit rounds into 4 ungreased 4-inch tart pans with removable bottoms. (Or, roll pastry to an 11-inch round; fit pastry into a 9-inch tart pan with removable bottom.) Line pastry in pan(s) with a double thickness of foil. Place on a baking sheet.

2 Bake in a 350°F oven for 15 minutes; remove foil. Bake for 5 to 6 minutes more for small tarts (12 to 15 minutes for large tart) or until golden. Cool in pan(s) on a wire rack.

3 For filling, in a saucepan combine ½ cup of the sugar, fruit puree, and butter. Bring just to boiling over medium heat, stirring occasionally. Beat the 3 eggs slightly with a fork. Slowly add fruit mixture, beating continuously. Return to saucepan; heat and stir over medium heat 4 to 5 minutes until slightly thickened (do not boil). Strain; cover. Keep warm.

4 For meringue, in a large mixing bowl combine the egg whites, vanilla, and cream of tartar. Beat with an electric mixer on high speed until soft peaks form (tips curl). Gradually add the remaining sugar, beating on high speed until stiff peaks form (tips stand straight).

5 To assemble, remove pastry shell(s) from pan(s). Place shell(s) on a baking sheet. Spoon fruit filling into shells. Spoon meringue into a pastry bag fitted with a large star tip. Pipe meringue onto the top of tart(s) in a woven pattern. Bake in a 350°F oven for 10 to 12 minutes for small tarts (15 minutes for large tart) or until meringue edges are golden. Cool 30 minutes on a wire rack. Chill in the refrigerator for 3 to 6 hours.

Nutrition Facts per serving: 766 cal., 44 g total fat (25 g sat. fat), 368 mg chol., 316 mg sodium, 83 g carbo., 2 g fiber, 12 g pro. **Daily Values:** 60% vit. A, 15% vit. C, 4% calcium, 17% iron

Passion Fruit Tarts:
End dinner on a passionate note. With their buttery crusts, fragrant fruit fillings, and light pipings of meringue, these little gems are seductive indeed.

PASTRIES FOR SPECTACULAR DESSERTS

Patterned after the rich, buttery French pastries, pâte brisée (short pastry) and pâte sucrée (sweetened short pastry), the following tart pastries result in short, crisp, and buttery crusts (unlike the flaky crust the piecrust pastry on page 190 provides). The key ingredients: butter and egg yolk.

Rich Tart Pastry: In a medium mixing bowl cut ½ cup cold butter into 1¼ cups all-purpose flour until pieces are the size of small peas. In a small bowl, combine 1 beaten egg yolk and 1 tablespoon ice water. Gradually stir egg yolk mixture into flour mixture. Add 1 to 2 tablespoons ice water, 1 tablespoon at a time, until all of the dough is moistened. Using your fingers, gently knead the dough just until a ball forms. If necessary, cover dough with plastic wrap and chill in the refrigerator for 30 to 60 minutes or until dough is easy to handle.

Sweet Tart Pastry: In a medium bowl stir together 1¼ cups all-purpose flour and ¼ cup sugar. Using a pastry blender, cut in ½ cup cold butter until pieces are pea-size. In a small bowl stir together 2 beaten egg yolks and 1 tablespoon water. Gradually stir egg yolk mixture into dry mixture. Using your fingers, gently knead dough just until a ball forms. If necessary, cover with plastic wrap and chill in refrigerator for 30 to 60 minutes or until dough is easy to handle.

RASPBERRY MARZIPAN TART

Prep: 30 minutes Bake: 48 minutes
Makes: 12 servings Oven: 350°F

Decadent chocolate and raspberry jam meet up with a generously nutty marzipan filling—with marvelous results in this company-special dessert.

 1 recipe Sweet Tart Pastry
   (see tip, above)
½ cup slivered almonds
⅔ cup sugar
 3 tablespoons all-purpose flour
⅓ cup butter, softened
 2 eggs
 1 teaspoon vanilla
½ teaspoon almond extract
⅓ cup unsalted pistachio nuts,
   chopped
⅓ cup seedless raspberry jam
 2 ounces semisweet chocolate, cut up
   Raspberries and pistachio nuts for
   garnish (optional)

1 **Prepare pastry.** Grease a 9-inch fluted tart pan with removable bottom. Press dough evenly into bottom and sides of prepared pan. Bake in a 350°F oven 18 to 20 minutes or until just lightly browned. Place pan on a wire rack.

2 **In food processor/blender container,** combine almonds, sugar, and flour. Cover; process or blend 1 minute or until almonds are finely ground. Add butter and 1 of the eggs. Process until smooth. Add the remaining egg, vanilla, and almond extract. Process until blended. Add the nuts and process with on-off turns until mixed in. Spread the jam over the bottom of the tart shell. Spoon the filling over the jam and spread evenly to cover. Bake in 350°F oven 30 to 35 minutes or until the filling is golden brown and firm when lightly touched. Cool in pan on wire rack. In a small saucepan melt the chocolate over low heat. Spread over the filling. If desired, arrange raspberries and nuts around edge and in center to garnish. Refrigerate tart 10 minutes or until chocolate sets.

Nutrition Facts per serving: 344 cal., 21 g total fat (10 g sat. fat), 105 mg chol., 143 mg sodium, 37 g carbo., 2 g fiber, 5 g pro. **Daily Values:** 18% vit. A, 0% vit. C, 3% calcium, 10% iron

Della Robbia Fruit Tart:
This artistic pastry ring, with its hand-painted array of fruits, resembles a della Robbia wreath. Originally, in the 15th and 16th centuries, the della Robbias were a family of sculptors. Today, they are known as much for their fruit designs as their sculptures.

DELLA ROBBIA FRUIT TART

BEST-LOVED

Prep: 1 hour   Bake: 30 minutes
Makes: 10 servings   Oven: 375°F

**2 recipes Rich Tart Pastry
(see tip, page 187)**
**3 ripe medium nectarines, peaches,
apples, or pears (about 1 pound)**
¼ cup sugar
1 tablespoon all-purpose flour
¼ teaspoon ground nutmeg
¼ cup chopped pecans
¼ cup dried tart cherries or raisins
**1 recipe Pastry Paint (see page 189)
or 1 slightly beaten egg yolk and
1 tablespoon water**
**Vanilla ice cream or 1 recipe
custard sauce (optional) (see
recipe, page 197)**

1 Divide pastry dough in half. Shape each half into a ball. For bottom pastry, on a lightly floured surface, use hands to slightly flatten 1 ball.

Roll dough from center to edges, forming an 11-inch circle. Trim circle to 10 inches; reserve scraps. Transfer to an ungreased baking sheet; set aside.

2 If using peaches, apples, or pears, peel. Cut fruit in half. Remove and discard pits or seeds. With cut sides down, cut each fruit half into 16 slices. Do not separate slices. Set fruit aside. Stir together sugar, flour, and nutmeg. Sprinkle about half of the sugar mixture over pastry circle on baking sheet to within ½ inch of edge. Sprinkle with pecans and cherries. Arrange fruit halves, cut sides down, in a circle about 1 inch from edge of pastry. (Leave center open.) Press down on the fruit halves to slightly fan out slices. Sprinkle with remaining sugar mixture.

3 For top pastry, on lightly floured surface, use hands to slightly flatten remaining ball of dough. Roll from center to edges, forming 12½-inch circle. Trim to 11½ inches; reserve scraps. Moisten edge of bottom pastry. Drape top pastry over fruit, aligning edges. Press pastry around fruit, being careful not to stretch pastry. Fold edges of top pastry under bottom pastry. Seal; make petal edge (see photo, page 46). If desired, cut 1½-inch circle from center of top and bottom pastries to form ring. Seal; crimp inside ring.

4 **Roll dough scraps** to ⅛-inch thickness. Using a knife or small cookie cutters, cut fruit and leaf shapes from the dough. Brush bottoms of pastry cutouts with a little water. Press cutouts onto the top pastry. Brush cutouts with the Pastry Paint or a mixture of the 1 egg yolk and 1 tablespoon water.

5 **Bake in a 375°F oven** 30 to 40 minutes or until fruit is tender. (If necessary, to prevent overbrowning, cover with foil after 25 minutes.) Cool on baking sheet for 10 minutes. Carefully transfer tart from baking sheet to serving plate. Serve warm. If desired, serve with ice cream or Custard Sauce.

Pastry Paint: Combine 2 slightly beaten egg yolks and 2 teaspoons water; divide mixture among 3 or 4 custard cups. To each cup, stir in a few drops food coloring. Makes about 2 tablespoons.

Nutrition Facts per serving: 359 cal., 23 g total fat (12 g sat. fat), 134 mg chol., 189 mg sodium, 35 g carbo., 2 g fiber, 5 g pro. **Daily Values:** 34% vit. A, 3% vit. C, 1% calcium, 11% iron

PEANUT BUTTER AND CHOCOLATE SHORTBREAD TART

Prep: 30 minutes   Bake: 15 minutes
Freeze: 30 minutes   Chill: 30 minutes
Makes: 20 servings   Oven: 350°F

> 1 recipe Chocolate Shortbread Crust
> 1 8-ounce package cream cheese, softened
> 1 cup sifted powdered sugar
> ¾ cup creamy peanut butter
> 1½ cups whipping cream
> ¾ cup chocolate-covered peanuts, coarsely chopped
> ¾ cup semisweet chocolate pieces
> 3 tablespoons creamy peanut butter
> 3 tablespoons whipping cream

1 **Prepare Chocolate Shortbread Crust.** Press dough evenly into bottom and sides of a 10- to 11-inch tart pan with removable bottom. Prick bottom and sides of tart shell with a fork. Bake in a 350°F oven for 15 to 18 minutes or until crisp and edges are beginning to brown. Cool on a wire rack.

2 **For filling,** beat cream cheese, powdered sugar, and the ¾ cup peanut butter with an electric mixer on medium speed until light. Beat in ¼ cup of the cream. In a medium mixing bowl beat ¾ cup of the cream with electric mixer on high speed just until soft peaks form. Gently fold whipped cream into peanut butter mixture. Fold in chopped peanuts. Pour filling into the cooled pastry shell and spread evenly. Freeze the tart 30 minutes or until firm.

3 **For glaze,** heat remaining ½ cup sifted cream over medium-low heat until hot. Add chocolate pieces; remove from heat. Whisk until melted and smooth. Set glaze aside to cool for 3 to 5 minutes.

4 **Meanwhile,** beat the 3 tablespoons peanut butter and 3 tablespoons cream until smooth. Place peanut butter mixture in a heavy-duty plastic bag. Spread chocolate glaze in a thin layer over filling. Cut a tiny corner from bag containing peanut butter mixture; squeeze to pipe concentric circles on top of chocolate. Using a wooden toothpick or tip of a sharp knife, pull tip through peanut butter, starting from center and pulling to edge of pan. Repeat to create 8 to 10 evenly-spaced lines in a weblike pattern. Chill 30 minutes or until glaze sets.

Chocolate Shortbread Crust: In a food processor bowl* combine 1 cup all-purpose flour, ½ cup powdered sugar, 3 tablespoons unsweetened cocoa powder, and ⅛ teaspoon salt. Cover and process until combined. Add 6 tablespoons cold butter, cut into 8 pieces. Process until mixture is the texture of cornmeal. In a small bowl beat together 1 egg yolk and 1 teaspoon vanilla. Drizzle egg mixture over flour mixture. Process just until dough begins to pull away from sides of bowl.

*Note: For hand-mixed method, in a medium bowl, combine 1 cup all-purpose flour, ½ cup sifted powdered sugar, 3 tablespoons unsweetened cocoa powder, and ⅛ teaspoon salt. Using a pastry blender, cut in 6 tablespoons cold butter until mixture resembles fine crumbs and starts to cling. In a small bowl beat together 1 egg yolk and 1 teaspoon vanilla. Drizzle egg mixture over flour mixture. Form the mixture into a ball and knead until smooth.

Nutrition Facts per serving: 325 cal., 25 g total fat (11 g sat. fat), 60 mg chol., 150 mg sodium, 23 g carbo., 1 g fiber, 6 g pro. **Daily Values:** 18% vit. A, 3% calcium, 6% iron

ULTIMATE NUT AND CHOCOLATE CHIP TART

Prep: 35 minutes   Bake: 40 minutes
Makes: 8 to 10 servings   Oven: 350°F

> 1 **recipe Pastry for Single-Crust Pie (see recipe, page 45)**
> 3 **eggs**
> 1 **cup light-colored corn syrup**
> ½ **cup packed brown sugar**
> ⅓ **cup butter, melted and cooled**
> 1 **teaspoon vanilla**
> 1 **cup coarsely chopped salted mixed nuts**
> ½ **cup miniature semisweet chocolate pieces**
> ⅓ **cup miniature semisweet chocolate pieces**
> 1 **tablespoon shortening**
> **Vanilla ice cream (optional)**

1 Prepare Pastry for Single-Crust Pie. On a lightly floured surface, flatten dough with your hands. Roll pastry from center to edge, forming a circle about 12 inches in diameter. Ease pastry into 11-inch tart pan with removable bottom. Trim pastry even with the rim of pan. Do not prick pastry.

2 For filling, in a large bowl beat eggs slightly with a rotary beater or a fork. Stir in the corn syrup. Add the brown sugar, butter, and vanilla, stirring until brown sugar is dissolved. Stir in the nuts and the ½ cup chocolate pieces.

3 Place the pastry-lined tart pan on a baking sheet on the oven rack. Carefully pour filling into pan. Bake in a 350°F oven for 40 minutes or until a knife inserted near the center comes out clean. Cool on a wire rack.

4 Before serving, place the ⅓ cup chocolate pieces and the shortening in a small heavy saucepan over very low heat, stirring constantly just until it begins to melt. Immediately remove from heat and stir until smooth. Cool slightly. Transfer chocolate mixture to a clean, small, heavy plastic bag. Snip a tiny hole in a corner of the bag. Drizzle the melted chocolate in zigzag lines across servings of tart, overlapping onto the plate. If desired, serve with vanilla ice cream.

Nutrition Facts per serving: 616 cal., 34 g total fat (9 g sat. fat), 100 mg chol., 340 mg sodium, 74 g carbo., 1 g fiber, 8 g pro. **Daily Values:** 10% vit. A, 7% calcium, 25% iron

Ultimate Nut and Chocolate Chip Tart: Reminiscent of an all-time favorite—pecan pie—this tart mixes several kinds of nuts and chocolate pieces in a caramel custard filling. Served with a scoop of ice cream, it's heavenly.

ENGLISH TRIFLE

Prep: 40 minutes   Chill: 5 hours
Makes: 8 to 10 servings

The sun never sets on this quintessentially Victorian dessert, for it travels the world in a variety of versions, including this time-honored one.

> 1 **recipe Hot Milk Sponge Cake (see below right)**
> 1⅓ **cups whipping cream**
> 1 **vanilla bean, split lengthwise, or 1 teaspoon vanilla**
> 2 **egg yolks**
> ⅔ **cup sugar**
> 2 **tablespoons cream sherry or orange juice**
> ¼ **cup seedless red raspberry or strawberry preserves**
> ¼ **cup toasted sliced almonds (see tip, page 181)**
> 1 **recipe Sweetened Whipped Cream (see recipe, page 133)**
> 1 **cup fresh raspberries or 1½ cups small fresh strawberries**

1 Prepare cake; cool completely. To prepare crème anglaise, in a heavy saucepan bring 1⅓ cups whipping cream and vanilla bean, if using, just to boiling, stirring frequently. Remove from heat. In a mixing bowl, combine a small amount of the hot cream, egg yolks, and sugar. Beat with an electric mixer on high speed for 2 to 3 minutes or until thick and lemon-colored. Gradually stir about half of the remaining cream mixture into the egg yolk mixture. Return all of the egg yolk mixture to the saucepan. Cook and stir over medium heat just until mixture returns to boiling. Remove from heat. Remove and discard vanilla bean or stir in liquid vanilla, if using. Cover surface with plastic wrap. Chill for at least 2 hours or overnight.

2 Cut or tear the cake layer into 1-inch pieces. In a 1½-quart clear glass serving bowl with straight sides, a soufflé dish, or a serving bowl, place half of the cake pieces. Sprinkle with half of the sherry. Spoon on half of the raspberry or strawberry preserves by small teaspoons. Sprinkle with the almonds. Pour half of the crème anglaise over all. Repeat layers using the remaining cake pieces, sherry, preserves, and crème anglaise. Cover and chill 3 to 24 hours before serving.

3 Just before serving, spread about half of the Sweetened Whipped Cream over top. Arrange raspberries or strawberries on top, reserving some berries to garnish. To garnish, spoon the remaining Sweetened Whipped Cream into a pastry bag fitted with a medium star tip (about ¼-inch opening). Pipe stars around the outer edge of the trifle. Place a berry in the center of each star.

Nutrition Facts per serving: 491 cal., 31 g total fat (18 g sat. fat), 179 mg chol., 96 mg sodium, 49 g carbo., 1 g fiber, 5 g pro. **Daily Values:** 41% vit. A, 7% vit. C, 8% calcium, 6% iron

HOT MILK SPONGE CAKE

Prep: 15 minutes   Bake: 18 minutes
Makes: 8 servings   Oven: 350°F

> ½ **cup all-purpose flour**
> ½ **teaspoon baking powder**
> **Dash salt**
> 1 **egg**
> ½ **cup sugar**
> ¼ **cup milk**
> 1 **tablespoon butter**

1 Grease and lightly flour a 9×1½-inch or 8×1½-inch round baking pan; set aside. Stir together flour, baking powder, and salt; set aside.

2 Beat egg with an electric mixer on high speed 3 to 4 minutes or until thick and lemon-colored. Gradually add sugar, beating on medium speed 4 to 5 minutes or until sugar is almost dissolved. Add flour mixture. Beat on low to medium speed just until combined. Heat the milk and butter just until butter melts. Stir warm milk mixture into egg mixture. Pour batter into prepared pan; spread evenly.

3 Bake in a 350°F oven 18 minutes or until top springs back when touched. Cool cake in pan on a wire rack for 10 minutes. Remove cake and cool completely on wire rack.

Nutrition Facts per serving: 100 cal., 2 g total fat (1 g sat. fat), 31 mg chol., 66 mg sodium, 18 g carbo., 0 g fiber, 2 g pro. **Daily Values:** 2% vit. A, 2% calcium, 3% iron

DEVONSHIRE CREAM TRIFLE

Prep: 35 minutes   **Cool:** 30 minutes
Chill: 2½ hours   **Makes:** 12 servings

We've matched the effect of England's beloved Devonshire cream—a thick, rich ingredient also known as clotted cream—by combining gelatin, whipping cream, and sour cream. Try this recipe when you're blessed with a bounty of summer fruits.

  1 teaspoon unflavored gelatin
  1 cup whipping cream
  ¼ cup sugar
  2 teaspoons vanilla
  1 8-ounce carton dairy sour cream
  4 cups assorted fresh fruit such as
      raspberries, sliced strawberries,
      chopped peeled nectarines or
      peaches,* and cut-up peeled
      kiwifruit
  2 tablespoons sugar
  1 recipe Hot Milk Sponge Cake
      (see recipe, page 191) or one
      10¾-ounce frozen loaf pound
      cake, thawed
  ¼ cup peach brandy, amaretto,
      orange liqueur, or orange juice
      Grated chocolate (optional)

1 For Devonshire cream, in a small saucepan combine gelatin and ½ cup cold water; let stand 5 minutes to soften. Heat and stir over medium heat until gelatin dissolves; cool.

2 In a chilled medium mixing bowl beat whipping cream, the ¼ cup sugar, and vanilla with an electric mixer on medium-low speed until soft peaks form (tips curl). Do not overbeat.

3 Combine cooled gelatin mixture and sour cream; mix well. Fold sour cream mixture into whipped cream. Chill for 30 to 45 minutes or until mixture thickens and will mound on a spoon.

4 Meanwhile, for fruit filling, in a large bowl combine the fresh fruit and the 2 tablespoons sugar. Let stand for 10 minutes.

5 Cut the Hot Milk Sponge Cake or pound cake into 2×½-inch strips. In a 2½- or 3-quart clear glass serving bowl or a soufflé dish, arrange half of the cake strips on the bottom. Arrange half of the fruit atop the cake strips. Sprinkle with 2 tablespoons of the brandy. Spoon half of the Devonshire cream on top. Repeat layers, piping or spooning remaining Devonshire cream on top.

6 Cover and chill 2 to 24 hours. If desired, sprinkle with chocolate.

*Note: If using peaches or nectarines, dip slices in a mixture of 1 cup water and 1 tablespoon lemon juice to prevent them from discoloring.

Nutrition Facts per serving: 235 cal., 13 g total fat
(8 g sat. fat), 56 mg chol., 62 mg sodium,
25 g carbo., 2 g fiber, 3 g pro. **Daily Values:**
15% vit. A, 17% vit. C, 5% calcium, 3% iron

MERINGUE MAGIC

Q Is the kind of meringue that goes on top of a tart or pie the same kind of meringue used to make shells for holding fillings?

A Yes, although the length of time the meringue spends in the oven gives it a different texture. Meringue toppings are baked only until they are cooked and their tops are slightly golden brown. Their interiors are still soft.

Meringue shells are baked until they are cooked and are left in the oven to cool and dry out until crisp enough to stand up to fruit or custard fillings.

To ensure the success of either kind of meringue:

■ Let the egg whites stand at room temperature for 30 minutes so they'll beat more readily and with heightened volume.

■ Use a clean glass or metal bowl. A plastic bowl will not work, as it may contain a film of oil, which can inhibit beating.

■ Make sure no yolk or other fat gets into the egg whites. Fat can reduce the meringue's volume.

■ Pipe or shape the meringue immediately after beating; then bake so that none of the volume is lost.

Berries in a Cloud:
Ever hear of cloud nine?
With baked meringue,
a generous mound of
creamy cocoa mousse,
and a crown of sweet ripe
strawberries, this is it.

BERRIES IN A CLOUD

Prep: 45 minutes   Bake: 45 minutes
Stand: 1 hour   Makes: 12 servings   Oven: 300°F

  3 **egg whites**
  1 **teaspoon vanilla**
  ¼ **teaspoon cream of tartar**
  1 **cup granulated sugar**
  ½ **cup toasted, finely chopped**
       almonds (see tip, page 181)
  1 **3-ounce package cream cheese,**
       softened
  ½ **cup packed brown sugar**
  ½ **cup unsweetened cocoa powder**
  2 **tablespoons milk**
  ½ **teaspoon vanilla**
  1 **cup whipping cream**
  3 **cups fresh whole strawberries,**
       stems and caps removed
  1 **ounce semisweet chocolate, cut up**
  1 **teaspoon shortening**

1 **Allow egg whites to stand** at room temperature for 30 minutes. Cover a baking sheet with plain brown paper or parchment paper. Draw a 9-inch circle on the paper; set aside.

2 **In a large mixing bowl combine** egg whites, the 1 teaspoon vanilla, and cream of tartar. Beat with an electric mixer on medium speed until soft peaks form (tips curl). Gradually add the granulated

sugar, 1 tablespoon at a time, beating on high speed until stiff peaks form (tips stand straight) and sugar is almost dissolved. Fold in the almonds.

3 **Spread meringue mixture** over circle drawn on paper, building sides up taller than the center to form a shell. Bake in a 300°F oven 45 minutes. Turn off oven; let meringue dry in oven with door closed at least 1 hour (do not open oven door). Remove baking sheet from oven. Lift meringue and carefully peel off paper; transfer to a flat serving platter. (Or, store shell in a flat, airtight container overnight).

4 **For cocoa mousse,** in a small mixing bowl beat cream cheese and brown sugar until smooth. Add cocoa powder, milk, and the ½ teaspoon vanilla; beat until smooth. In another small chilled mixing bowl beat whipping cream with chilled beaters of an electric mixer on medium speed until soft peaks form; fold into cocoa mixture. Carefully spoon cocoa mousse into meringue shell. Press whole berries, stemmed side down, into the mousse. In a small heavy saucepan melt semisweet chocolate and shortening over low heat, stirring constantly. With a small spoon, lightly drizzle over filling and meringue.

5 **Serve immediately** or cover and chill up to 2 hours. To serve, cut into wedges, dipping knife in water between cuts.

Nutrition Facts per serving: 265 cal., 14 g total fat
(7 g sat. fat), 35 mg chol., 47 mg sodium,
32 g carbo., 1 g fiber, 4 g pro. **Daily Values:**
12% vit. A, 35% vit. C, 7% calcium, 7% iron

Crème Brûlée:
The caramelized sugar
process is simplified; it's
now done on top of the
stove. But the dessert—with
its ever-so-thin glaze of
melted sugar on top of a
smooth, rich custard—is as
delectable as ever.

CRÈME BRÛLÉE *EASY*

Prep: 20 minutes   **Bake:** 18 minutes
Cool: 20 minutes   **Chill:** 1 hour   **Stand:** 20 minutes
Makes: 4 servings   **Oven:** 325°F

> 2 cups half-and-half or light cream
> 5 slightly beaten egg yolks
> ⅓ cup sugar
> 1 teaspoon vanilla
> ⅓ cup sugar

1 **In a small heavy saucepan heat** half-and-half over medium-low heat just until bubbly. Remove from heat; set aside.

2 **In a medium bowl** combine egg yolks, the ⅓ cup sugar, vanilla, and ¼ teaspoon salt. Beat with a wire whisk or rotary beater just until combined. Slowly whisk or stir the hot cream into the egg mixture.

3 **Place four ungreased 4-inch quiche dishes** or oval or round tart pans without removable bottoms into a 13×9×2-inch baking pan. Set the baking pan on oven rack in a 325°F oven. Pour the custard mixture evenly into the four dishes. Pour very hot water into the baking pan around and about halfway up the sides of the dishes.

4 **Bake in the 325°F oven** for 18 to 24 minutes or until a knife inserted near the center of each dish comes out clean. Remove dishes from the water bath; let cool on a wire rack. Cover and chill for at least 1 hour or up to 8 hours.

5 **Before serving,** let the custards stand at room temperature for 20 minutes.

6 **Place the ⅓ cup sugar** in a heavy 10-inch skillet. Heat skillet over medium-high heat until sugar begins to melt, shaking skillet occasionally to heat sugar evenly. Do not stir. Once sugar starts to melt, reduce heat to low; cook until sugar is completely melted and golden (3 to 5 minutes more), stirring as needed.

7 **Spoon melted sugar** quickly over custards in a lacy pattern or in a solid piece. If melted sugar starts to harden in pan, return to heat, stirring until it melts. If it starts to form clumps, carefully stir in 1 to 2 teaspoons water. Serve immediately.

Nutrition Facts per serving: 364 cal., 20 g total fat
(11 g sat. fat), 311 mg chol., 192 mg sodium,
39 g carbo., 0 g fiber, 7 g pro. **Daily Values:**
56% vit. A, 1% vit. C, 13% calcium, 5% iron

TIRAMISU

Prep: 30 minutes Chill: 11 hours
Makes: 9 servings

  1 **cup milk**
½ **cup granulated sugar**
  2 **tablespoons cornstarch**
  4 **egg yolks**
  2 **tablespoons light rum or brandy**
  2 **tablespoons butter, cut up**
  2 **teaspoons vanilla**
  8 **ounces mascarpone cheese**
½ **cup whipping cream**
  1 **tablespoon instant coffee crystals**
  2 **tablespoons coffee liqueur**
  1 **recipe Ladyfingers (see recipe, right)***
  2 **ounces semisweet chocolate, grated**
  1 **tablespoon sifted powdered sugar**

1 **Heat ¾ cup of the milk** over low heat. In a saucepan combine granulated sugar and cornstarch. Add remaining ¼ cup milk and the egg yolks. Whisk until smooth. Gradually stir in hot milk. Cook and stir over medium heat until thick and bubbly. Reduce heat. Cook and stir 2 minutes more. Stir in rum, butter, and vanilla. Cover surface with plastic wrap; cool. Refrigerate until cold, about 3 hours (mixture will be very thick). Allow mascarpone to stand at room temperature for 30 minutes.

2 **Stir mascarpone** until smooth; fold in custard. In a chilled small mixing ladyfingers bowl, beat whipping cream just until stiff peaks form. Fold into custard mixture. In a small bowl dissolve coffee crystals in ¾ cup water; add liqueur. Brush 12 Ladyfingers with half of coffee mixture. Arrange in the bottom of a 2-quart square baking dish. Spread half of custard mixture on top and sprinkle with half of grated chocolate. Repeat with remaining Ladyfingers, coffee, custard, and chocolate. Cover; chill 8 hours or overnight. To serve, sprinkle powdered sugar over top. Cut into squares.

***Note:** Commercial ladyfingers are available in some supermarkets and Italian food shops. To substitute for the homemade Ladyfingers, purchase two 3-ounce packages (24 ladyfingers total).

Nutrition Facts per serving: 457 cal., 27 g total fat (14 g sat. fat), 248 mg chol., 151 mg sodium, 44 g carbo., 1 g fiber, 12 g pro. **Daily Values:** 38% vit. A, 6% calcium, 10% iron

LADYFINGERS

Prep: 45 minutes Bake: 12 minutes
Makes: 24 ladyfingers Oven: 350°F

These cakelike cookies, resembling a plump finger, often are found in layered desserts. Try them in the Tiramisu at left.

  4 **egg yolks**
¼ **cup granulated sugar**
  1 **tablespoon hot water**
1½ **teaspoons vanilla**
  4 **egg whites**
¼ **teaspoon salt**
¼ **cup granulated sugar**
  1 **cup all-purpose flour**
  2 **tablespoons sifted powdered sugar**

1 **Grease and** flour 2 large baking sheets. In a medium mixing bowl combine egg yolks, the ¼ cup granulated sugar, the water, and vanilla. Beat with an electric mixer on medium speed 2 minutes, until thickened and pale yellow.

2 **Thoroughly wash beaters.** In a large mixing bowl beat egg whites and salt with mixer on medium to high speed until soft peaks form (tips curl). Gradually add the ¼ cup granulated sugar, beating until stiff peaks form (tips stand straight). Add the yolk mixture and fold in by hand just until blended. Sift ⅓ cup of the flour over egg mixture. Fold flour in gently, until just blended. Repeat with remaining flour, ⅓ cup at a time; do not overfold.

3 **Place mixture** in a pastry bag fitted with a ½-inch round tip. Pipe batter into 24 ladyfinger shapes (about 4 inches long and 1 inch wide) on prepared baking sheets, 1 inch apart. Sift powdered sugar over ladyfingers.

4 **Bake in a 350°F oven** 12 to 15 minutes or until set and golden brown. Let cool on sheets 10 minutes. Remove with spatula to wire racks to cool completely.

Nutrition Facts per ladyfinger: 49 cal., 1 g total fat (0 g sat. fat), 36 mg chol., 33 mg sodium, 9 g carbo., 0 g fiber, 2 g pro. **Daily Values:** 5% vit. A, 0% calcium, 2% iron

THE STRUDEL DEFINED

Q Sometimes a strudel pastry is light and flaky; other times it's a rich, dense pastry. Which is the real strudel?

A They both are. A strudel is defined by the method by which it's made: It's an elongated pastry wrapped around a filling, typically made of fruit or cheese. Its name speaks of its shape—"strudel" means "whirlpool" in German. Traditional strudels are made with layers of tissue-thin dough (making flaky pastry), but the Fall Fruit Strudel also fits the definition. It uses a cream-cheese dough that is simply rolled instead of pulled and offers a heartier pastry, ideal for the mixed-fruit filling.

FALL FRUIT STRUDEL

Prep: 30 minutes   Bake: 35 minutes
Chill: 1 hour   Makes: 8 servings   Oven: 375°F

- 1½ **cups all-purpose flour**
- 2 **tablespoons sugar**
- ¼ **teaspoon salt**
- ¼ **cup cold butter, cut up**
- 1 **3-ounce package cream cheese, chilled and cut into ½-inch pieces**
- 3 to 4 **tablespoons cold water**
- ½ **cup golden raisins**
- ½ **cup dried tart cherries**
- ¼ **cup snipped dried apricots**
- 3 **tablespoons dark rum, cream sherry, or apple juice**
- 1 **large firm ripe pear, peeled, cored, and diced**
- ¼ **cup chopped walnuts or pecans**
- 3 **gingersnaps, coarsely crushed**
- 3 **tablespoons sugar**
- ¼ **teaspoon ground cinnamon**
- 1 **tablespoon sugar**
- 1 **recipe Eggnog Custard Sauce or vanilla ice cream**

1 Lightly grease a 15×10×1-inch baking pan. In a large bowl stir together flour, the 2 tablespoons sugar, and the salt. Using a pastry blender, cut in the butter and cream cheese until pieces are the size of small peas. Sprinkle water gradually over dough, tossing with a fork until dough is moistened. Gather dough into a ball. Flatten dough into a disk, wrap in plastic wrap, and refrigerate 1 hour.

2 Meanwhile, for filling, in a bowl stir together raisins, cherries, apricots, and rum. Let stand 1 hour. Add pear, walnuts, gingersnaps, the 3 tablespoons sugar, and the cinnamon. Toss until blended.

3 On a lightly floured surface roll dough with a floured rolling pin to a 14×8-inch rectangle. Trim rough edges. Place the filling in a lengthwise strip down center of the rectangle to about 2 inches from the ends. Brush the edges of the dough lightly with water. Fold a long side of pastry up over the filling. Brush the edge lightly with water and fold the other side over, overlapping slightly. Press gently to seal. Bring the ends of the pastry up to the top and press gently to seal.

4 Place the prepared baking pan next to strudel. Ease the strudel into pan, seam side down. Brush top lightly with water and sprinkle with the 1 tablespoon sugar. Bake in a 375°F oven for 35 minutes or until golden. Cool on baking sheet on a wire rack. Cut into slices with a serrated knife. Serve with Eggnog Custard Sauce or ice cream.

Eggnog Custard Sauce: In a small saucepan heat 1 cup milk over medium-low heat. In a small bowl stir together 3 tablespoons sugar, ½ teaspoon cornstarch, and ⅛ teaspoon ground nutmeg. Add 2 beaten egg yolks and whisk until smooth. Gradually whisk about half of the hot milk into the yolk mixture. Pour all of the yolk mixture into the hot milk. Cook over low heat, stirring constantly until the custard thickens slightly and coats a metal spoon. Remove from heat. Stir in 2 teaspoons dark rum and ½ teaspoon vanilla. Cover surface with plastic wrap. Cool; chill in refrigerator up to 3 days.

Nutrition Facts per serving: 383 cal., 14 g total fat (5 g sat. fat), 75 mg chol., 186 mg sodium, 55 g carbo., 2 g fiber, 6 g pro. **Daily Values:** 27% vit. A, 2% vit. C, 5% calcium, 13% iron

index

MY FAVORITE RECIPES   PAGE NUMBER

Numbers in italics indicate photo pages.

A

Almonds.
Almond Filling, 81
Almond Frosting, *149*
Apricot-Almond Breakfast Pastries, *83* BEST-LOVED
Caramel-Almond Torte, *120* BEST-LOVED
Dutch Letters, 87 BEST-LOVED
Fruit Tart with Amaretto Creme, Mixed, *68–69*
Ginger-Almond Filling, 26
Lemon-Almond Tea Cookies, 154 LOW-FAT
Nutty Spritz, 147
Peach and Almond Crisp, *34* BEST-LOVED
Peach-Filled Almond Puffs, 90
Raspberry Twirls, Red, *154–155* LOW-FAT
Sherry-Almond Sponge Cake, 110-*111*
Strawberry-Filled Almond Puffs, 90
Torte, Linzer, 72-73
Altitudes, baking at high, 9
Angel food cakes.
Angel Food Cake, 106 LOW-FAT
Angel Food Cake, Marble, *108* LOW-FAT
Chocolate Angel Cake with Coffee Liqueur Glaze, 107 LOW-FAT
defined, 109
Honey Angel Food Cake, 106 LOW-FAT
marbling method, *108*
preparing, *106*
tips, 107
Apples.
Apple-Cherry Pandowdy, 28
Apple-Cinnamon Rolls, 41
Apple Cobbler, 29
Apple-Cranberry Deep-Dish Pie, *46–47*
Apple-Cranberry Streusel Pie, *50*
Apple Pie, 48
Apple Pie, No-Peel, *48–49* EASY
apple pie, history of, 48
Apple Strudel, 93 BEST-LOVED
Apple Tartlets, Sunrise, 82
Apple-Walnut Filling, 26
Baked Apples, Best-Ever, *26–27* LOW-FAT
for pies, 51
Pineapple Crisp, Hawaiian, *33*
selecting, 26, 51

Tarte Tatin, *43-64*
Apricots.
Apricot-Almond Breakfast Pastries, *83* BEST-LOVED
Apricot-Cardamom Bars, *169* LOW-FAT
Apricot-Hazelnut Biscotti, *141*
Apricot Icing, 169
Apricot-Oatmeal Cookies, 140
Apricot Roses, 178
Brandied Apricot-Pear Dumplings, *25* BEST-LOVED
Brandied Cranberry-Apricot Bars, *172* BEST-LOVED
Cherry and Apricot Tart, Country, *70*
Sacher Torte, 178–*179*

B

Baklava, *94-95*
Bananas.
Banana Cream Napoleons, 84
Banana Cream Pie, 61
Banana Layer Cake, 104
Banana Nut Roll, Amazing, 116–*117* BEST-LOVED
Banana Split Cake, 104-105
Banana Streusel Pie, *56*
Cake, Granny, *118* BEST-LOVED
Bar cookies. *See also* Brownies
Apricot-Cardamom Bars, *169* LOW-FAT
Bar Cookies, Ultimate, *157, 162*
Blondies, 167 EASY
Brandied Cranberry-Apricot Bars, *172* BEST-LOVED
Brickle Bars, *159* EASY
Carrot-Pumpkin Bars with Orange Icing, 170-*171*
Chocolate Chip Cookie Bars, 137
Chocolate-Peanut Butter Bars, Layered, 166
cleanup tip, 169
Cranberry-Macadamia Bars, *165*
cutting, 161
freezing, 162
Hazelnut Bars, 162
Lemon Bars Deluxe, 164 BEST-LOVED
Mocha Cheesecake Dreams, *168*
Nut Bars, Mixed, 170
Oatmeal-Caramel Bars, 167
pans for, 166
Piña Colada Squares, 172
Raspberry-Citrus Bars, *164*
toppings for, 170
Berries. *See also* specific kinds
Berries in a Cloud, *193*

Berry Pie, Mixed, 51 BEST-LOVED
Brown Butter Tart 69 BEST-LOVED
Betties, about, 29
Betty, Strawberry-Rhubarb, 30
Biscotti.
about, 141
Apricot-Hazelnut Biscotti, *141*
slicing and baking tips, 141
Biscuits.
Peach Cobbler with Cinnamon-Swirl Biscuits, *23*, 29
Blackberries.
Berry Pie, Mixed, 51 BEST-LOVED
Blackberry Cobbler, 30
Blueberries.
Berry Pie, Mixed, 51 BEST-LOVED
Blueberry Crisp, 32
Blueberry Filling, 81
Blueberry Pie, 52
Blueberry Tart, Fresh, 71
Cherry-Blueberry Cobbler Supreme, 28
history of, 52
Bread pudding.
leftovers, 31
Orange Bread Pudding with Warm Maple Sauce, *35* LOW-FAT
Whiskey-Sauced Bread Pudding, 34
Brickle Bars, *159* EASY
Brownie Pudding Cake, 38 EASY
Brownies. *See also* Bar cookies
Brownies, history of, 159
Brownies, Irish Cream, 160
Brownies, Trilevel, 161 BEST-LOVED
cleanup tip, 169
Creamy, Fudgy, Nutty Brownies, *157, 163*
cutting tips, 161
Fudge Brownies, Easy, *159* EASY
Fudge Brownie Tarts, 160
Butter.
Brown Butter Tart, 69 BEST-LOVED
Browned Butter Cookies, *138*
Browned Butter Frosting, *133*
Browned Butter Icing, *138*
Buttercream, 134
Buttercream, White Chocolate, 134
Butter-Pecan Shortbread, 159
Butter Frosting, 131
Chocolate Butter Frosting, *131*

METRIC COOKING HINTS

By making a few conversions, cooks in Australia, Canada, and the United Kingdom can use the recipes in *Better Homes and Gardens® Amazing Desserts for Every Occasion* with confidence. The charts on this page provide a guide for converting measurements from the U.S. customary system, which is used throughout this book, to the imperial and metric systems. There also is a conversion table for oven temperatures to accommodate the differences in oven calibrations.

Product Differences: Most of the ingredients called for in the recipes in this book are available in English-speaking countries. However, some are known by different names. Here are some common American ingredients and their possible counterparts:

- Sugar is granulated or castor sugar.
- Powdered sugar is icing sugar.
- All-purpose flour is plain household flour or white flour. When self-rising flour is used in place of all-purpose flour in a recipe that calls for leavening, omit the leavening agent (baking soda or baking powder) and salt.
- Light-colored corn syrup is golden syrup.
- Cornstarch is cornflour.
- Baking soda is bicarbonate of soda.
- Vanilla is vanilla essence.
- Green, red, or yellow sweet peppers are capsicums.
- Golden raisins are sultanas.

Volume and Weight: Americans traditionally use cup measures for liquid and solid ingredients. The chart, below, shows the approximate imperial and metric equivalents. If you are accustomed to weighing solid ingredients, the following approximate equivalents will help.

- 1 cup butter, castor sugar, or rice = 8 ounces = about 250 grams
- 1 cup flour = 4 ounces = about 125 grams
- 1 cup icing sugar = 5 ounces = about 150 grams

Spoon measures are used for smaller amounts of ingredients. Although the size of the tablespoon varies slightly in different countries, for practical purposes and for recipes in this book, a straight substitution is all that's necessary.

Measurements made using cups or spoons always should be level unless stated otherwise.

EQUIVALENTS: U.S. = AUSTRALIA/U.K.

⅛ teaspoon = 0.5 ml
¼ teaspoon = 1 ml
½ teaspoon = 2 ml
1 teaspoon = 5 ml
1 tablespoon = 1 tablespoon
¼ cup = 2 tablespoons = 2 fluid ounces = 60 ml
⅓ cup = ¼ cup = 3 fluid ounces = 90 ml
½ cup = ⅓ cup = 4 fluid ounces = 120 ml
⅔ cup = ½ cup = 5 fluid ounces = 150 ml
¾ cup = ⅔ cup = 6 fluid ounces = 180 ml
1 cup = ¾ cup = 8 fluid ounces = 240 ml
1¼ cups = 1 cup
2 cups = 1 pint
1 quart = 1 liter
½ inch = 1.27 cm
1 inch = 2.54 cm

BAKING PAN SIZES

American	Metric
8×1½-inch round baking pan	20×4-cm cake tin
9×1½-inch round baking pan	23×3.5-cm cake tin
11×7×1½-inch baking pan	28×18×4-cm baking tin
13×9×2-inch baking pan	30×20×3-cm baking tin
2-quart rectangular baking dish	30×20×3-cm baking tin
15×10×1-inch baking pan	30×25×2-cm baking tin (Swiss roll tin)
9-inch pie plate	22×4- or 23×4-cm pie plate
7- or 8-inch springform pan	18- or 20-cm springform or loose-bottom cake tin
9×5×3-inch loaf pan	23×13×7-cm or 2-pound narrow loaf tin or pâté tin
1½-quart casserole	1.5-liter casserole
2-quart casserole	2-liter casserole

OVEN TEMPERATURE EQUIVALENTS

Fahrenheit Setting	Celsius Setting*	Gas Setting
300°F	150°C	Gas Mark 2 (slow)
325°F	160°C	Gas Mark 3 (moderately slow)
350°F	180°C	Gas Mark 4 (moderate)
375°F	190°C	Gas Mark 5 (moderately hot)
400°F	200°C	Gas Mark 6 (hot)
425°F	220°C	Gas Mark 7
450°F	230°C	Gas Mark 8 (very hot)
Broil		Grill

*Electric and gas ovens may be calibrated using Celsius. However, for an electric oven, increase the Celsius setting 10 to 20 degrees when cooking above 160°C. For convection or forced-air ovens (gas or electric), lower the temperature setting 10°C when cooking at all heat levels.

MICROWAVE HINTS

■ **Butter, melting:** In a bowl heat butter, uncovered, on 100% power (high) 35 to 45 seconds for 2 tablespoons, 45 to 60 seconds for $\frac{1}{4}$ cup, or 1 to $1\frac{1}{2}$ minutes (about 45 seconds in high-wattage ovens) for $\frac{1}{2}$ cup.

■ **Butter, softening:** In a bowl heat $\frac{1}{2}$ cup butter, uncovered, on 10% power (low) for $1\frac{1}{2}$ to $2\frac{1}{2}$ minutes (about 45 seconds in high-wattage ovens) or until softened.

■ **Chocolate, melting:** In a bowl heat chocolate, uncovered, on 100% power (high) 1 to 2 minutes for 1 ounce ($1\frac{1}{2}$ to $2\frac{1}{2}$ minutes for 1 cup chocolate pieces) or until soft enough to stir smooth, stirring every minute during cooking time.

■ **Coconut, toasting:** In a 2-cup measure cook 1 cup coconut, uncovered, on 100% power (high) for $2\frac{1}{2}$ to $3\frac{1}{2}$ minutes or till toasted, stirring after 1 minute, then stirring every 30 seconds.

■ **Cream cheese, softening:** In a bowl heat cream cheese, uncovered, on 100% power (high) 15 to 30 seconds for 3 ounces (30 to 60 seconds for 8 ounces) or till softened.

■ **Lemons, juicing:** Halve or quarter 1 lemon. Heat on 100% power (high) 20 to 45 seconds. Squeeze lemon to release juice.

■ **Sauces, reheating:** Heat chilled topping, uncovered, on 100% power (high) 30 seconds to $1\frac{1}{2}$ minutes for $\frac{1}{2}$ cup or 60 seconds to 2 minutes for 1 cup.

■ **Muffins and rolls, warming:** Place muffins or rolls on a plate. Heat, uncovered, on 100% power (high) for 10 to 20 seconds for 1 or 2 muffins or 30 to 60 seconds for 4 muffins or until heated through.

■ **Nuts, toasting:** In a 2-cup measure cook nuts, uncovered, on 100% power (high) till toasted, stirring every minute for the first 2 minutes, then stirring every 30 seconds. Allow 2 to 3 minutes for $\frac{1}{2}$ cup almonds or pecans, 2 to 3 minutes for 1 cup almonds, 3 to 4 minutes for 1 cup pecans, 3 to 4 minutes for $\frac{1}{2}$ cup raw peanuts or walnuts, and $3\frac{1}{2}$ to 5 minutes for 1 cup raw peanuts or walnuts. Whole nuts may toast first on the inside, so open a few to check for doneness. At the first sign of toasting, spread whole or chopped nuts on paper towels to cool. They will continue to toast as they stand. Let them stand for at least 15 minutes.

■ **Pie (fruit), warming:** Place 1 slice of fruit pie on a plate. Heat, uncovered, on 100% power (high) 45 to 60 seconds (about 20 seconds in high-wattage ovens) or until heated through.

FREEZER STORAGE

Brownies and Bars (unfrosted)	Up to 3 months
Layer Cakes (unfrosted)	Up to 4 months
Angel Food, Sponge, and Chiffon Cakes (unfrosted)	Up to 3 months
Cheesecakes	Up to 1 month (whole) Up to 2 weeks (pieces)
Cookie Dough	Up to 6 months
Cookies (unfrosted)	Up to 3 months
Cream Puff Pastry Shells	Up to 2 months
Croissant and Puff Pastry Dough	Up to 3 months
Croissants and Danishes	Up to 2 months
Fruit Pies (baked)	Up to 8 months
Fruit Pies (unbaked)	Up to 3 months
Muffins, Biscuits, and Scones	Up to 3 months
Pie Pastry Dough	Up to 3 months
Quick Breads	Up to 3 months
Yeast Breads	Up to 3 months

TOASTING NUTS, SEEDS, AND COCONUT

Toasting heightens the flavor of nuts, seeds, and coconut. To toast, spread the nuts, seeds, or coconut in a single layer in a shallow baking pan. Bake in a 350° oven for 5 to 10 minutes or until light golden brown, watching carefully and stirring once or twice to brown evenly.

WEIGHTS AND MEASURES

3 teaspoons = 1 tablespoon	1 tablespoon = ½ fluid ounce	1 teaspoon = 5 milliliters
4 tablespoons = ¼ cup	1 cup = 8 fluid ounces	1 tablespoon = 15 milliliters
5⅓ tablespoons = ⅓ cup	1 cup = ½ pint	1 cup = 240 milliliters
8 tablespoons = ½ cup	2 cups = 1 pint	1 quart = 1 liter
10⅔ tablespoons = ⅔ cup	4 cups = 1 quart	1 ounce = 28 grams
12 tablespoons = ¾ cup	2 pints = 1 quart	1 pound = 454 grams
16 tablespoons = 1 cup	4 quarts = 1 gallon	

EMERGENCY BAKING SUBSTITUTIONS

Use these substitutions only in a pinch, as they may affect the flavor or texture of your recipe.

If you don't have:	Substitute:
Apple pie spice, 1 teaspoon	½ teaspoon ground cinnamon plus ¼ teaspoon ground nutmeg, ⅛ teaspoon ground allspice, and dash ground cloves or ginger
Baking powder, 1 teaspoon	½ teaspoon cream of tartar plus ¼ teaspoon baking soda
Buttermilk, 1 cup	Sour milk: 1 tablespoon lemon juice or vinegar plus enough milk to make 1 cup (let stand 5 minutes before using); or 1 cup plain yogurt
Chocolate, semisweet, 1 ounce	3 tablespoons semisweet chocolate pieces; or 1 ounce unsweetened chocolate plus 1 tablespoon sugar
Chocolate, sweet baking, 4 ounces	¼ cup unsweetened cocoa powder plus ⅓ cup sugar and 3 tablespoons shortening
Chocolate, unsweetened, 1 ounce	3 tablespoons unsweetened cocoa powder plus 1 tablespoon cooking oil or shortening, melted
Cornstarch, 1 tablespoon (for thickening)	2 tablespoons all-purpose flour
Corn syrup, 1 cup	1 cup granulated sugar plus ¼ cup water
Egg, 1 whole	2 egg whites; 2 egg yolks; or ¼ cup frozen egg product, thawed
Flour, cake, 1 cup	1 cup minus 2 tablespoons all-purpose flour
Flour, self-rising, 1 cup	1 cup all-purpose flour plus 1 teaspoon baking powder, ½ teaspoon salt, and ¼ teaspoon baking soda
Fruit liqueur, 1 tablespoon	1 tablespoon fruit juice
Gingerroot, grated, 1 teaspoon	¼ teaspoon ground ginger
Half-and-half or light cream, 1 cup	1 tablespoon melted butter or margarine plus enough whole milk to make 1 cup
Honey, 1 cup	1¼ cups granulated sugar plus ¼ cup water
Mascarpone cheese, 8 ounces	8 ounces regular cream cheese
Milk, 1 cup	½ cup evaporated milk plus ½ cup water; or 1 cup water plus ⅓ cup nonfat dry milk powder
Molasses, 1 cup	1 cup honey
Pumpkin pie spice, 1 teaspoon	½ teaspoon ground cinnamon plus ¼ teaspoon ground ginger, ¼ teaspoon ground allspice, and ⅛ teaspoon ground nutmeg
Sour cream, dairy, 1 cup	1 cup plain yogurt
Sugar, granulated, 1 cup	1 cup packed brown sugar
Yeast, active dry, 1 package	1 cake compressed yeast